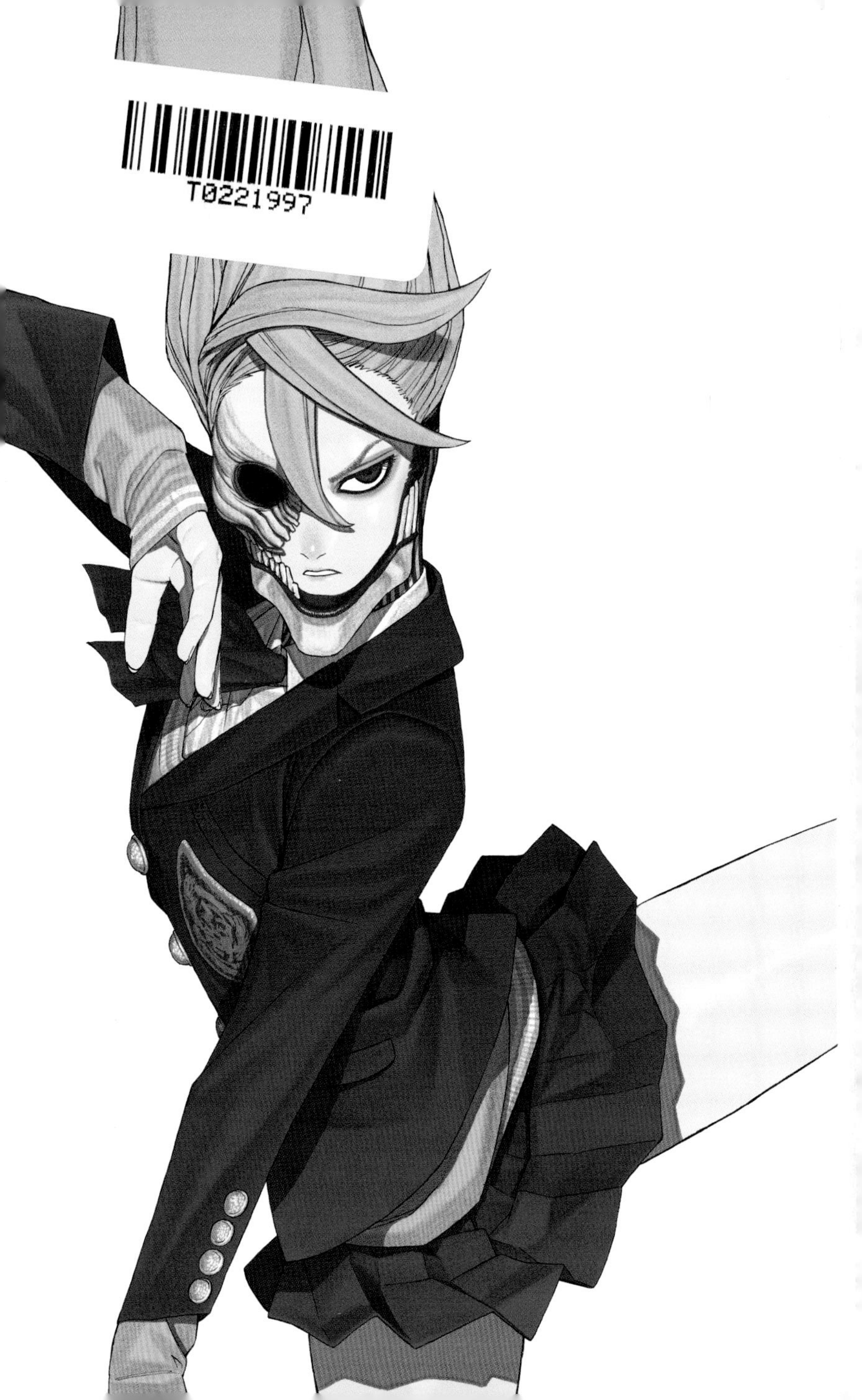

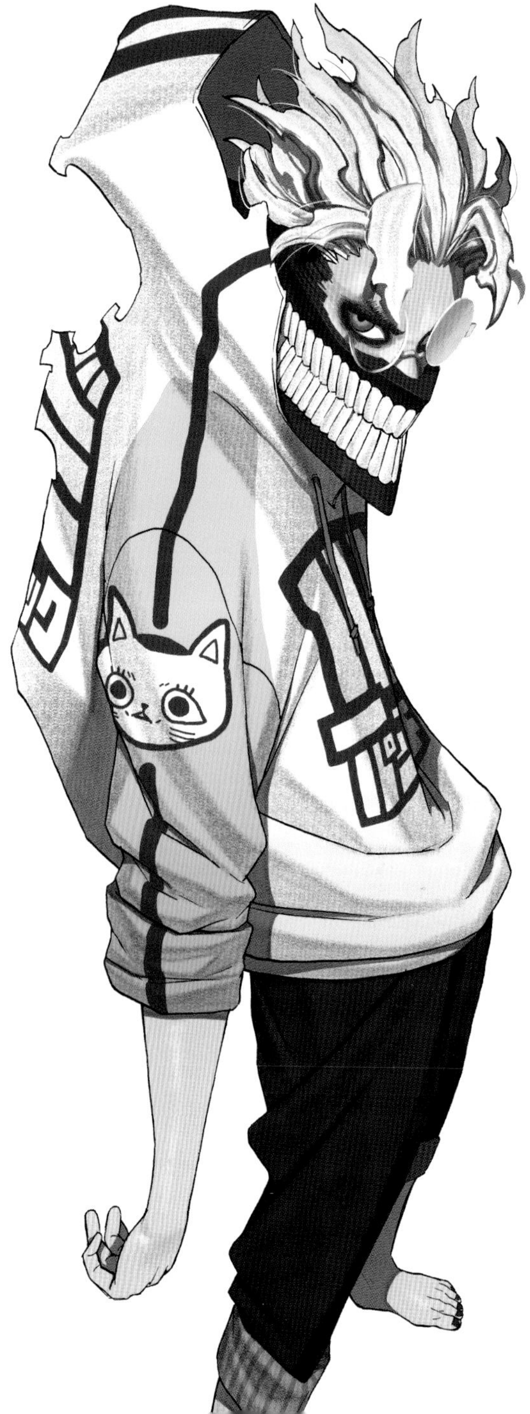

DANDADAN

STORY AND ART BY
**YUKINOBU
TATSU**

7

CHARACTERS

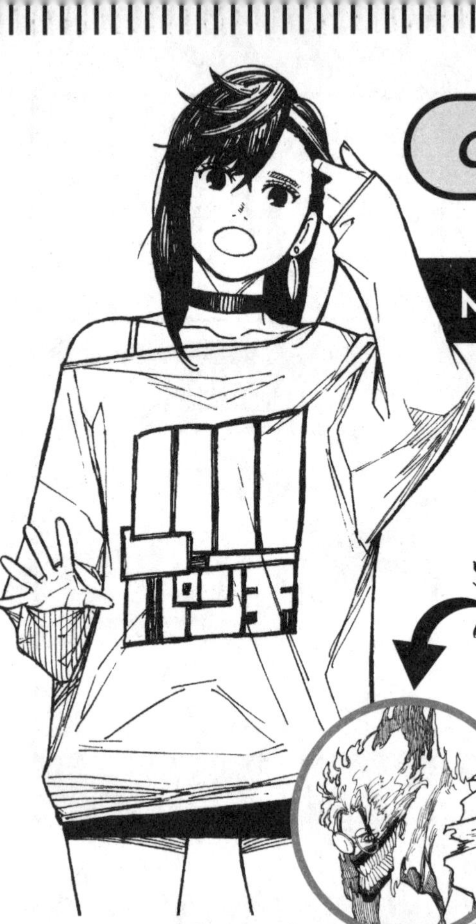

MOMO AYASE

A high school girl from a family of spirit mediums. Her powers awakened after she was abducted by aliens. Following the battle with Turbo Granny, she helps to search for Okarun's testicles.

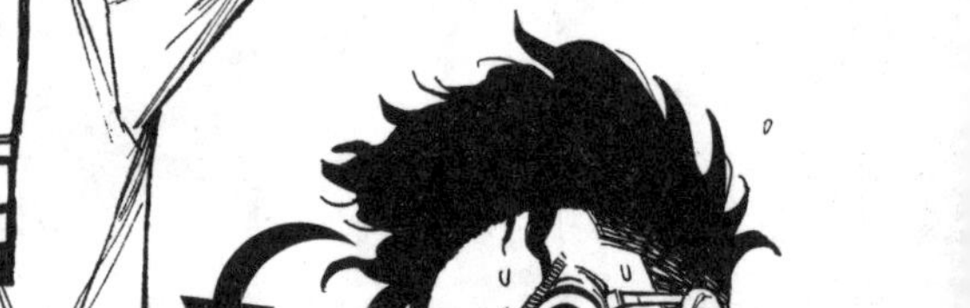

OKARUN (KEN TAKAKURA)

A geek for paranormal phenomena who lost his testicles in the fight against Turbo Granny and must now spend his time looking for them. He has developed feelings for Momo.

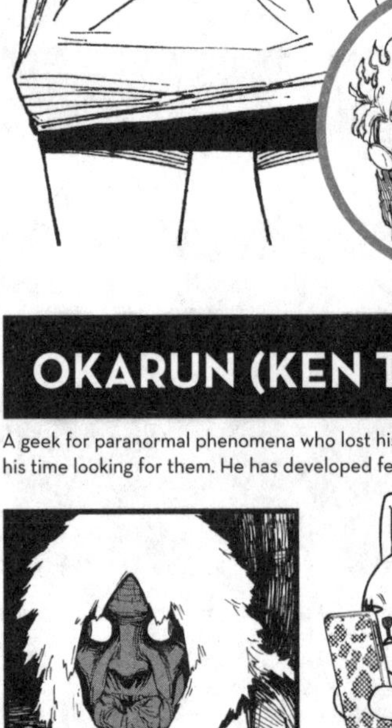

TURBO GRANNY

Appearing at unexpected times and places, she's a present-day yokai who ran riot throughout the country. Her power remains within Okarun, while her consciousness is stuck in a beckoning-cat figure that she uses to get around.

JIJI (JIN ENJOJI)

Momo's friend since childhood. He recruits Momo and Okarun to investigate and exorcise the spirits in his family's new house. But before they can, his body is possessed by the Evil Eye, a boy who'd been sacrificed under the house and became a yokai.

AIRA SHIRATORI

A popular, attractive girl at Momo's school whose powers awaken when she unknowingly picks up one of Okarun's family jewels. She ends up taking on the aura of the Acrobatic Silky.

TARO

An anatomical-model yokai who is dating anatomical model Hana. At present he has Jiji, currently possessed by the Evil Eye, trapped inside his own body.

MANJIRO

A priest at the Tsuchinoko Shrine near Jiji's home. He is also Seiko's disciple.

SEIKO

Momo's grandmother. She's active as the spirit medium Santa Dodoria. She's powerful enough to enclose their home in a mystical barrier, and she supports Momo and the others from the shadows.

STORY

Momo, a firm believer in spirits, comes to the rescue of a paranormal fanatic named Ken Takakura, aka Okarun, when he's getting bullied. After arguing about the validity of each other's interests, they decide to prove their respective beliefs, so Momo is sent to an abandoned hospital known for UFO sightings and Okarun heads to a supposedly haunted tunnel. Once there, Okarun gets cursed by a yokai called Turbo Granny! At the hospital, Momo ends up abducted by aliens called Serpoians, who are seeking a human female for reproduction. They take her aboard their ship, and Momo finds herself in big trouble. Suddenly, Okarun appears, and thanks to Turbo Granny's curse, he's able to transform. At the same time, Momo awakens to her paranormal abilities, and the two are able to escape the UFO. But Okarun's curse affects those around them, so they decide to have a showdown with Turbo Granny. Seiko sets up a barrier around Kamikoshi City, and Momo and Okarun subsequently beat Turbo Granny through a game of tag. Later, Jiji, Momo's old childhood friend and first crush, shows up troubled with supernatural problems of his own occurring in his family's new home, so Okarun and Momo head there to investigate. However, there are legends of a giant serpent in the area. In fact, the Kito clan has been secretly sacrificing humans to it under Jiji's new home, and they toss the young trio into an underground alternate reality as the latest offering. There the three find the serpent as well as a sacrificed child, now an Evil Eye yokai who goes on to possess Jiji. Suddenly, Seiko appears, sealing Jiji's possessed body inside the anatomical-model yokai Taro with a plan to exorcise it. Will Jiji get his body back, or is it too late to separate them?!

DAN DA DAN 7

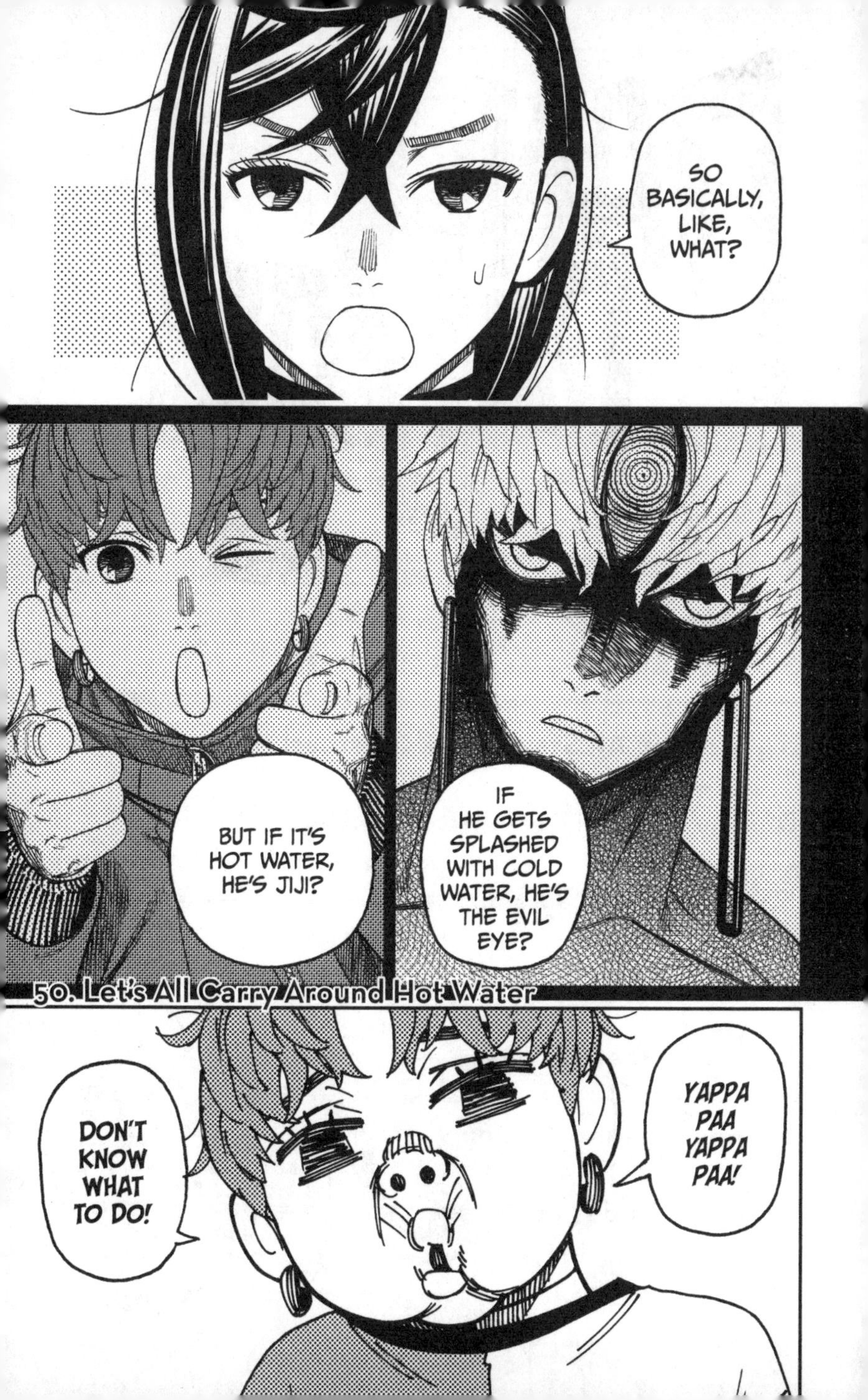
SO BASICALLY, LIKE, WHAT?
IF HE GETS SPLASHED WITH COLD WATER, HE'S THE EVIL EYE?
BUT IF IT'S HOT WATER, HE'S JIJI?
50. Let's All Carry Around Hot Water
YAPPA PAA YAPPA PAA!
DON'T KNOW WHAT TO DO!

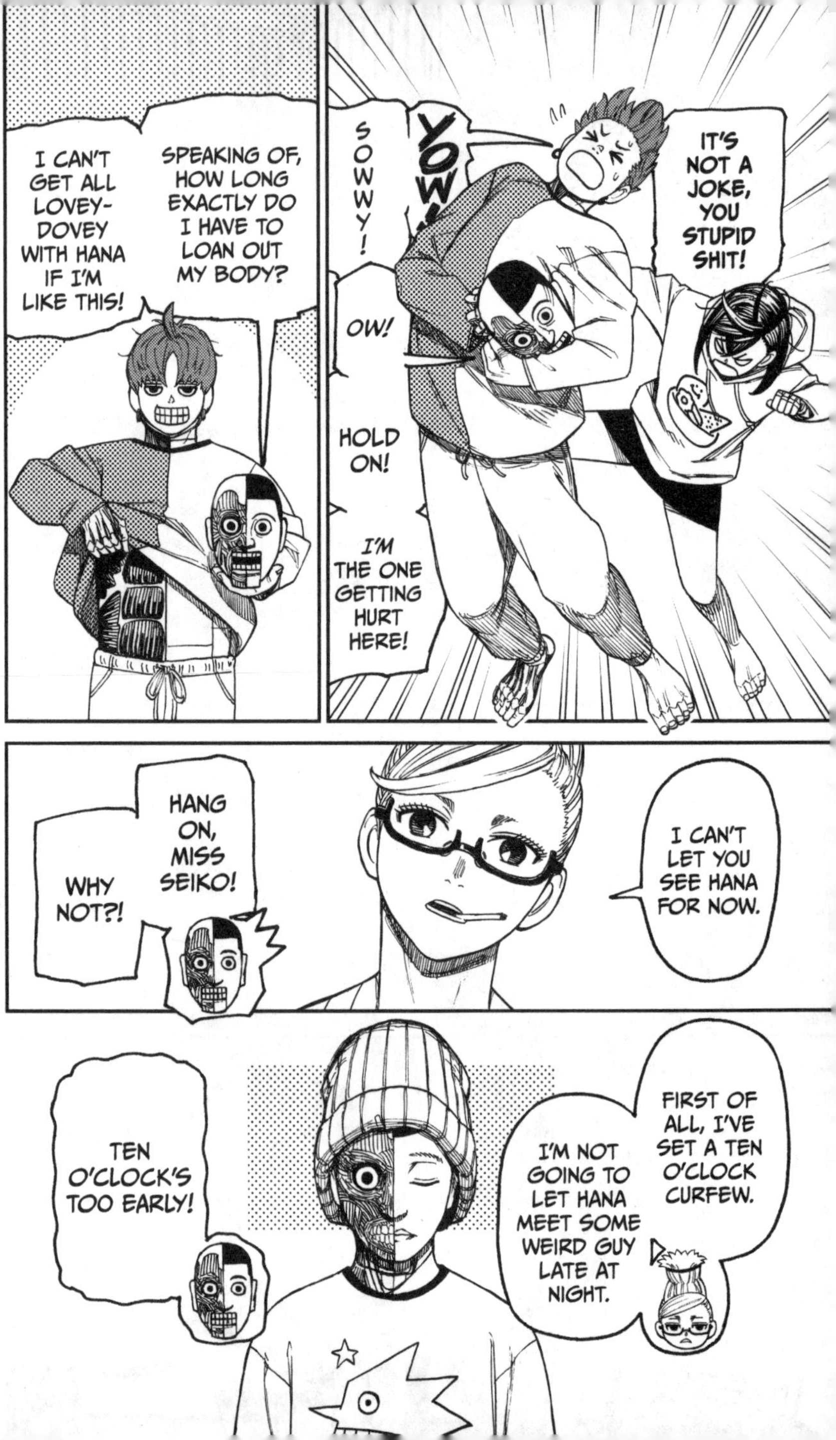
IT'S NOT A JOKE, YOU STUPID SHIT!
YOW!
SOWWY!
OW!
HOLD ON!
I'M THE ONE GETTING HURT HERE!
SPEAKING OF, HOW LONG EXACTLY DO I HAVE TO LOAN OUT MY BODY?
I CAN'T GET ALL LOVEY-DOVEY WITH HANA IF I'M LIKE THIS!
I CAN'T LET YOU SEE HANA FOR NOW.
HANG ON, MISS SEIKO!
WHY NOT?!
FIRST OF ALL, I'VE SET A TEN O'CLOCK CURFEW.
I'M NOT GOING TO LET HANA MEET SOME WEIRD GUY LATE AT NIGHT.
TEN O'CLOCK'S TOO EARLY!

YOU AND FOUR-EYES TOO, MOMO.

MORE IMPORTANTLY, JIJI...

HAD I KNOWN THE EVIL EYE WAS THERE...

...I WOULDN'T HAVE LET YOU GO ON YOUR OWN.

...I'M SORRY.

SORZ.

I'M RESPONSIBLE.

I'M THE ONE WHO ASKED FOR YOUR HELP.

PLEASE DON'T APOLOGIZE.

HEY, QUIT IT.

IT'S WEIRD.

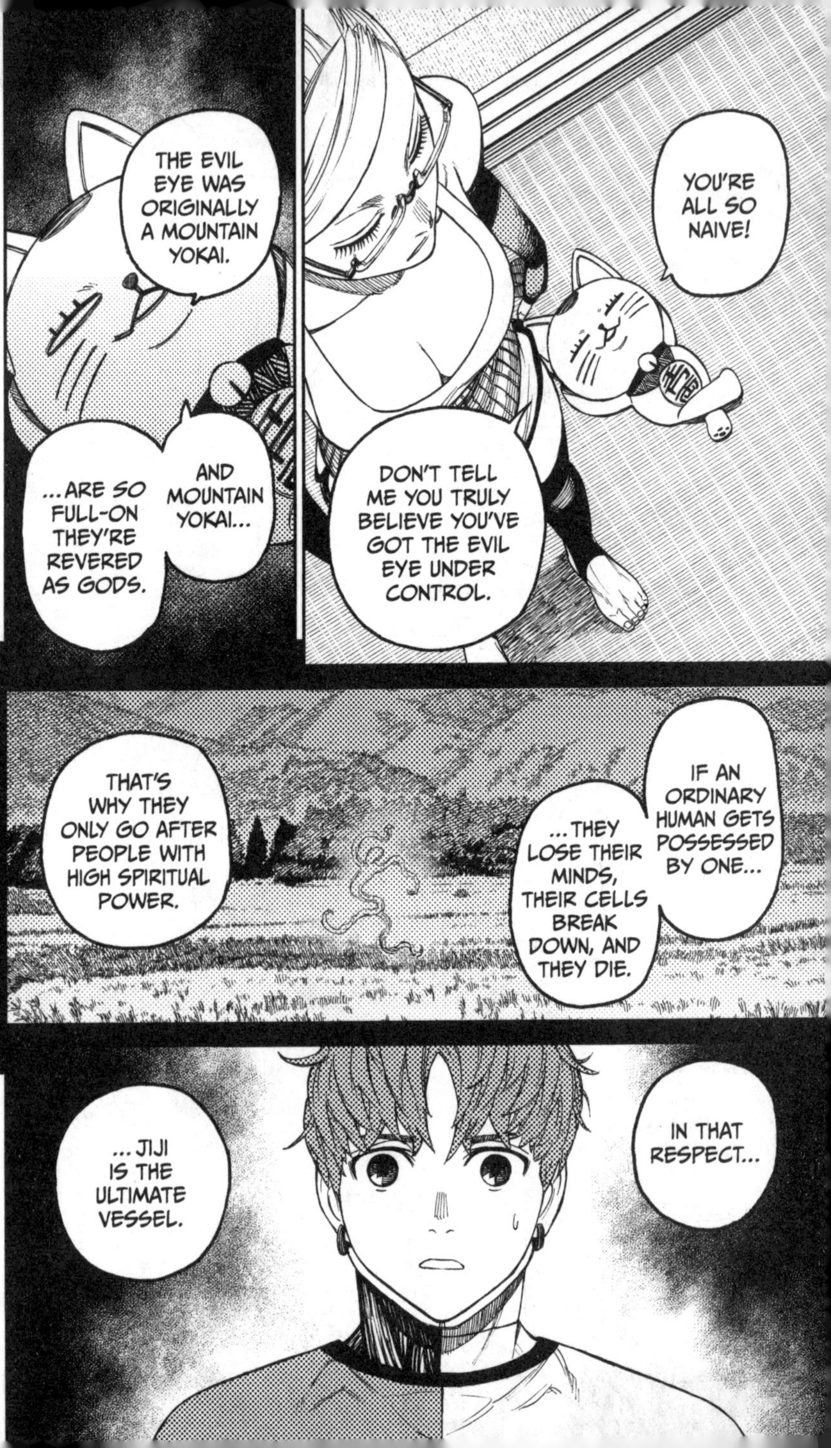
YOU'RE ALL SO NAIVE!
DON'T TELL ME YOU TRULY BELIEVE YOU'VE GOT THE EVIL EYE UNDER CONTROL.
THE EVIL EYE WAS ORIGINALLY A MOUNTAIN YOKAI.
AND MOUNTAIN YOKAI...
...ARE SO FULL-ON THEY'RE REVERED AS GODS.
IF AN ORDINARY HUMAN GETS POSSESSED BY ONE...
...THEY LOSE THEIR MINDS, THEIR CELLS BREAK DOWN, AND THEY DIE.
THAT'S WHY THEY ONLY GO AFTER PEOPLE WITH HIGH SPIRITUAL POWER.
IN THAT RESPECT...
...JIJI IS THE ULTIMATE VESSEL.

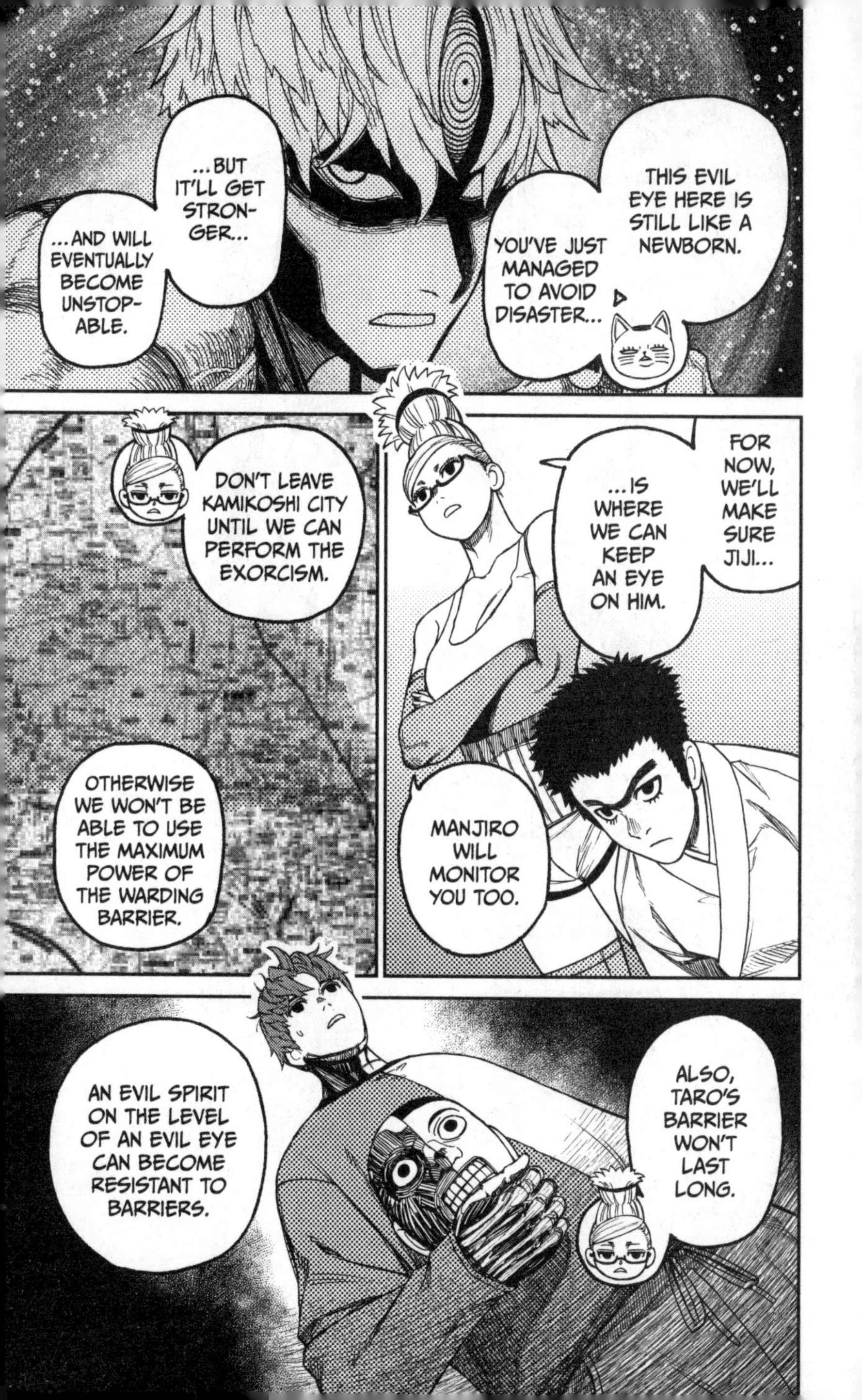
THIS EVIL EYE HERE IS STILL LIKE A NEWBORN.
YOU'VE JUST MANAGED TO AVOID DISASTER...
...BUT IT'LL GET STRONGER...
...AND WILL EVENTUALLY BECOME UNSTOPPABLE.
FOR NOW, WE'LL MAKE SURE JIJI...
...IS WHERE WE CAN KEEP AN EYE ON HIM.
MANJIRO WILL MONITOR YOU TOO.
DON'T LEAVE KAMIKOSHI CITY UNTIL WE CAN PERFORM THE EXORCISM.
OTHERWISE WE WON'T BE ABLE TO USE THE MAXIMUM POWER OF THE WARDING BARRIER.
ALSO, TARO'S BARRIER WON'T LAST LONG.
AN EVIL SPIRIT ON THE LEVEL OF AN EVIL EYE CAN BECOME RESISTANT TO BARRIERS.

EACH OF YOU...

...KEEP A HOT-WATER THERMOS ON YOU...

...SO YOU'RE PREPARED TO SPLASH HIM AT ANY TIME.

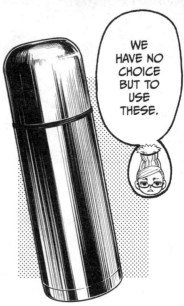

WE HAVE NO CHOICE BUT TO USE THESE.

WHEN YOU WASH YOUR HANDS, DRINK WATER, GO OUT IN THE RAIN...

YOU TAKE PLENTY OF CARE TOO, JIJI.

THE SLIGHTEST BIT OF COLD WATER WILL CAUSE YOU TO TRANSFORM.

WHERE WILL YOU LIVE, SHRIMP ALIEN?

I'LL BE LIVING AND WORKING AT A NEARBY DAIRY FARM.

THANKS TO MISS SEIKO.

IS IT AN ANTI-GRAVITY PROPULSION SYSTEM?!

HOW DOES THAT UFO ACTUALLY FLY?!

IT'S 🦐📶!

BY THE WAY, SHRIMP, SIR...

WHAT'S YOUR NAME?

ER...

ON EARTH IT WOULD BE PRONOUNCED...

IF ANYTHING COMES UP, FEEL FREE TO CALL ON ME AGAIN.

THANKS FOR COMING TO OUR RESCUE!

HOOH! HOOH!

UM, MR. SHRIMP?!

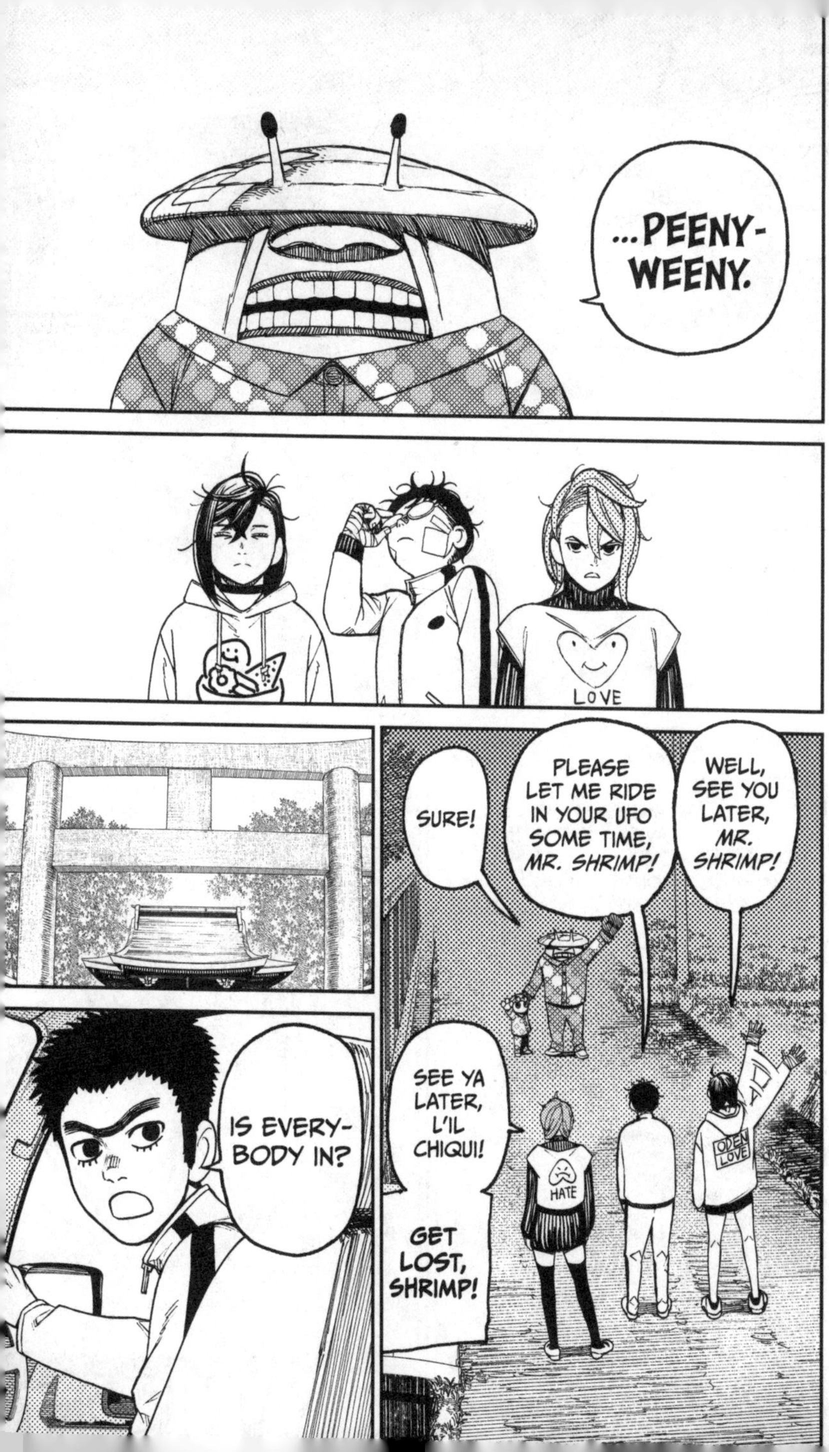
...PEENY-WEENY.
LOVE
WELL, SEE YOU LATER, MR. SHRIMP!
PLEASE LET ME RIDE IN YOUR UFO SOME TIME, MR. SHRIMP!
SURE!
SEE YA LATER, L'IL CHIQUI!
GET LOST, SHRIMP!
ODEN LOVE
HATE
IS EVERY-BODY IN?

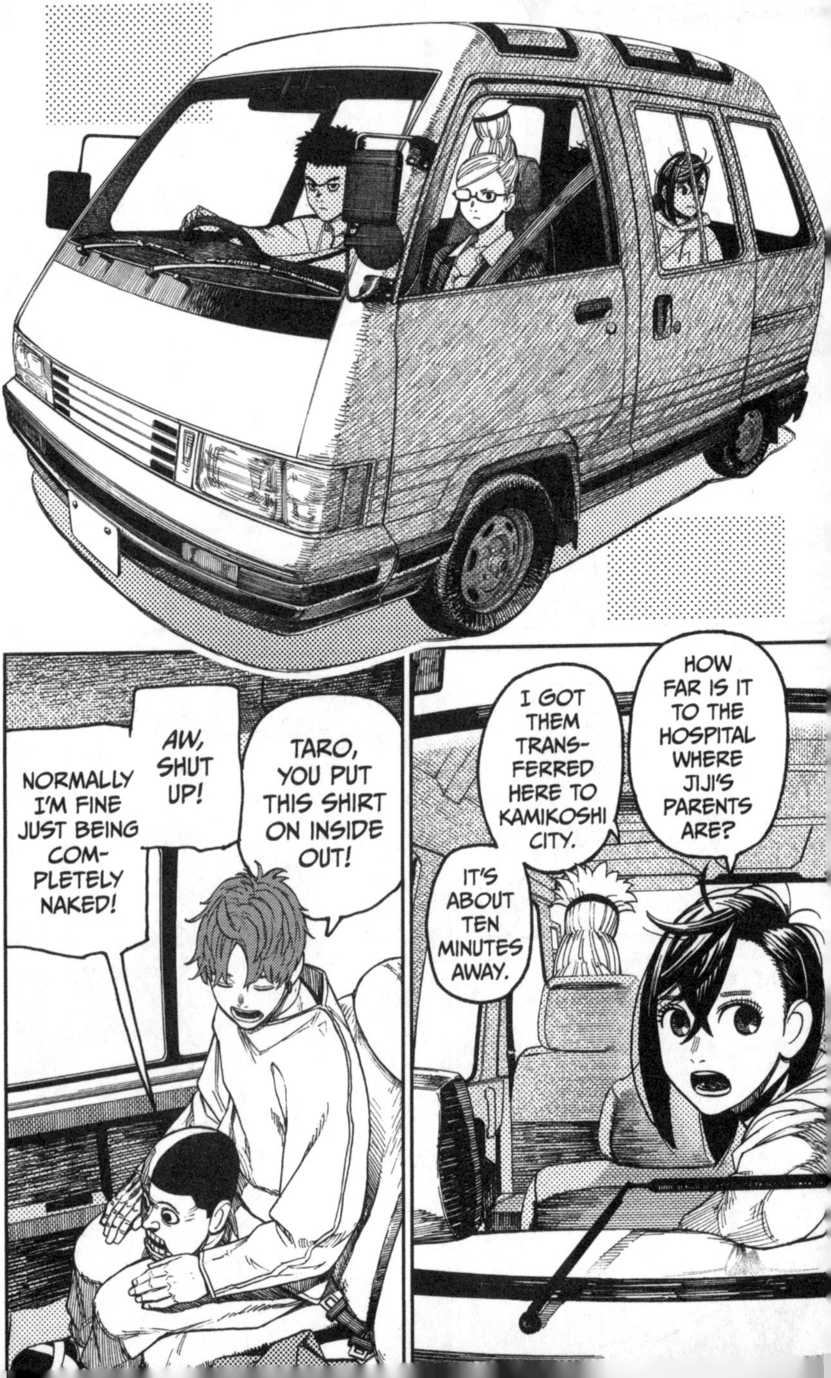
HOW FAR IS IT TO THE HOSPITAL WHERE JIJI'S PARENTS ARE?
I GOT THEM TRANSFERRED HERE TO KAMIKOSHI CITY.
IT'S ABOUT TEN MINUTES AWAY.
TARO, YOU PUT THIS SHIRT ON INSIDE OUT!
AW, SHUT UP!
NORMALLY I'M FINE JUST BEING COMPLETELY NAKED!

STEP

STEP

TAP

TAP

WHAT?

I'M NOT DOING ANYTHING.

UM... MISS AYASE...

WHAT ARE YOU DOING?

AW, SHUCKS, WHAT'RE YOU TALKING ABOUT?

I MEAN YOUR HAND...

WHATEVER THE GAME IS, I DON'T KNOW THE RULES...

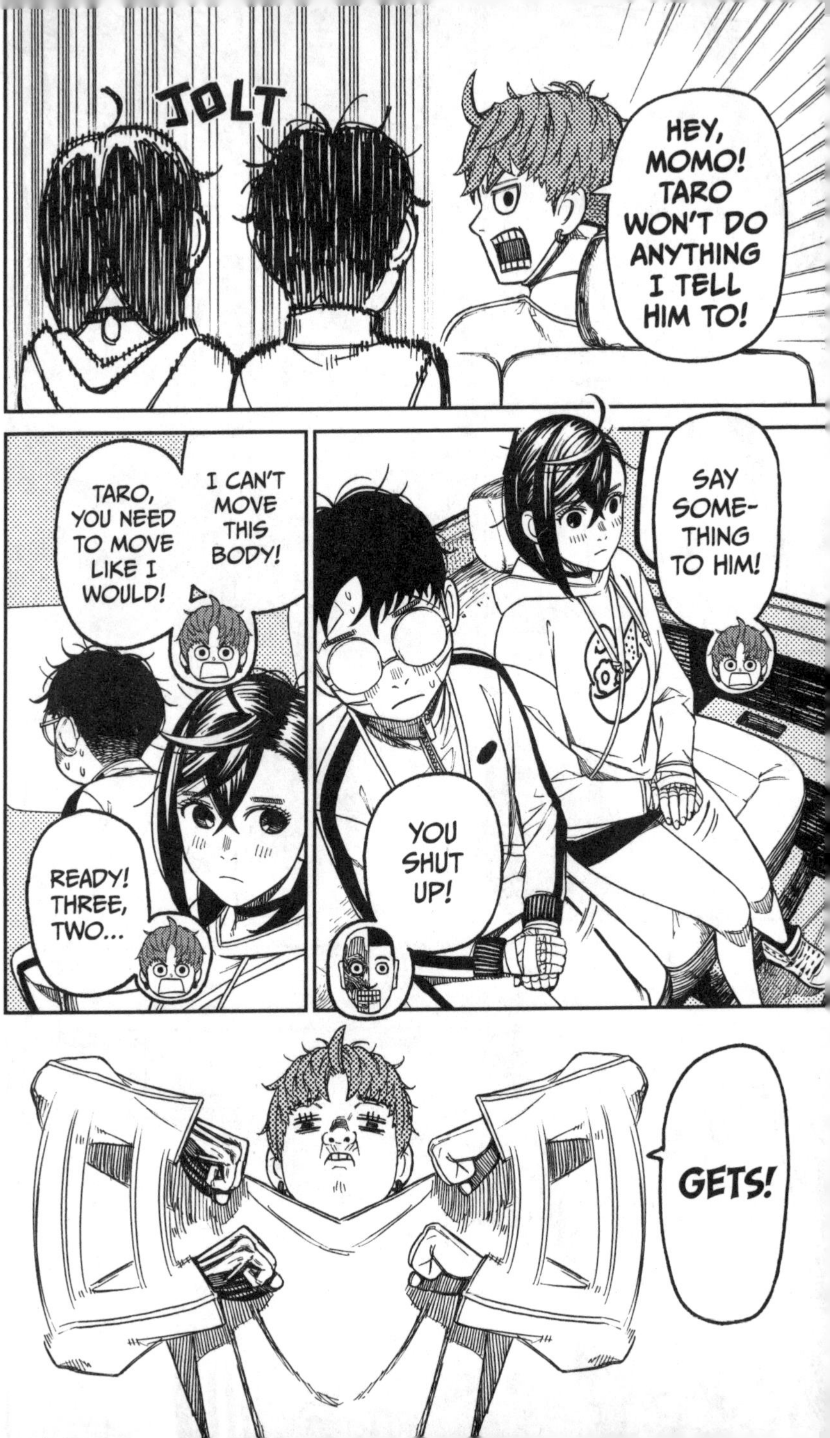
HEY, MOMO! TARO WON'T DO ANYTHING I TELL HIM TO!
JOLT
SAY SOME-THING TO HIM!
YOU SHUT UP!
I CAN'T MOVE THIS BODY!
TARO, YOU NEED TO MOVE LIKE I WOULD!
READY! THREE, TWO...
GETS!

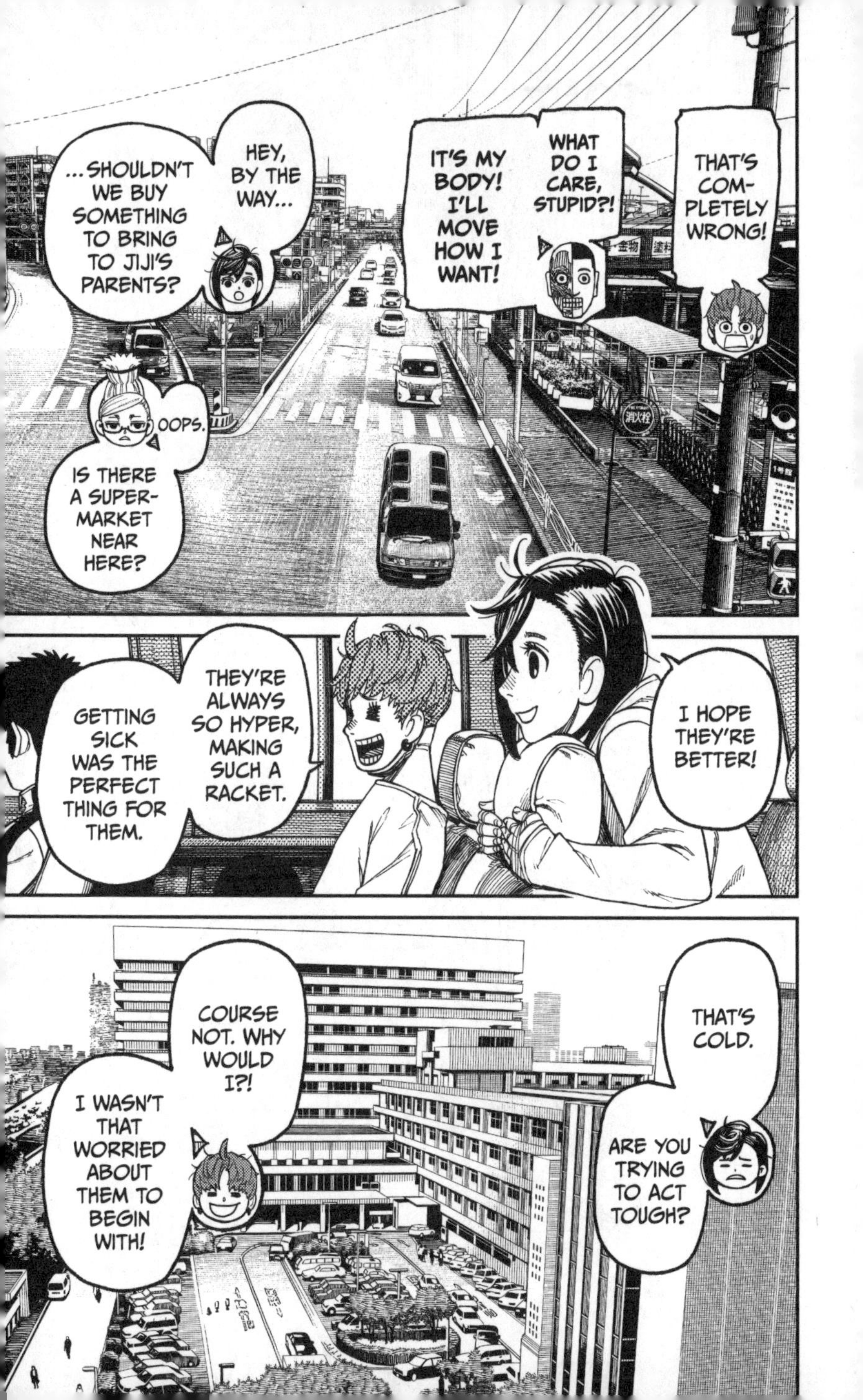
THAT'S COMPLETELY WRONG!
WHAT DO I CARE, STUPID?!
IT'S MY BODY! I'LL MOVE HOW I WANT!
消火栓
HEY, BY THE WAY...
...SHOULDN'T WE BUY SOMETHING TO BRING TO JIJI'S PARENTS?
OOPS.
IS THERE A SUPERMARKET NEAR HERE?
I HOPE THEY'RE BETTER!
THEY'RE ALWAYS SO HYPER, MAKING SUCH A RACKET.
GETTING SICK WAS THE PERFECT THING FOR THEM.
THAT'S COLD.
ARE YOU TRYING TO ACT TOUGH?
COURSE NOT. WHY WOULD I?!
I WASN'T THAT WORRIED ABOUT THEM TO BEGIN WITH!

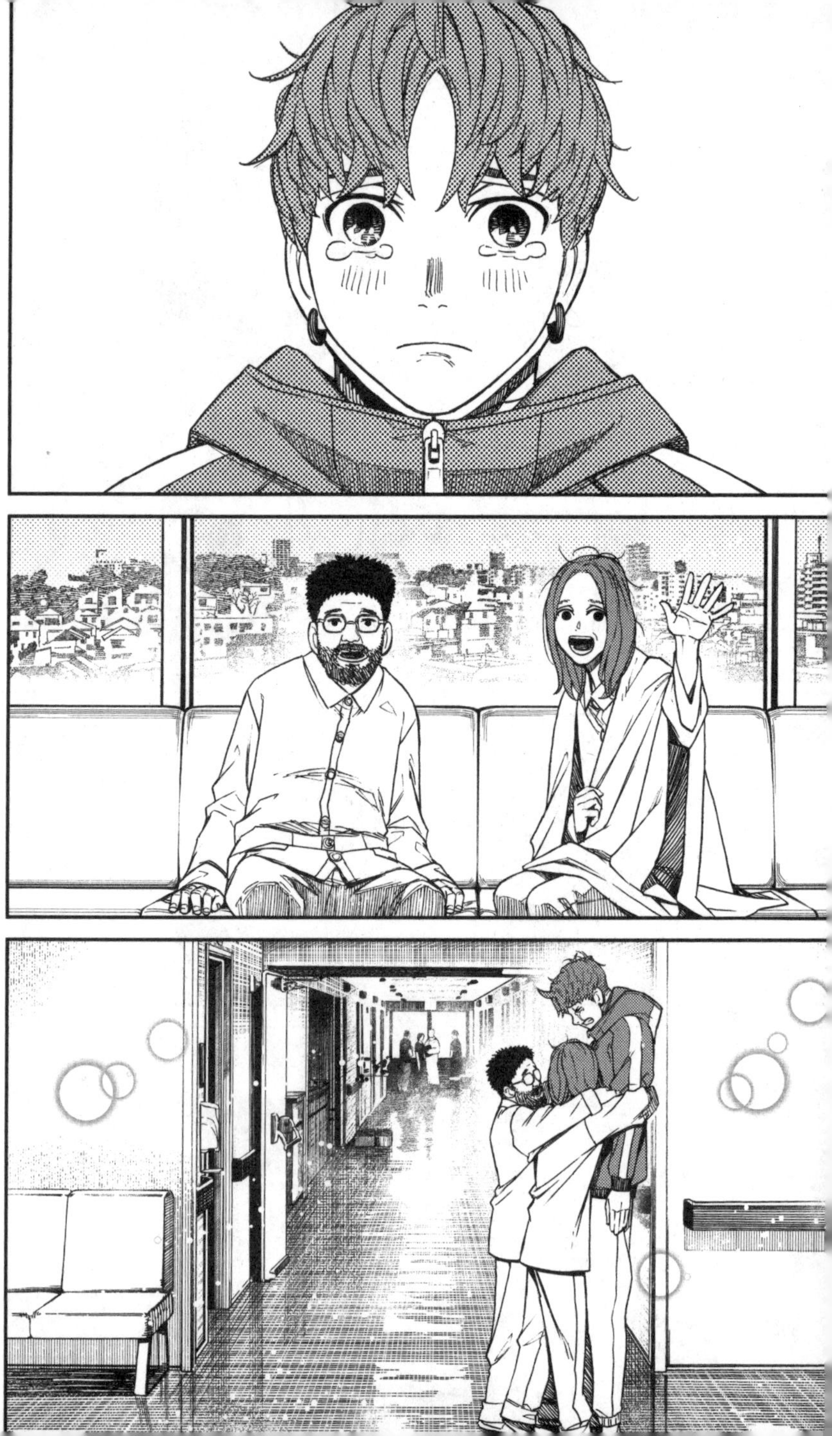

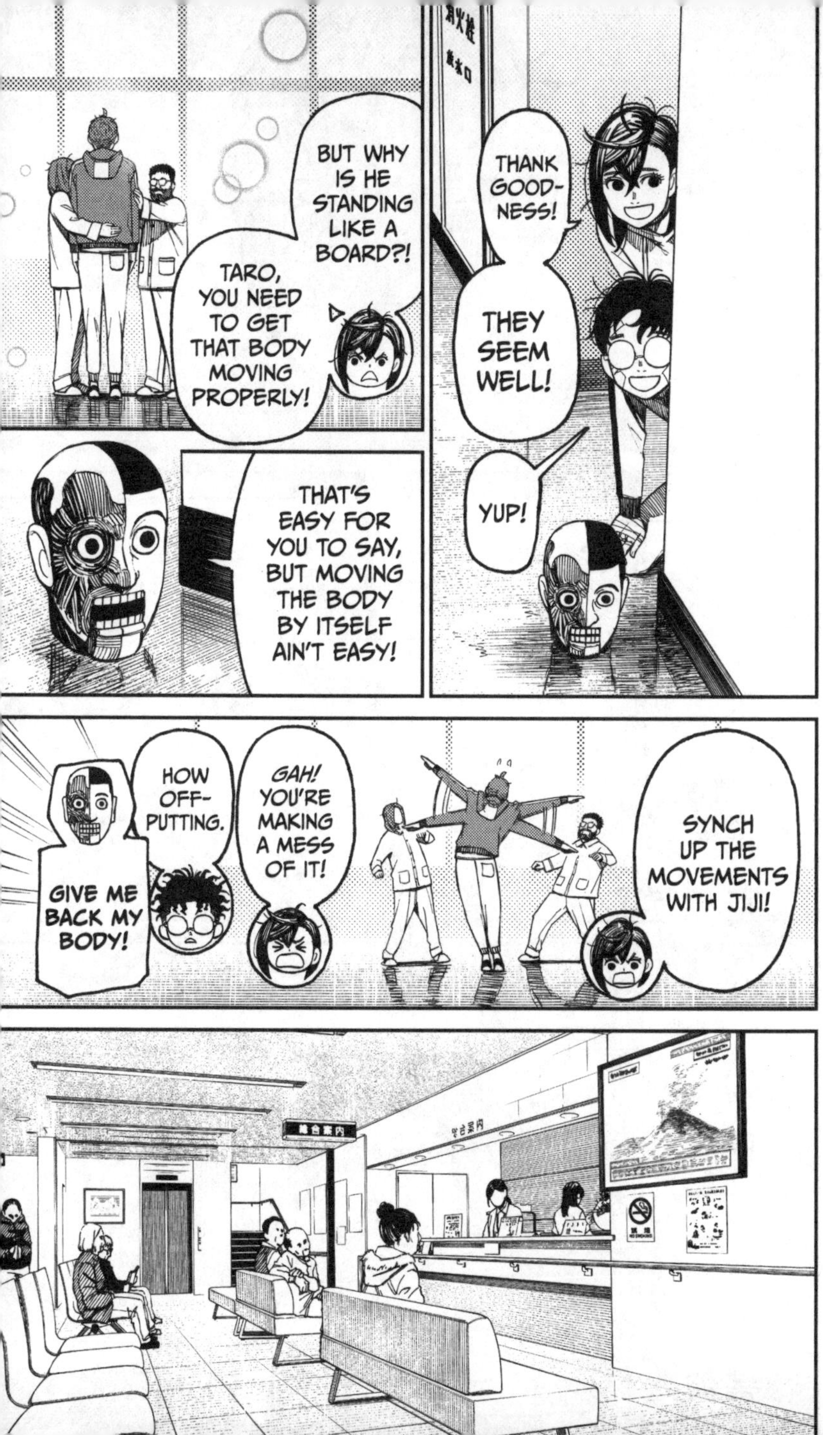
THANK GOODNESS!
THEY SEEM WELL!
YUP!
BUT WHY IS HE STANDING LIKE A BOARD?!
TARO, YOU NEED TO GET THAT BODY MOVING PROPERLY!
THAT'S EASY FOR YOU TO SAY, BUT MOVING THE BODY BY ITSELF AIN'T EASY!
SYNCH UP THE MOVEMENTS WITH JIJI!
GAH! YOU'RE MAKING A MESS OF IT!
HOW OFF-PUTTING.
GIVE ME BACK MY BODY!

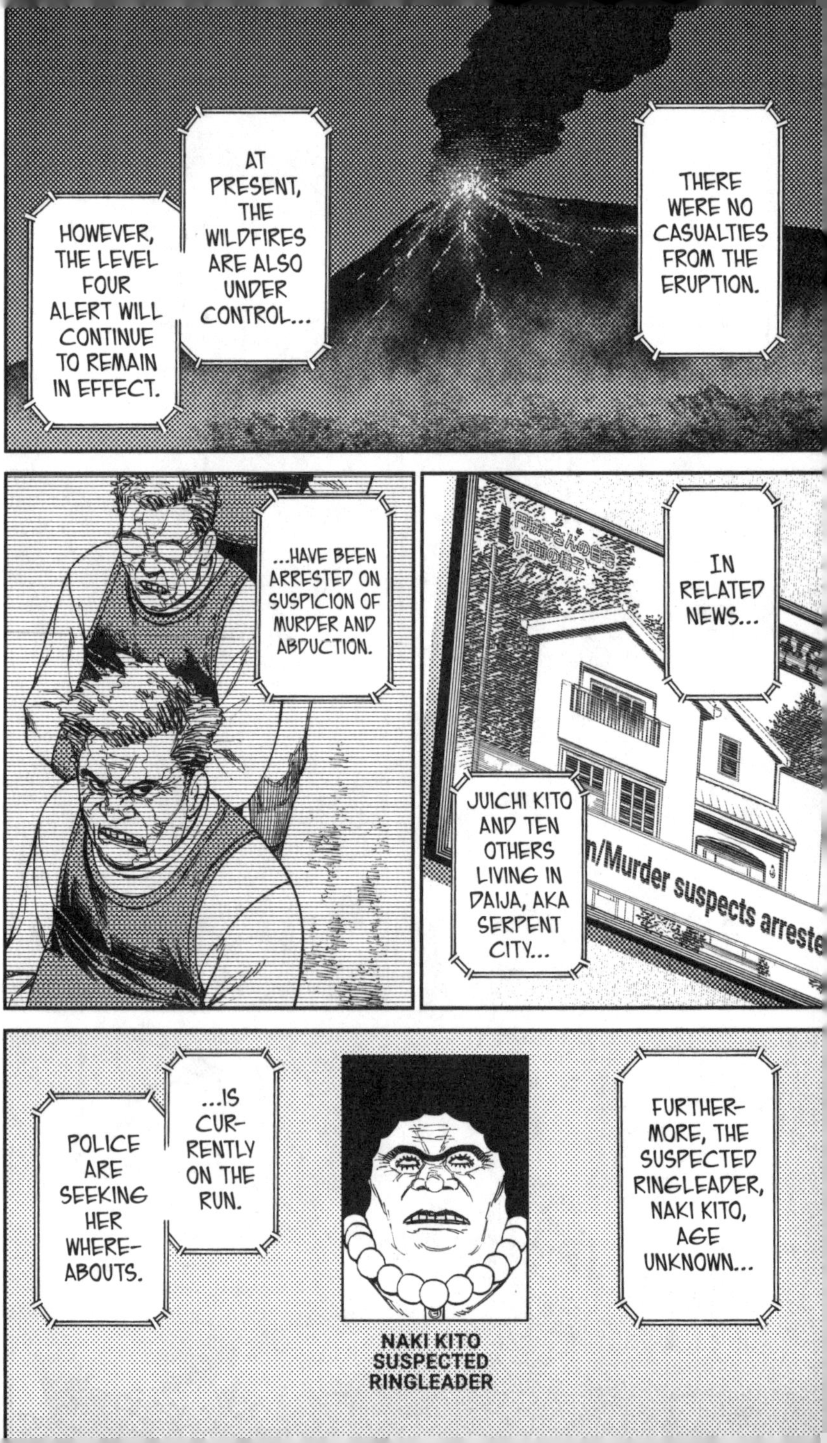
THERE WERE NO CASUALTIES FROM THE ERUPTION.
AT PRESENT, THE WILDFIRES ARE ALSO UNDER CONTROL...
HOWEVER, THE LEVEL FOUR ALERT WILL CONTINUE TO REMAIN IN EFFECT.
IN RELATED NEWS...
JUICHI KITO AND TEN OTHERS LIVING IN DAIJA, AKA SERPENT CITY...
n/Murder suspects arreste
...HAVE BEEN ARRESTED ON SUSPICION OF MURDER AND ABDUCTION.
FURTHER-MORE, THE SUSPECTED RINGLEADER, NAKI KITO, AGE UNKNOWN...
NAKI KITO SUSPECTED RINGLEADER
...IS CUR-RENTLY ON THE RUN.
POLICE ARE SEEKING HER WHERE-ABOUTS.

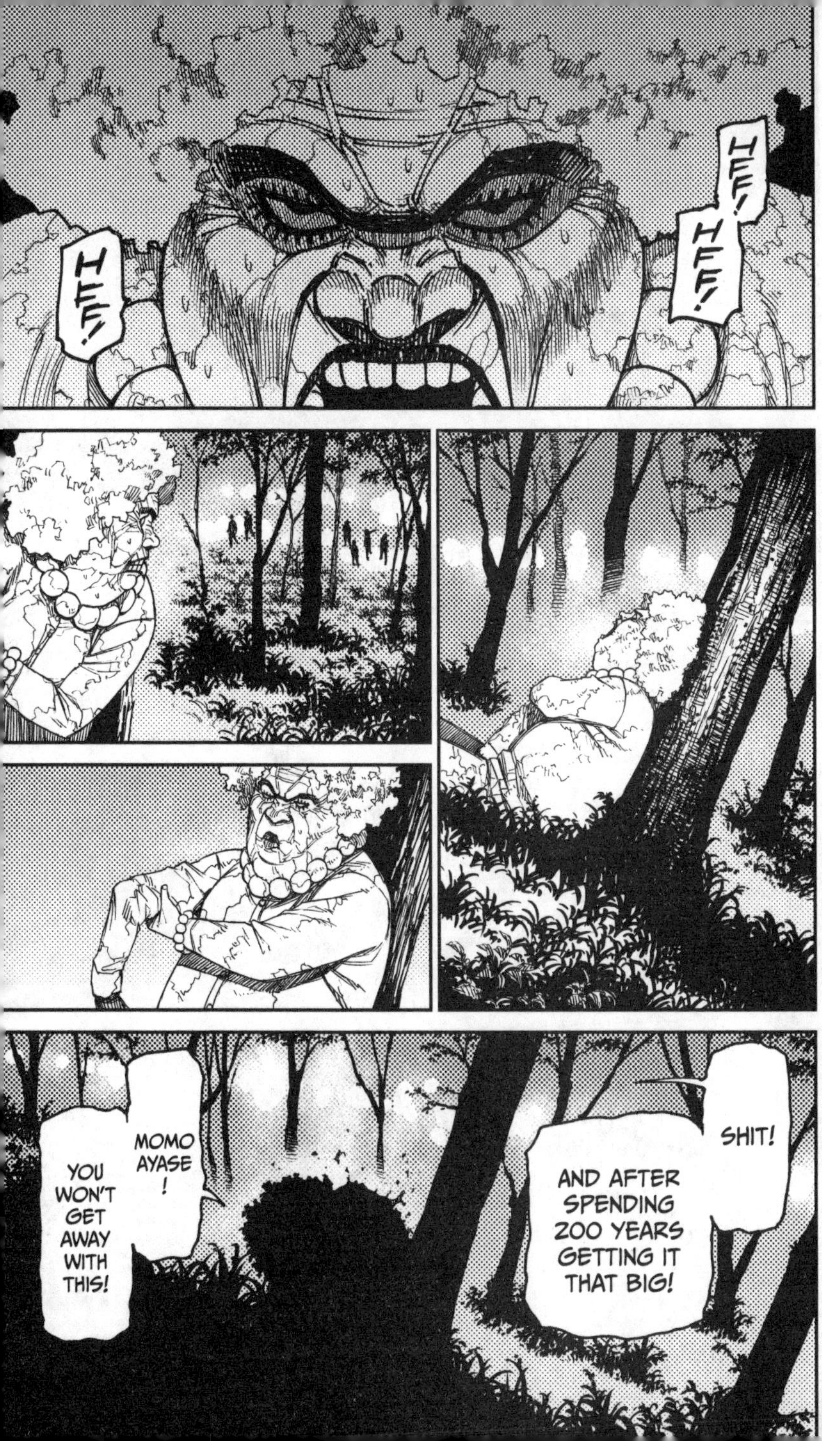
HEF! HEF!
HEF!
SHIT! AND AFTER SPENDING 200 YEARS GETTING IT THAT BIG!
MOMO AYASE! YOU WON'T GET AWAY WITH THIS!

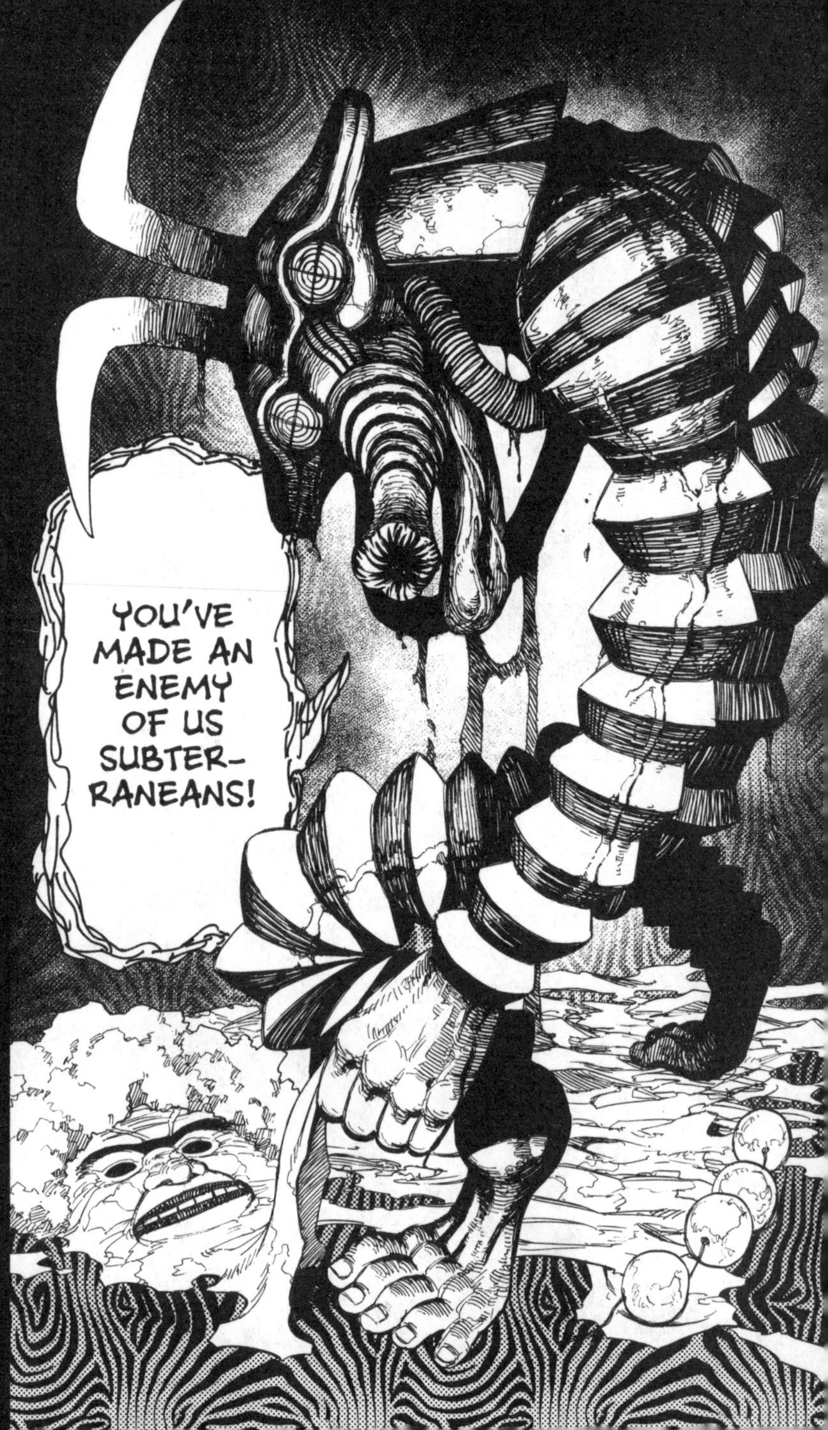
YOU'VE MADE AN ENEMY OF US SUBTER-RANEANS!

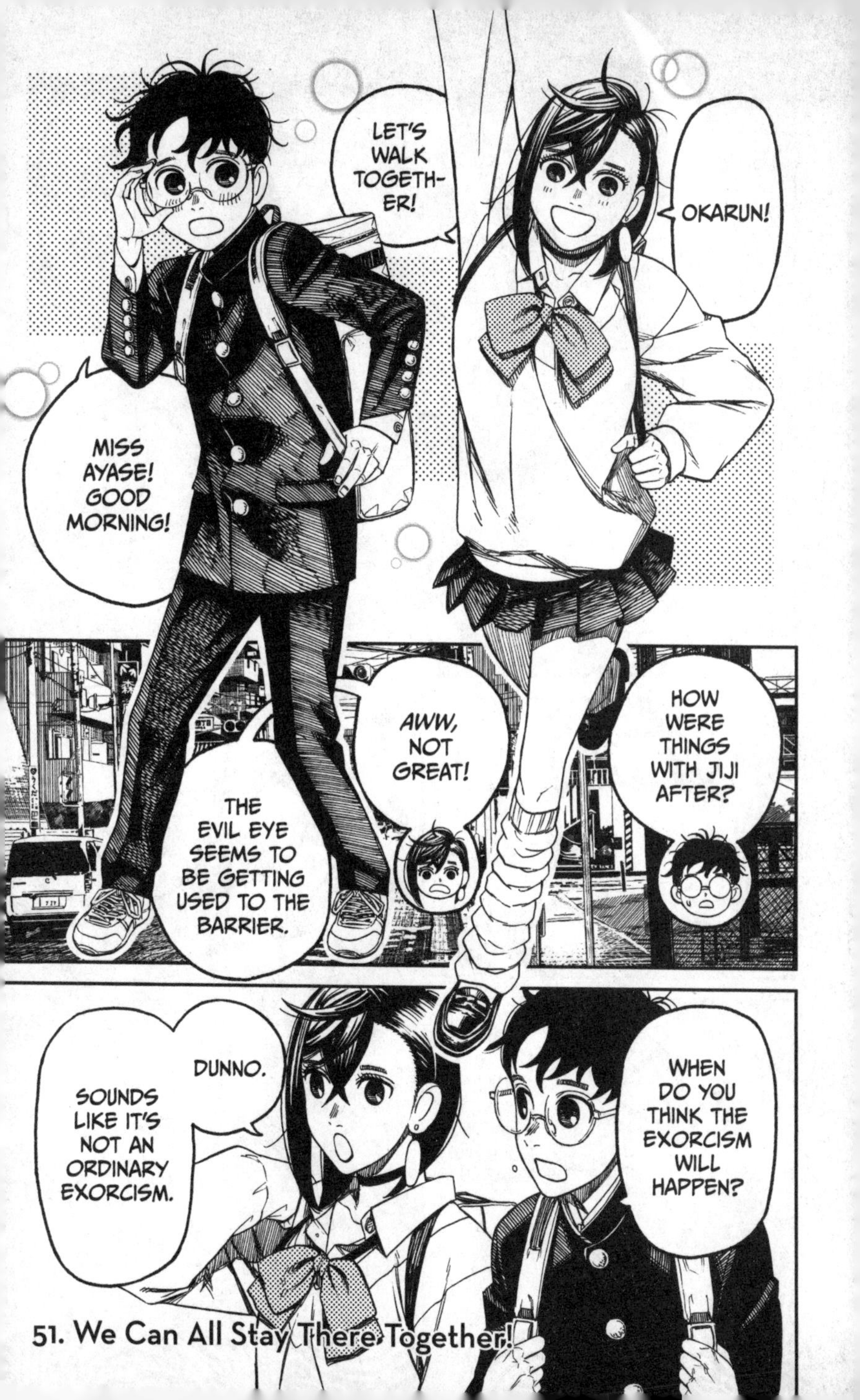
OKARUN!
LET'S WALK TOGETH-ER!
MISS AYASE! GOOD MORNING!
HOW WERE THINGS WITH JIJI AFTER?
AWW, NOT GREAT!
THE EVIL EYE SEEMS TO BE GETTING USED TO THE BARRIER.
WHEN DO YOU THINK THE EXORCISM WILL HAPPEN?
DUNNO.
SOUNDS LIKE IT'S NOT AN ORDINARY EXORCISM.

51. We Can All Stay There Together!

YOU KNOW THOSE HAYASHI PERFORMERS THEY HAVE AT, LIKE, FESTIVALS AND STUFF?

THEY'RE NEEDED IN ORDER TO KEEP THE EVIL EYE ENTERTAINED.

APPARENTLY THAT MAKES IT EASIER TO EXPEL IT FROM THE BODY.

WE'LL HAVE TO KEEP IT IN CHECK OURSELVES.

SO IF TARO'S BARRIER STOPS BEING EFFECTIVE, THEN WE'LL HAVE TO DEAL WITH THE EVIL EYE AGAIN?!

BUT IT SEEMS LIKE THERE AREN'T ANY AROUND TO PERFORM THE HAYASHI MUSIC FOR US.

BY THE WAY, THERE'S A FAVOR I WANTED TO ASK, OKARUN.

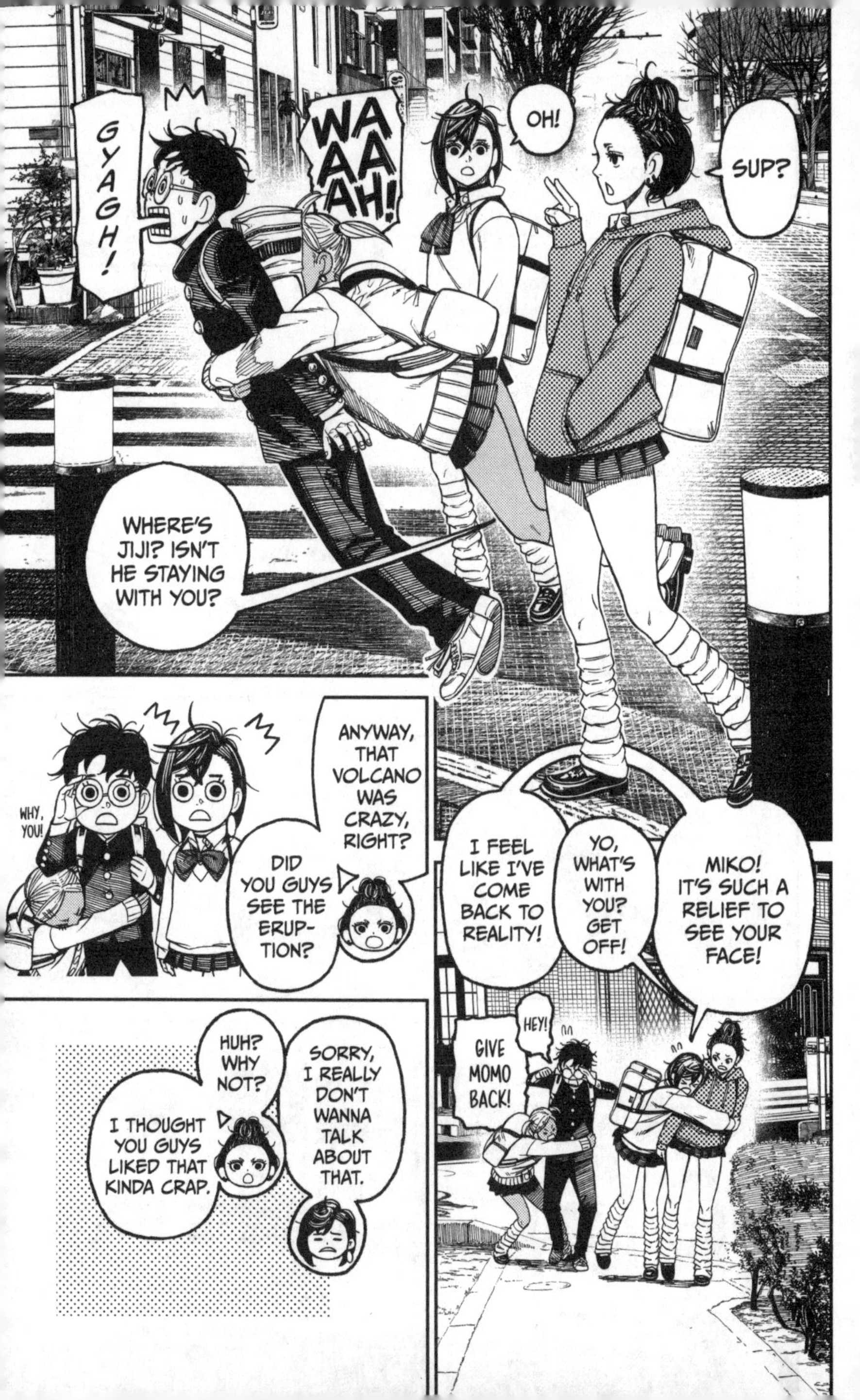
SUP?
OH!
WAAAAAH!
GYAGH!
WHERE'S JIJI? ISN'T HE STAYING WITH YOU?
MIKO! IT'S SUCH A RELIEF TO SEE YOUR FACE!
YO, WHAT'S WITH YOU? GET OFF!
I FEEL LIKE I'VE COME BACK TO REALITY!
HEY!
GIVE MOMO BACK!
ANYWAY, THAT VOLCANO WAS CRAZY, RIGHT?
DID YOU GUYS SEE THE ERUPTION?
WHY, YOU!
SORRY, I REALLY DON'T WANNA TALK ABOUT THAT.
HUH? WHY NOT?
I THOUGHT YOU GUYS LIKED THAT KINDA CRAP.

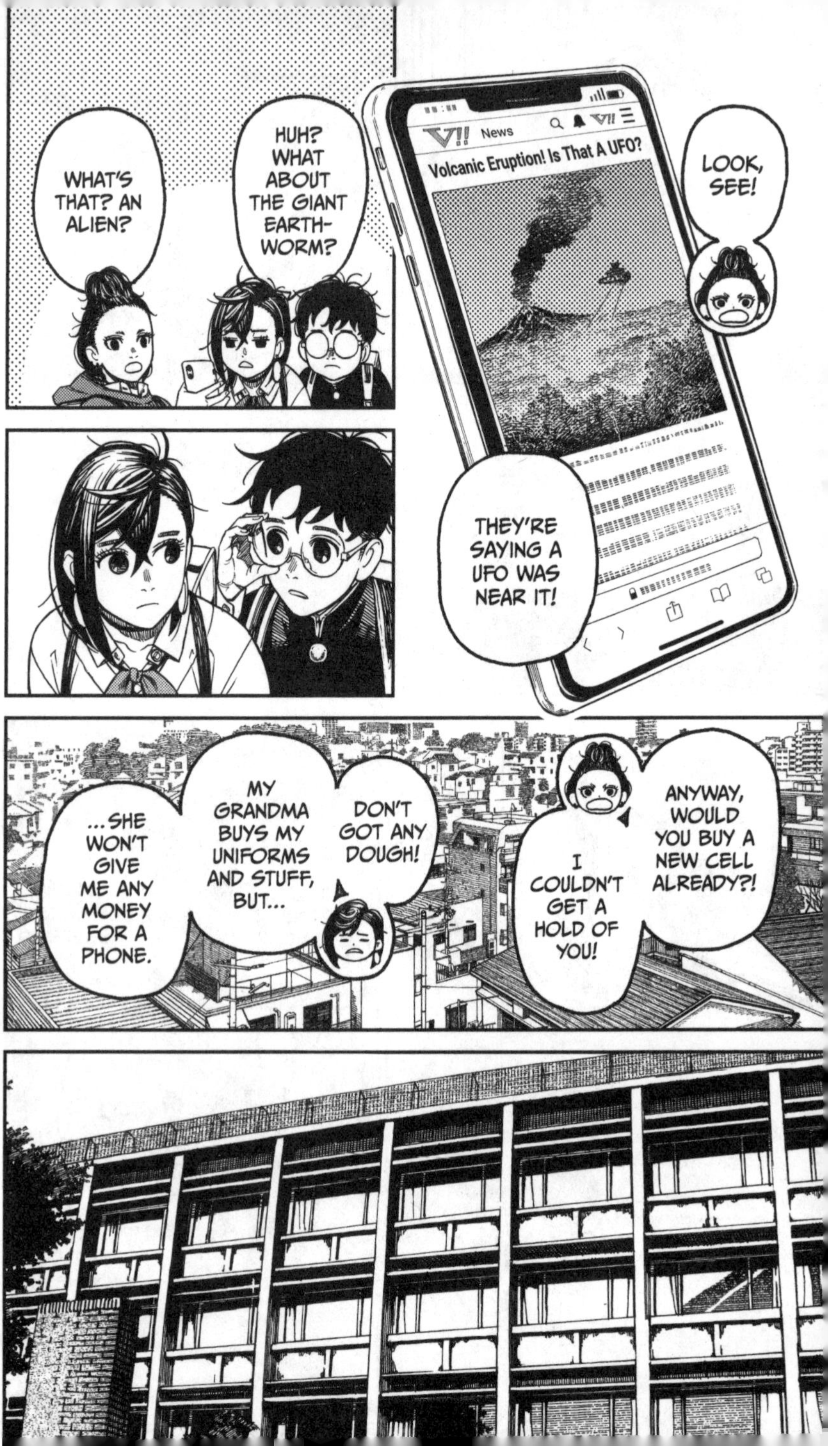
LOOK, SEE!
V!! News
Volcanic Eruption! Is That A UFO?
THEY'RE SAYING A UFO WAS NEAR IT!
HUH? WHAT ABOUT THE GIANT EARTH-WORM?
WHAT'S THAT? AN ALIEN?
ANYWAY, WOULD YOU BUY A NEW CELL ALREADY?!
I COULDN'T GET A HOLD OF YOU!
DON'T GOT ANY DOUGH!
MY GRANDMA BUYS MY UNIFORMS AND STUFF, BUT...
...SHE WON'T GIVE ME ANY MONEY FOR A PHONE.

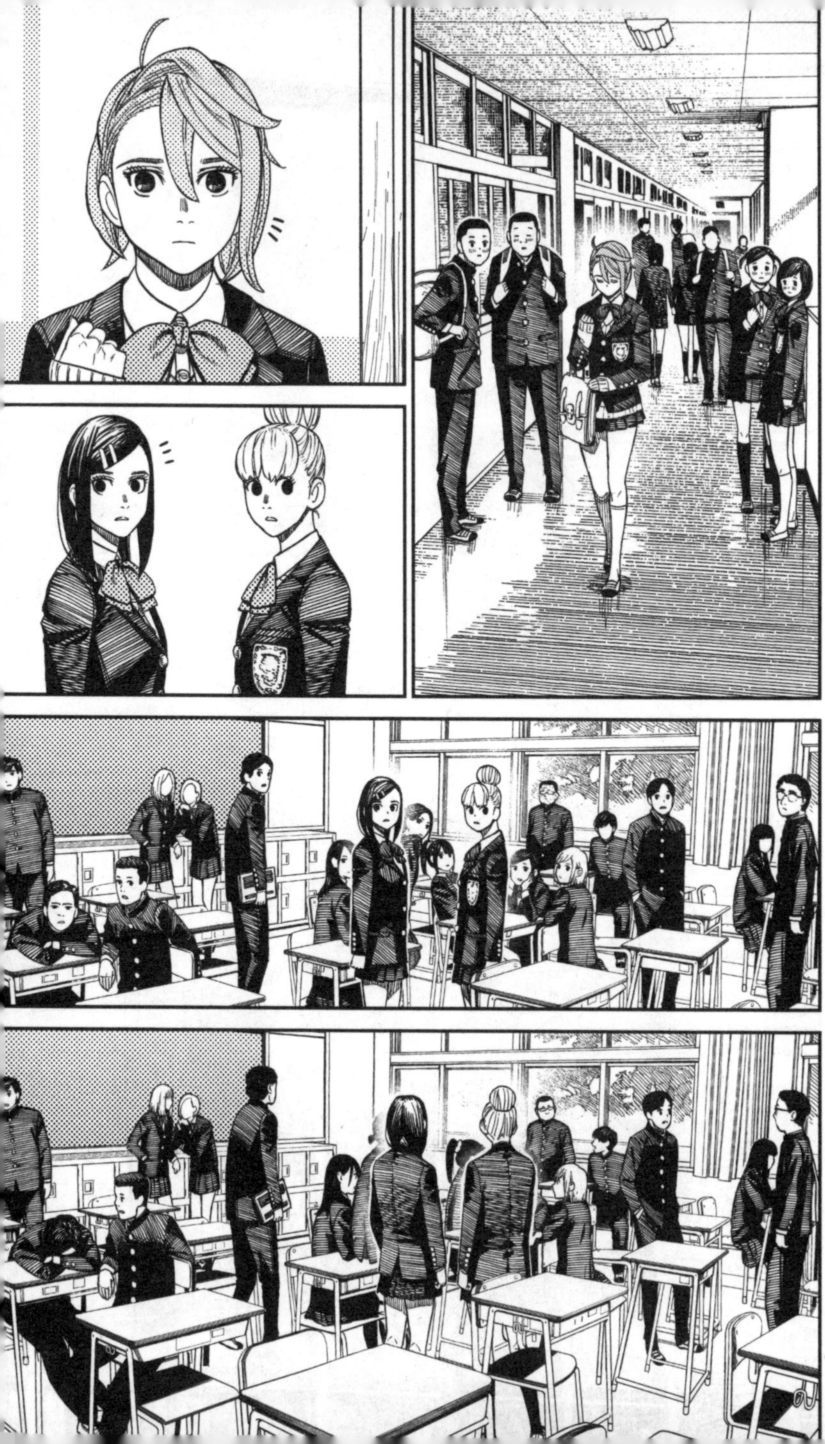

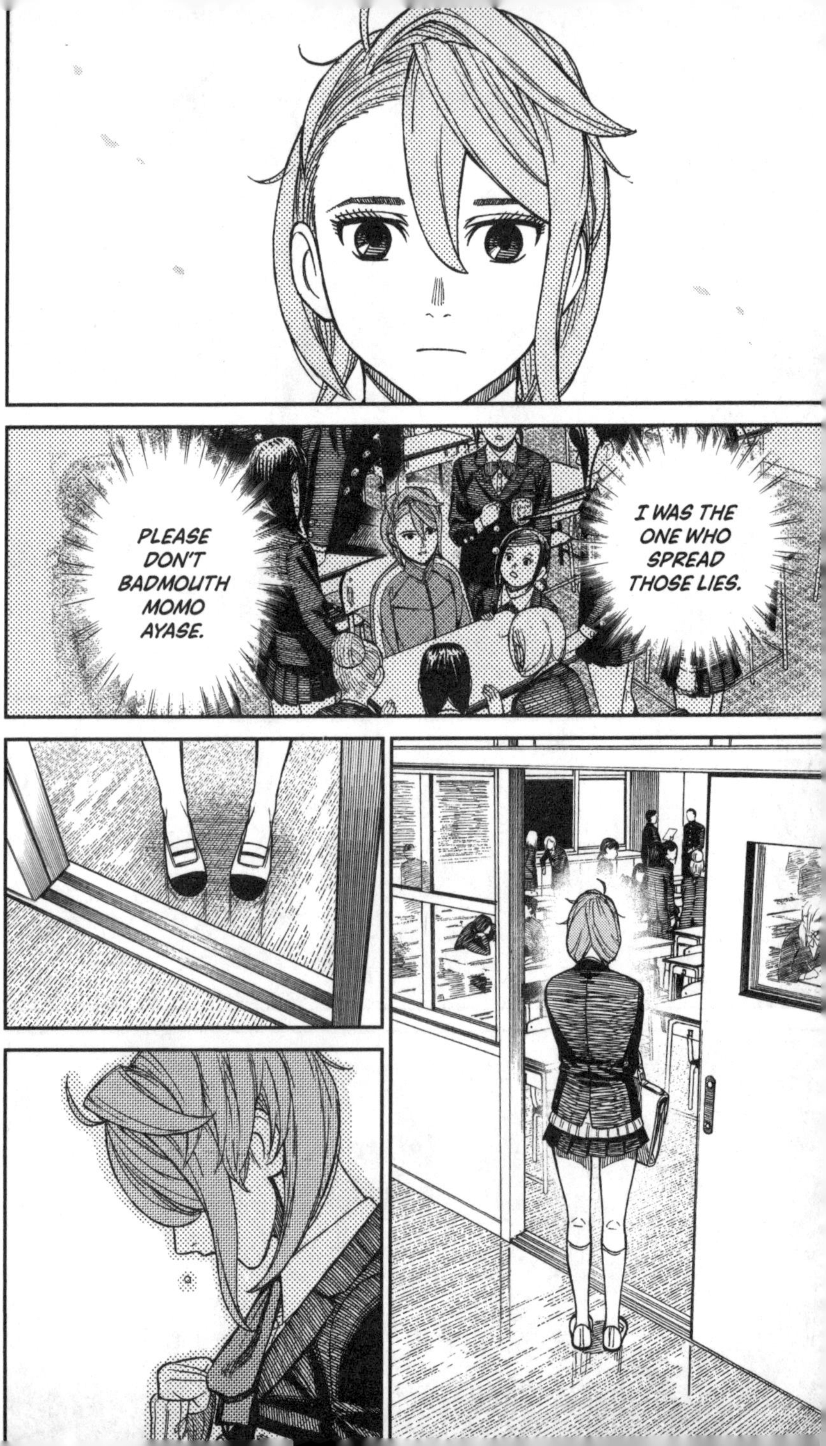
I WAS THE ONE WHO SPREAD THOSE LIES.
PLEASE DON'T BADMOUTH MOMO AYASE.

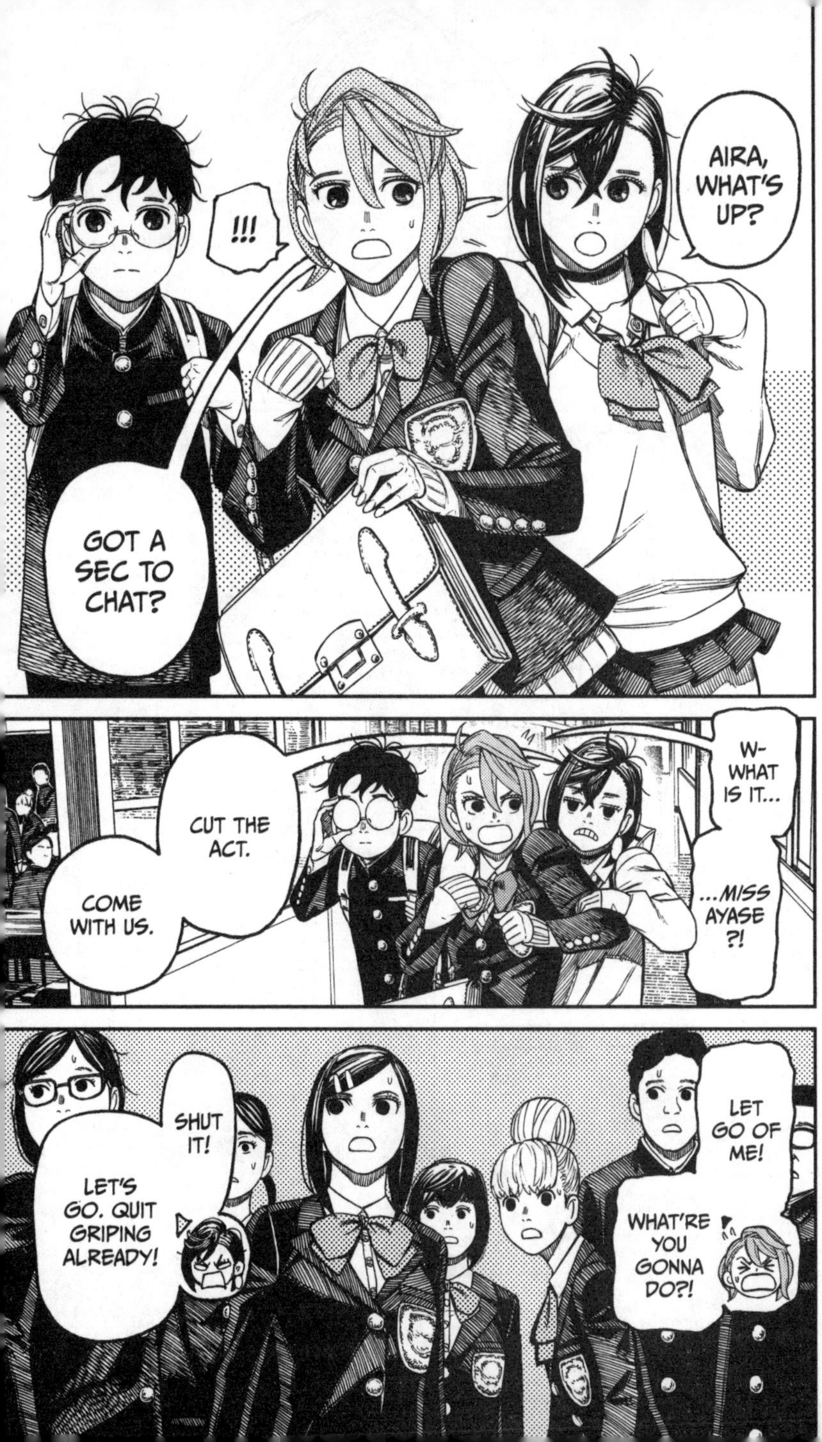
AIRA, WHAT'S UP?
!!!
GOT A SEC TO CHAT?
W- WHAT IS IT...
...MISS AYASE?!
CUT THE ACT.
COME WITH US.
LET GO OF ME!
WHAT'RE YOU GONNA DO?!
SHUT IT!
LET'S GO. QUIT GRIPING ALREADY!

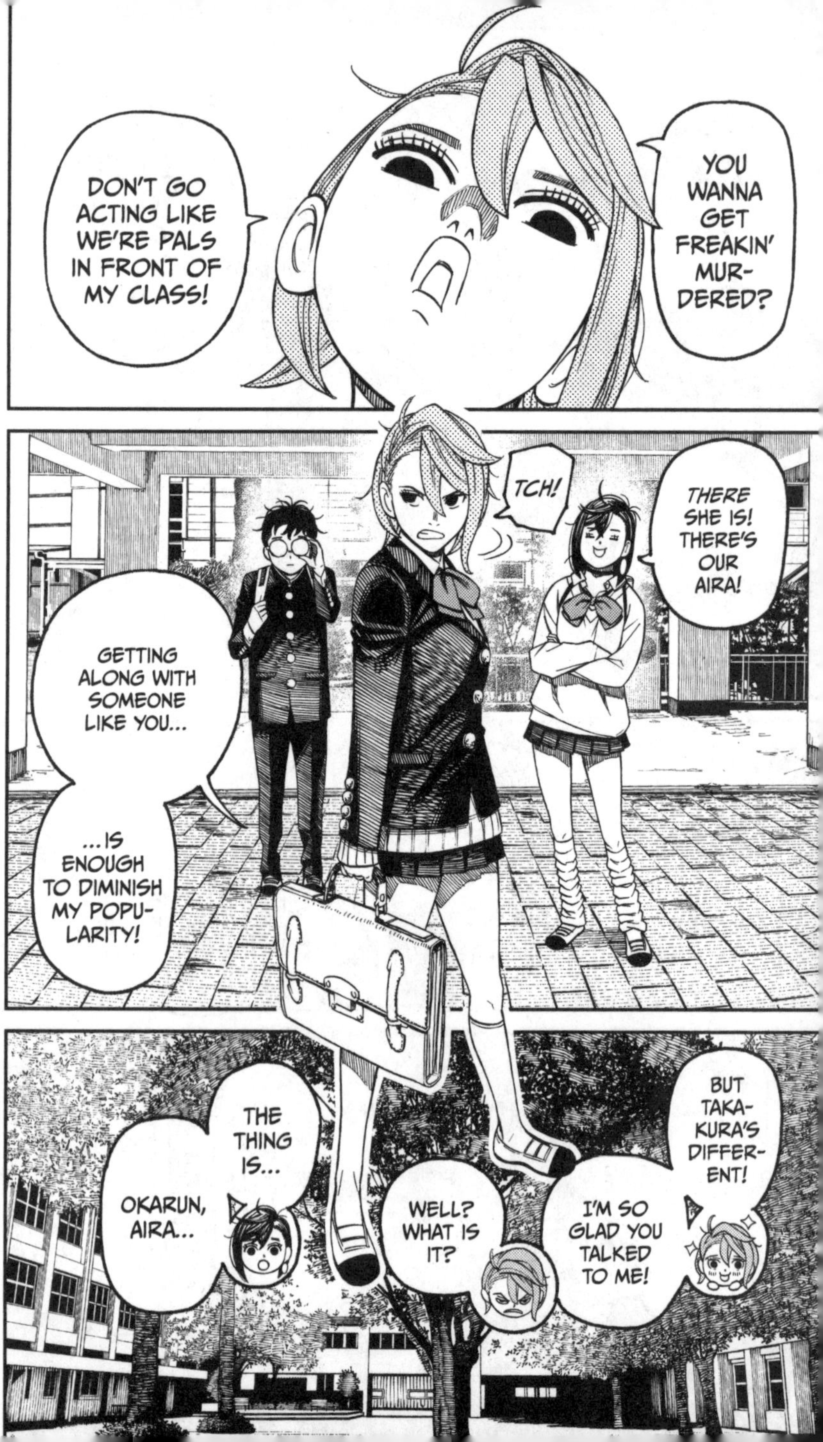
YOU WANNA GET FREAKIN' MUR-DERED?
DON'T GO ACTING LIKE WE'RE PALS IN FRONT OF MY CLASS!
THERE SHE IS! THERE'S OUR AIRA!
TCH!
GETTING ALONG WITH SOMEONE LIKE YOU...
...IS ENOUGH TO DIMINISH MY POPU-LARITY!
BUT TAKA-KURA'S DIFFER-ENT!
I'M SO GLAD YOU TALKED TO ME!
WELL? WHAT IS IT?
THE THING IS...
OKARUN, AIRA...

I MEAN, JUST THE THOUGHT OF IT ... ...MAKES ME SICK.

THIS IS THE WORST!

WELL, I GUESS THERE'S NO OTHER WAY...

CAN'T BE HELPED.

THIS TOTALLY SUCKS!

AGH! NO, NO, NO!

WHY HAS IT COME TO THIS?!

...

I GUESS IT'S UNAVOID-ABLE, HUH?

C'EST LA VIE, AS THEY SAY...

WE'LL DO IT!

IF YOU CAN'T, THAT'S FINE. I'LL—

AIRA, IF YOU'VE GOT PLANS WITH FRIENDS, YOU CAN COME OVER WHENEVER.

HOW ABOUT STARTING TONIGHT?

COOL!

TO-NIGHT ?!

HUH?! WHAT DO I DO?!

HUH?

...YOU DON'T HAVE TO FORCE YOURSELF TO HANG OUT WITH ME.

AIRA. IF SOMETHING'S GOING ON BETWEEN YOU AND YOUR FRIENDS BECAUSE OF ME...

NO...

I DON'T NEED TO HEAR THAT FROM YOU.

NOTHING LIKE THAT.

....

IT'S MY FAULT...

YOU'VE GOT NOTHING TO DO WITH IT.

AH!

THE ARM'S COME OFF.

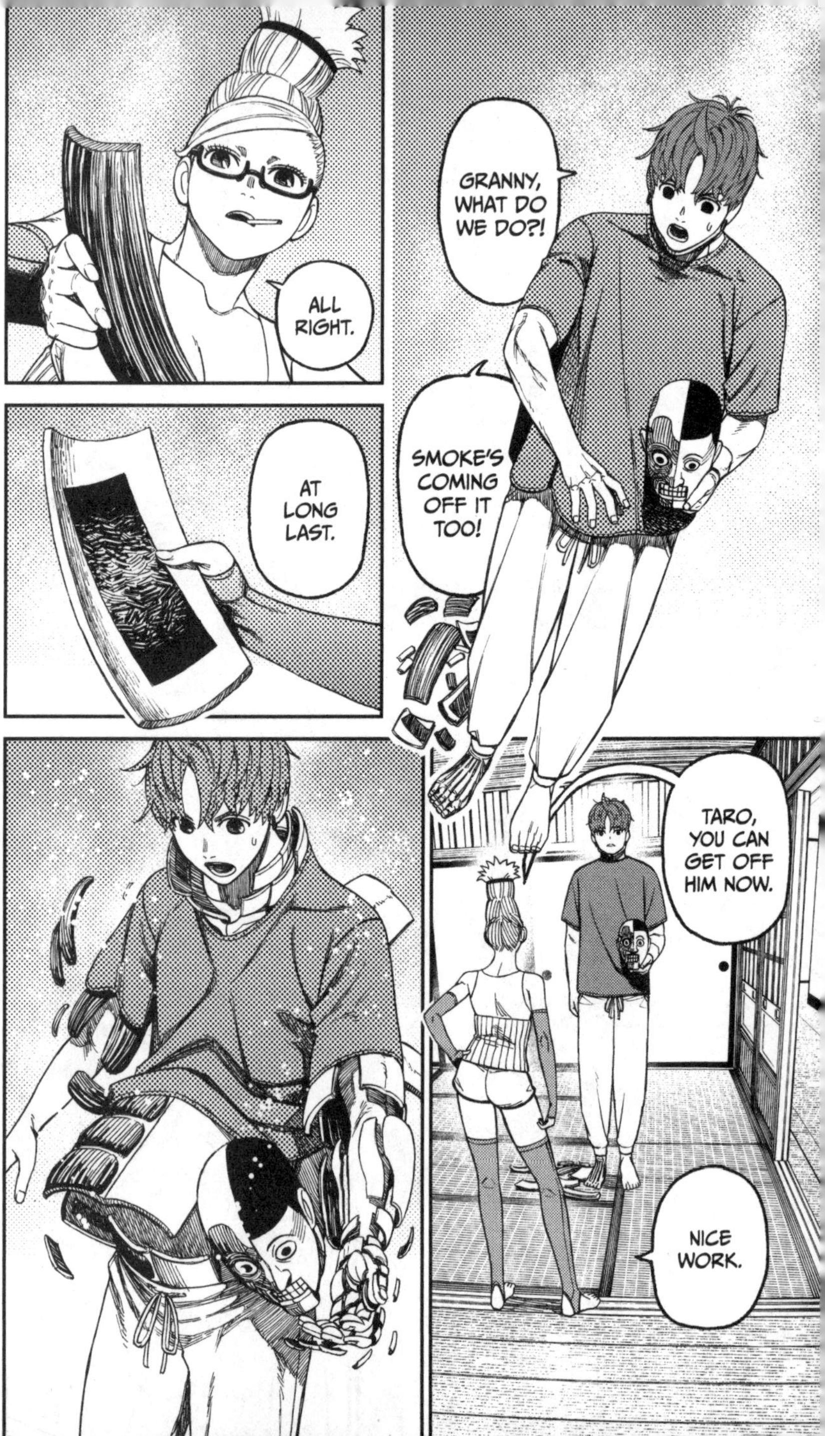
GRANNY, WHAT DO WE DO?!
SMOKE'S COMING OFF IT TOO!
ALL RIGHT.
AT LONG LAST.
TARO, YOU CAN GET OFF HIM NOW.
NICE WORK.

JIJI, FROM HERE ON OUT, YOU'LL HAVE NO SUPPORT.

YOU NEED TO BE EVEN MORE CAREFUL OF WATER THAN YOU HAVE BEEN.

ONLY WASH YOUR HANDS IN HOT WATER.

RIGHT!

YOU SAVED ME!

THANK YOU, TARO!

GEEZ, AM I BUSHED!

I'VE BROUGHT THE WHOLE GANG.

PARDON THE INTRUSION!

I'M HOME!

AH.

YOU'RE BACK. PERFECT.

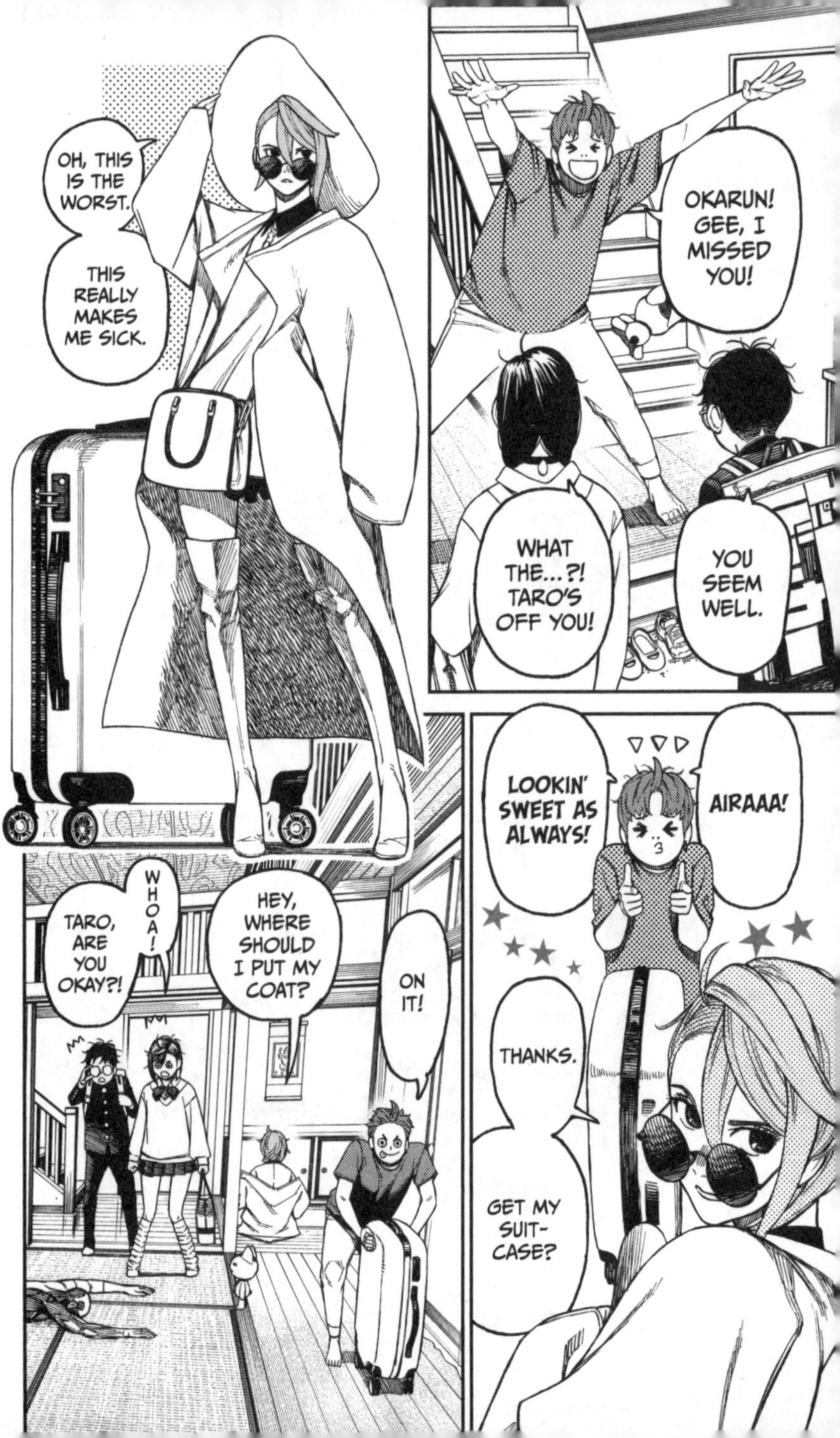
OKARUN! GEE, I MISSED YOU!
WHAT THE...?! TARO'S OFF YOU!
YOU SEEM WELL.
OH, THIS IS THE WORST.
THIS REALLY MAKES ME SICK.
AIRAAA!
LOOKIN' SWEET AS ALWAYS!
THANKS.
GET MY SUIT-CASE?
ON IT!
HEY, WHERE SHOULD I PUT MY COAT?
WHOA!
TARO, ARE YOU OKAY?!

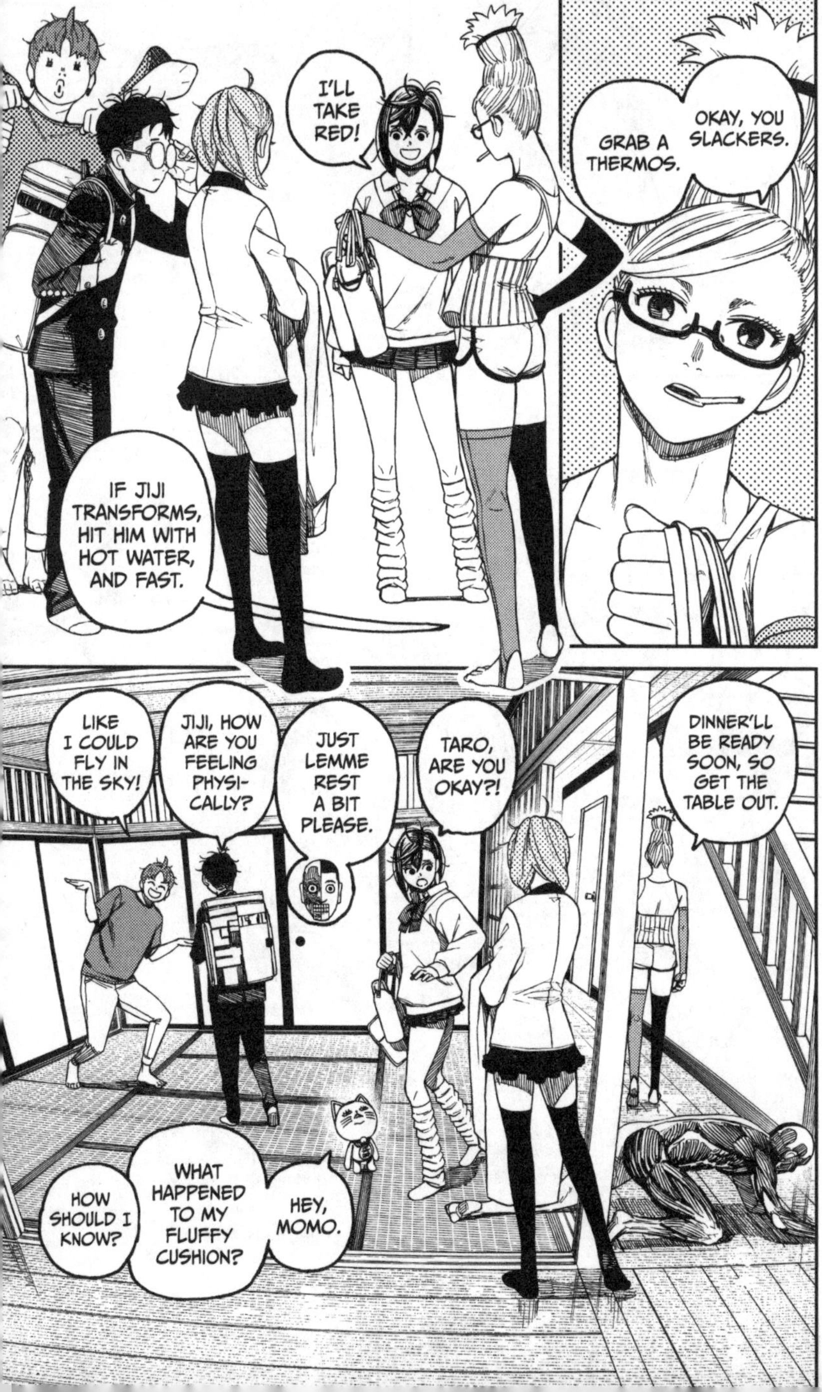
OKAY, YOU SLACKERS.
GRAB A THERMOS.
I'LL TAKE RED!
IF JIJI TRANSFORMS, HIT HIM WITH HOT WATER, AND FAST.
DINNER'LL BE READY SOON, SO GET THE TABLE OUT.
TARO, ARE YOU OKAY?!
JUST LEMME REST A BIT PLEASE.
JIJI, HOW ARE YOU FEELING PHYSI-CALLY?
LIKE I COULD FLY IN THE SKY!
HEY, MOMO.
WHAT HAPPENED TO MY FLUFFY CUSHION?
HOW SHOULD I KNOW?

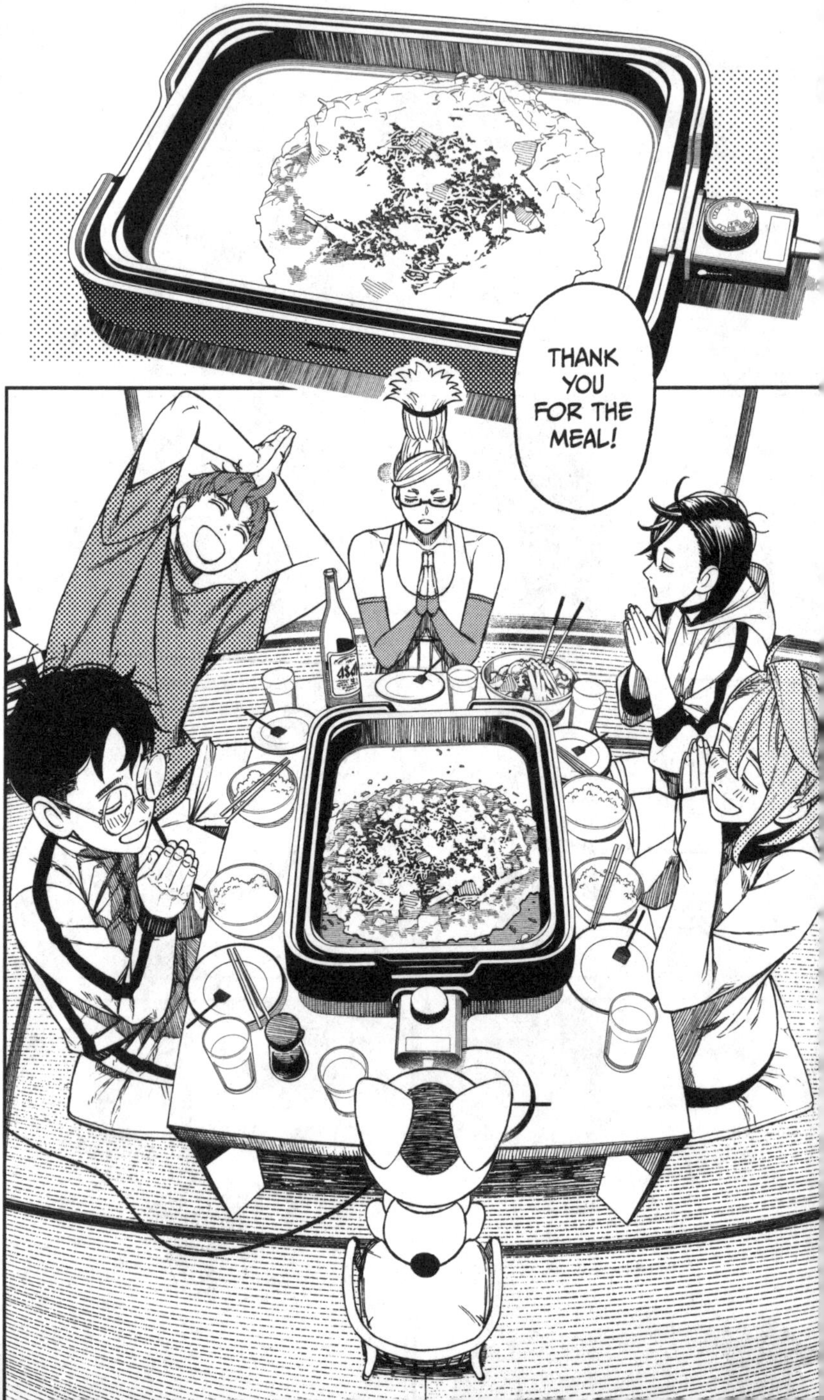
THANK YOU FOR THE MEAL!

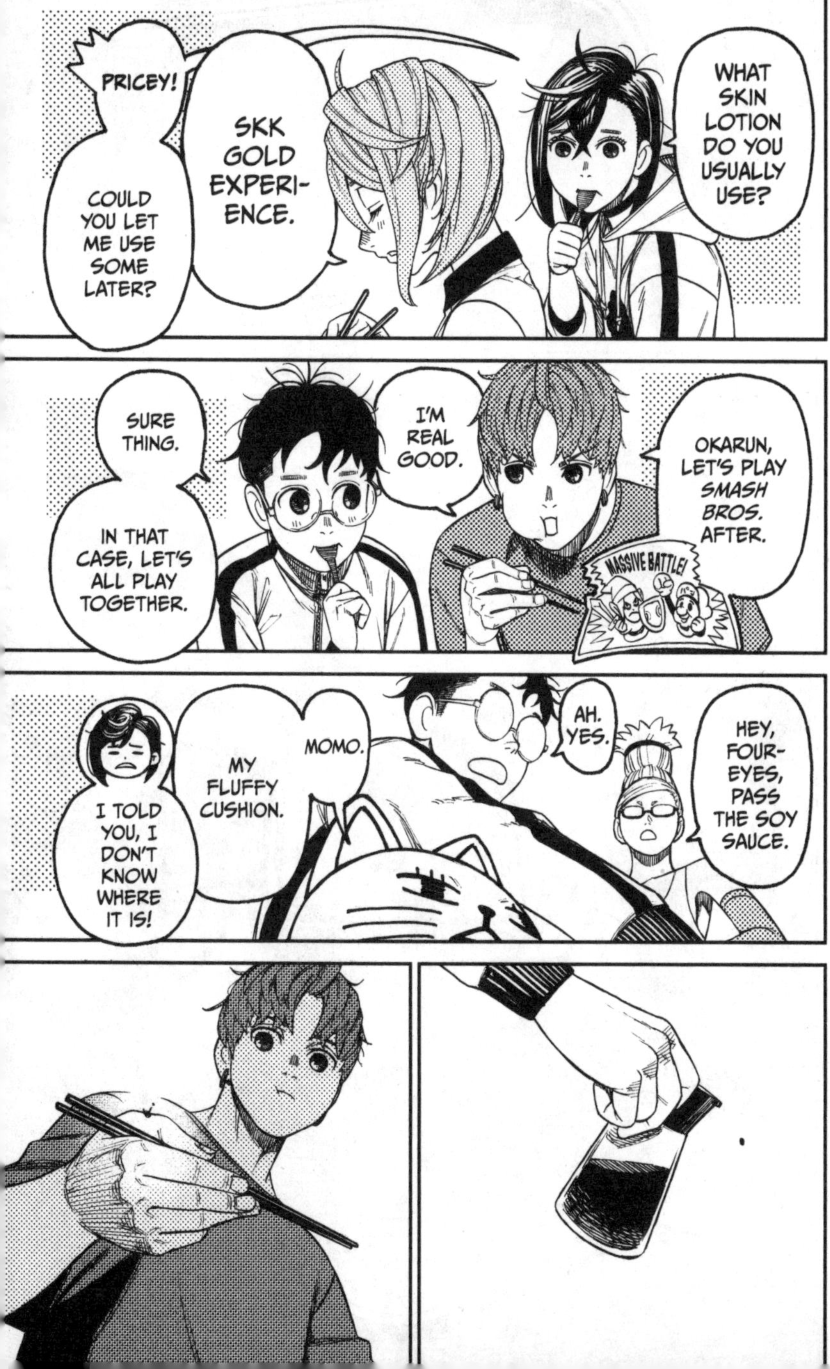
WHAT SKIN LOTION DO YOU USUALLY USE?
SKK GOLD EXPERI-ENCE.
PRICEY!
COULD YOU LET ME USE SOME LATER?
OKARUN, LET'S PLAY SMASH BROS. AFTER.
I'M REAL GOOD.
SURE THING.
IN THAT CASE, LET'S ALL PLAY TOGETHER.
MASSIVE BATTLE!
HEY, FOUR-EYES, PASS THE SOY SAUCE.
AH. YES.
MOMO.
MY FLUFFY CUSHION.
I TOLD YOU, I DON'T KNOW WHERE IT IS!

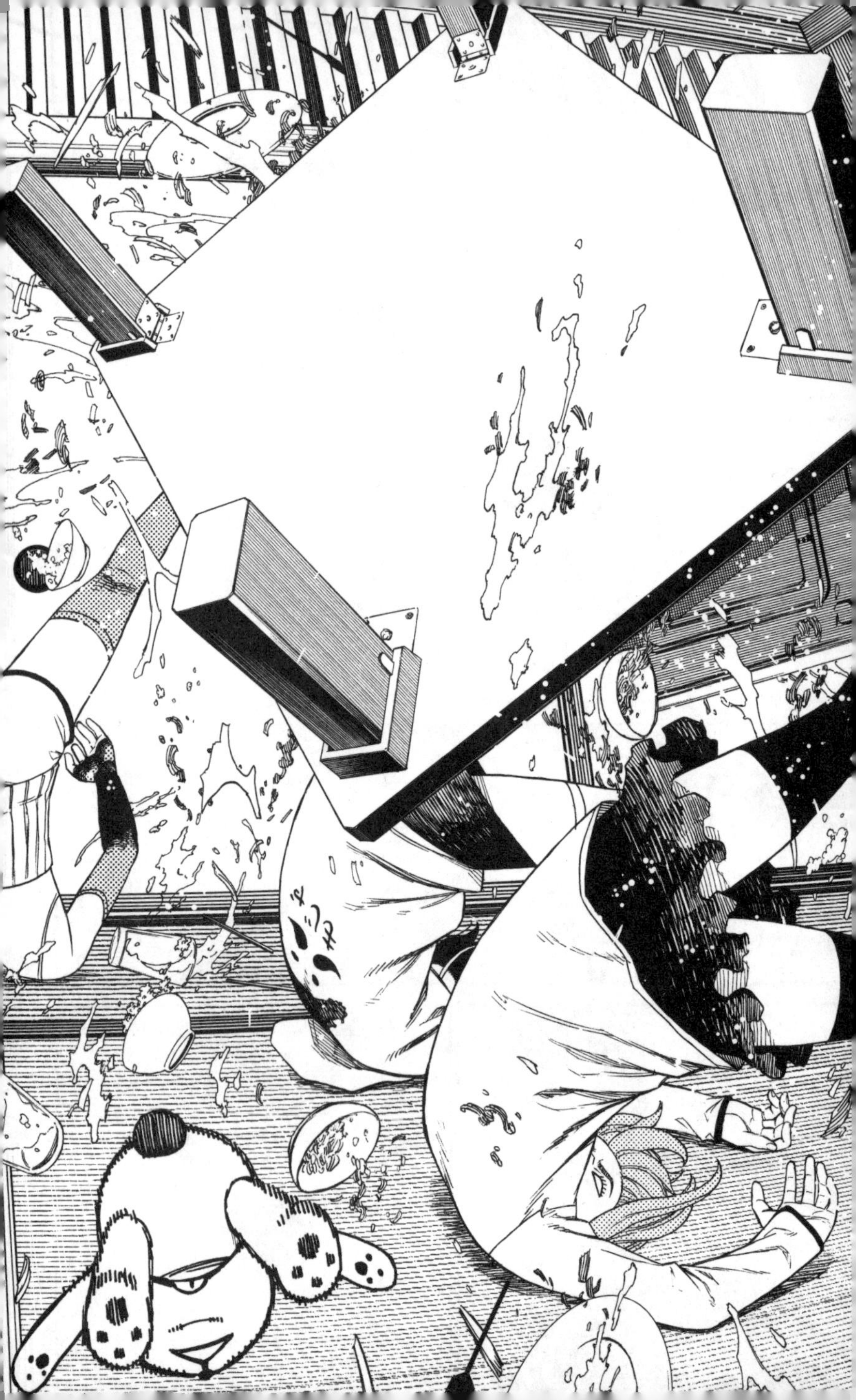

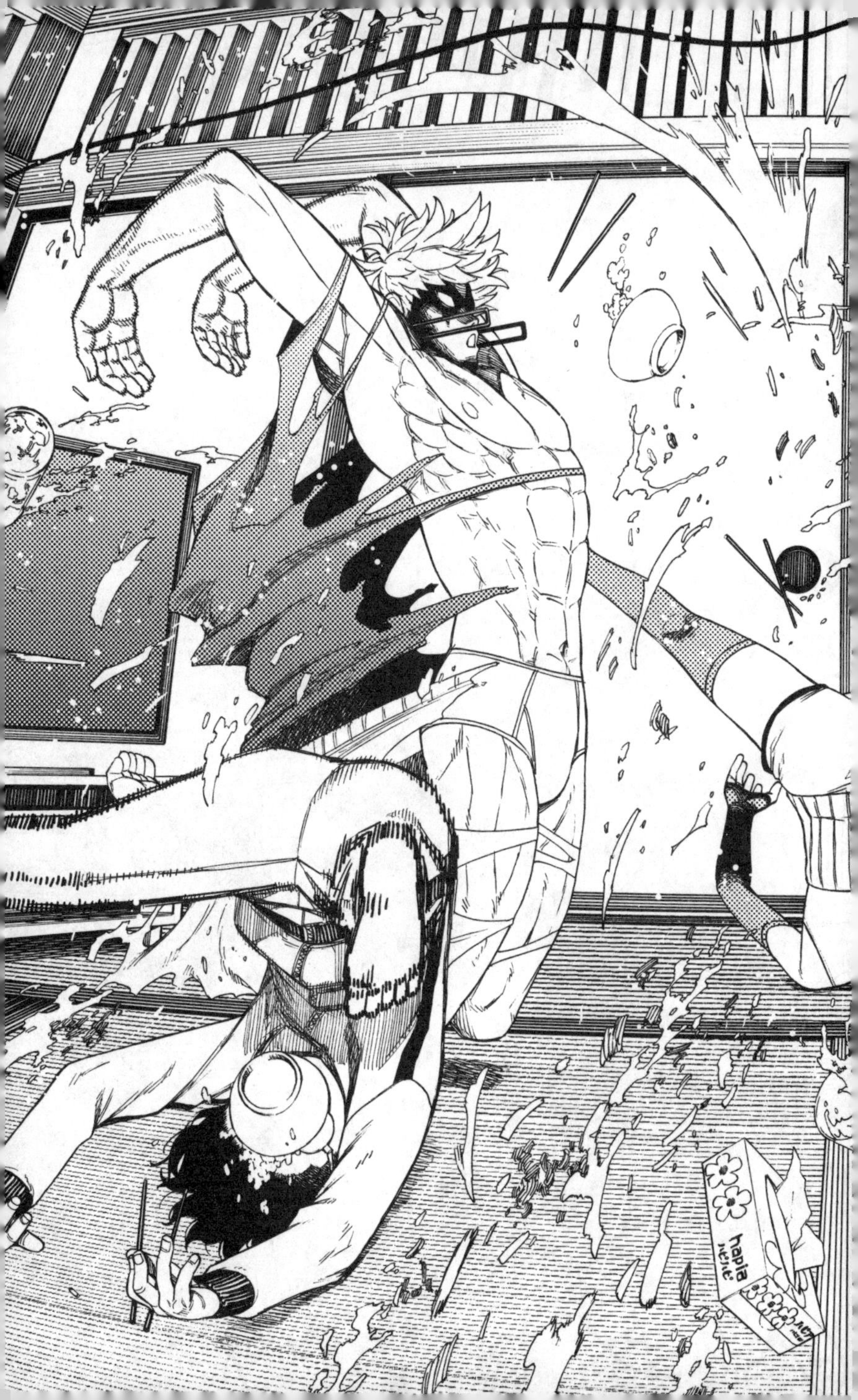
hapia

DAN
DA
DAN

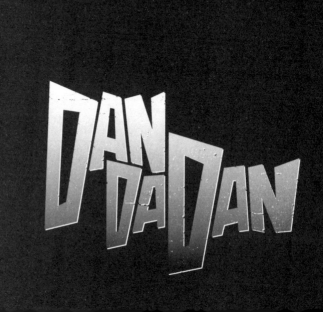

52. The Hayashi Performers Are Here

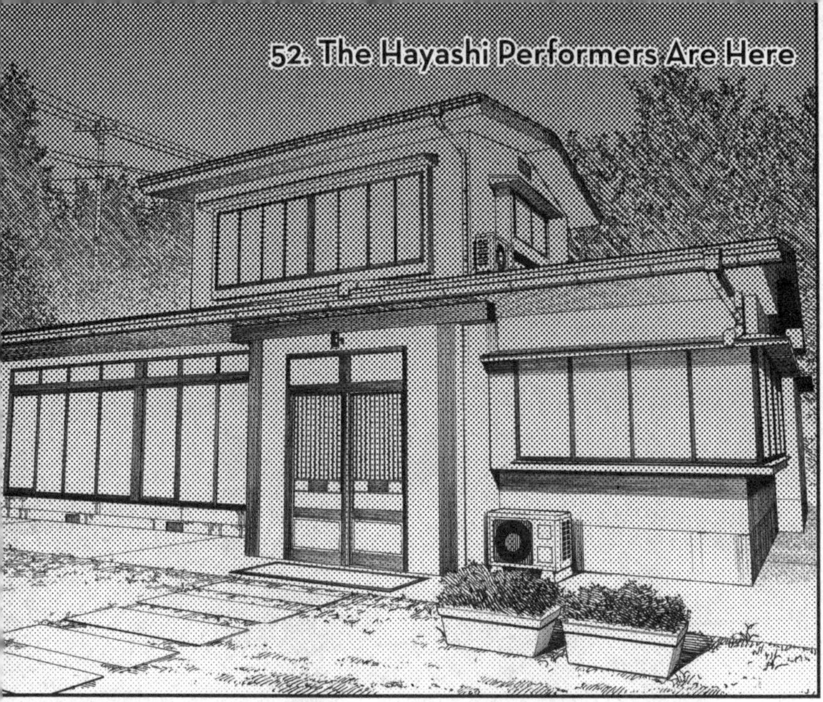

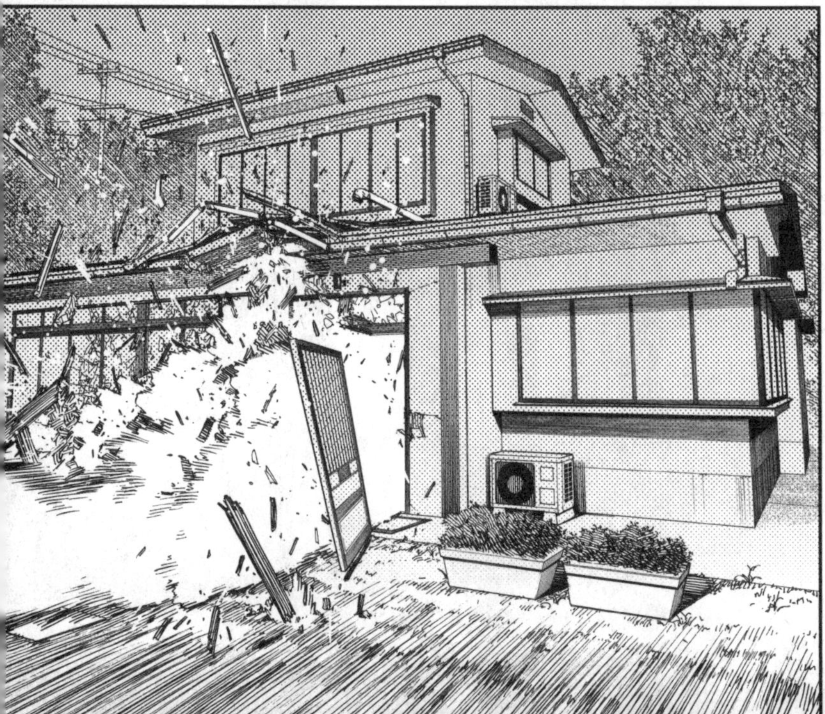

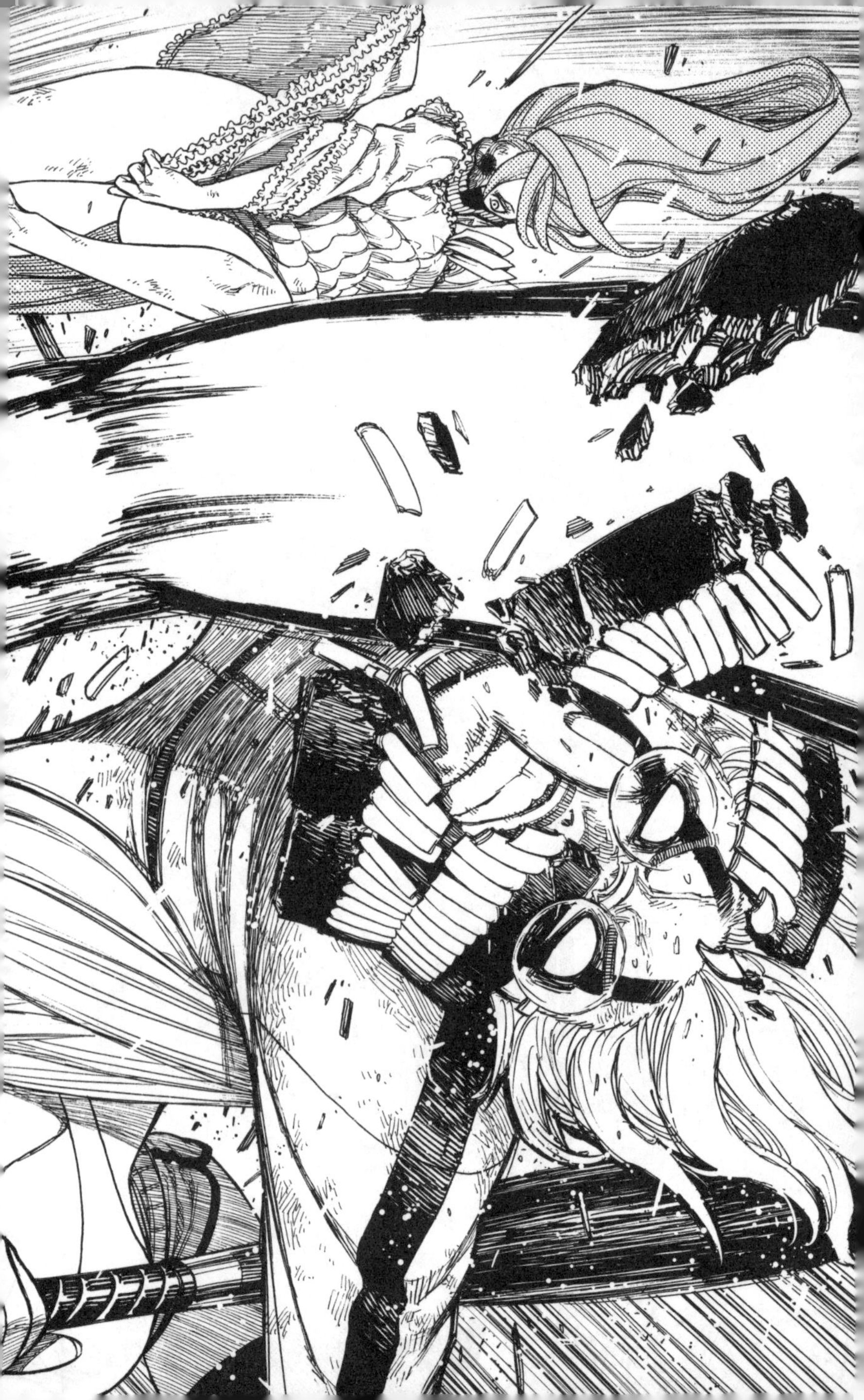

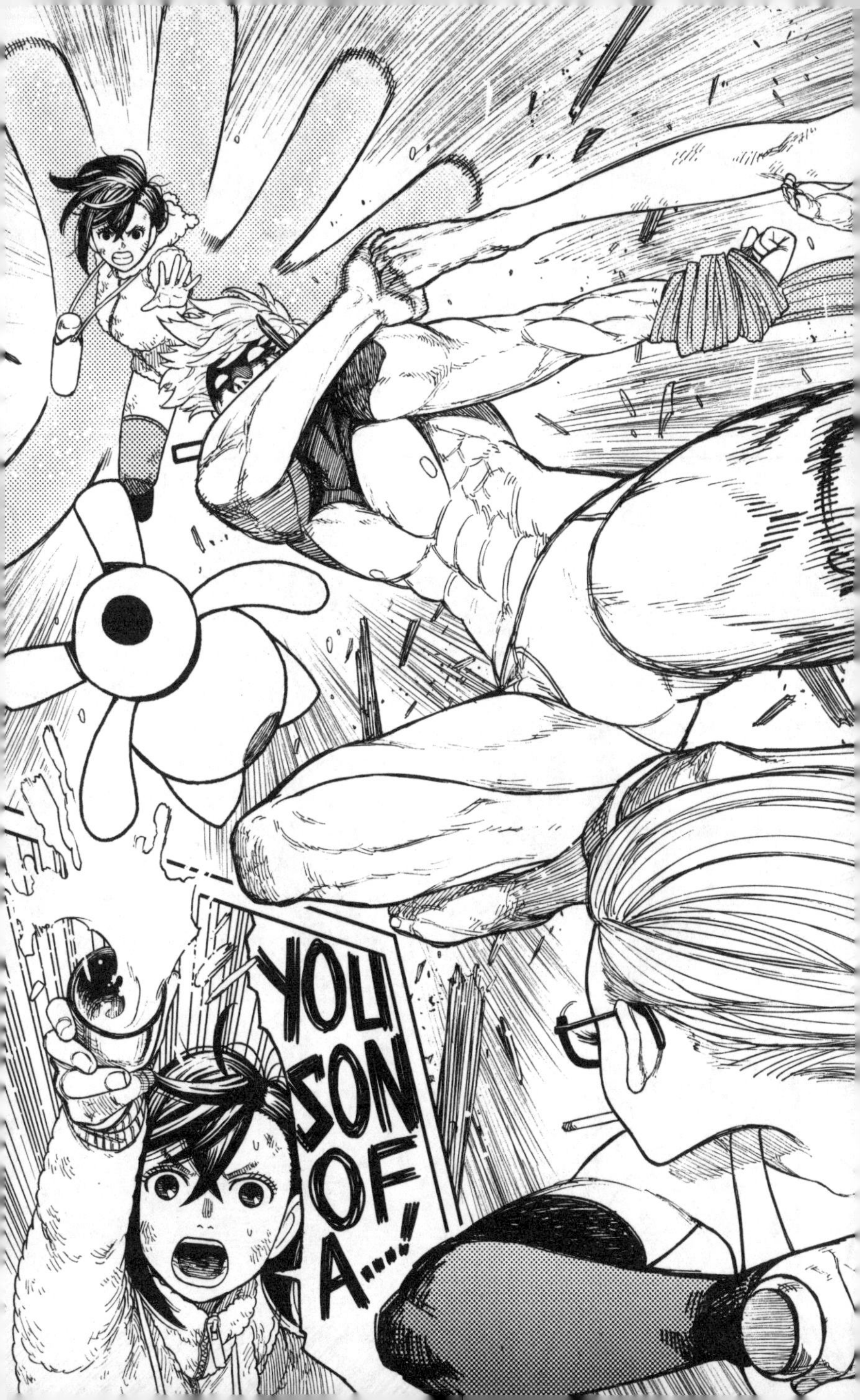
YOU SON OF A...!!

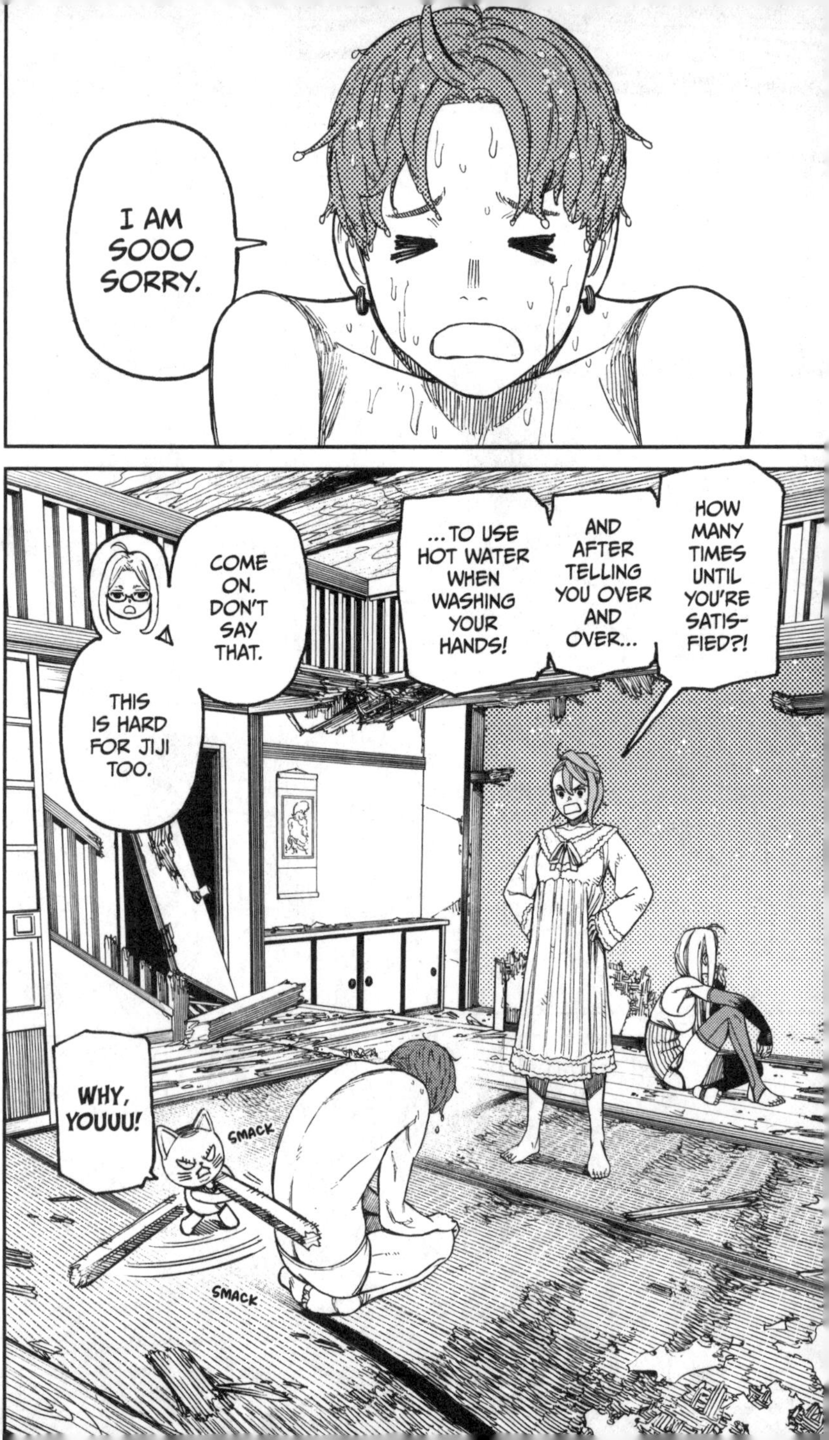
I AM SOOO SORRY.
HOW MANY TIMES UNTIL YOU'RE SATIS-FIED?!
AND AFTER TELLING YOU OVER AND OVER...
...TO USE HOT WATER WHEN WASHING YOUR HANDS!
COME ON. DON'T SAY THAT.
THIS IS HARD FOR JIJI TOO.
SMACK
WHY, YOUUU!
SMACK

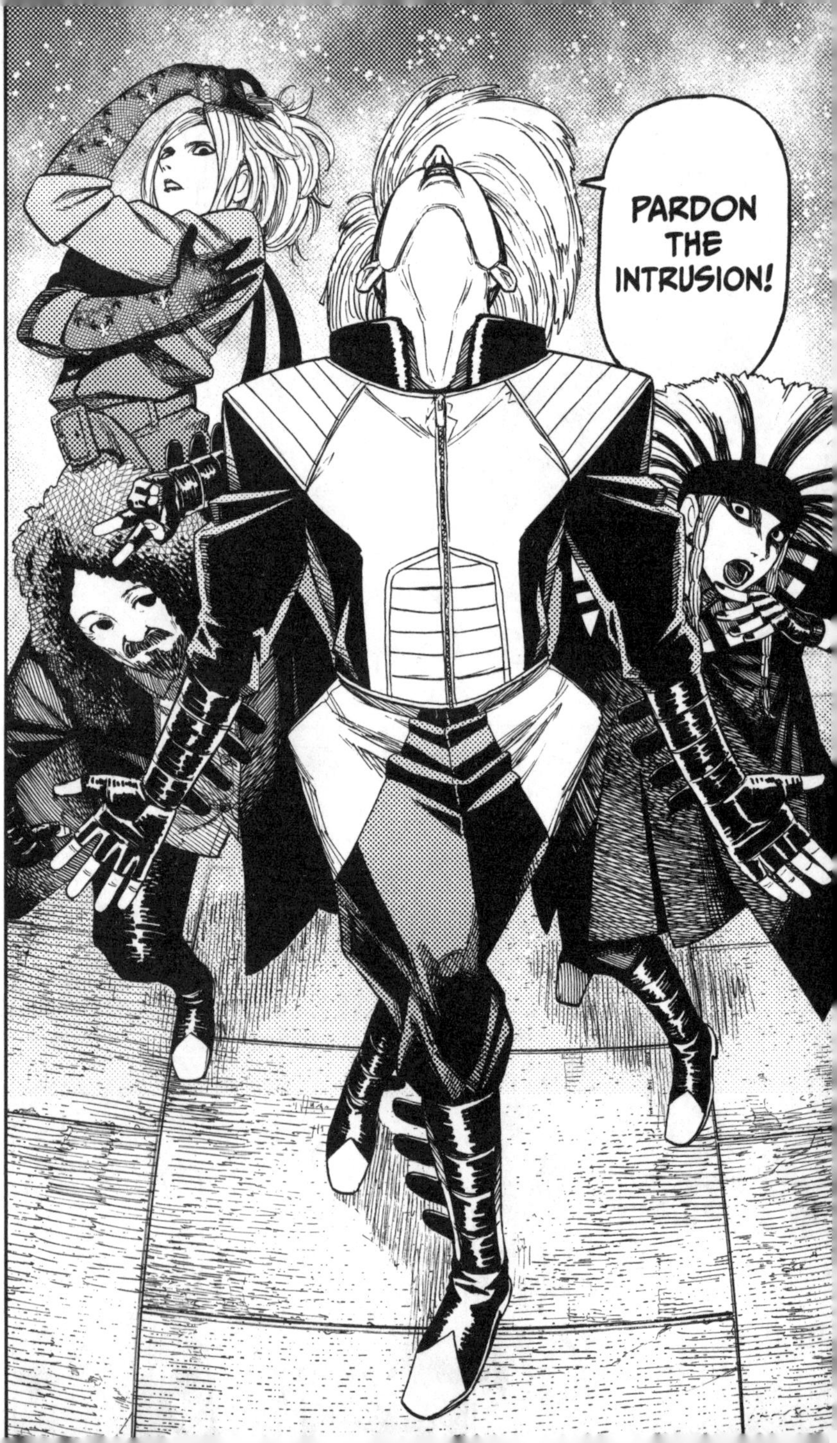
PARDON THE INTRUSION!

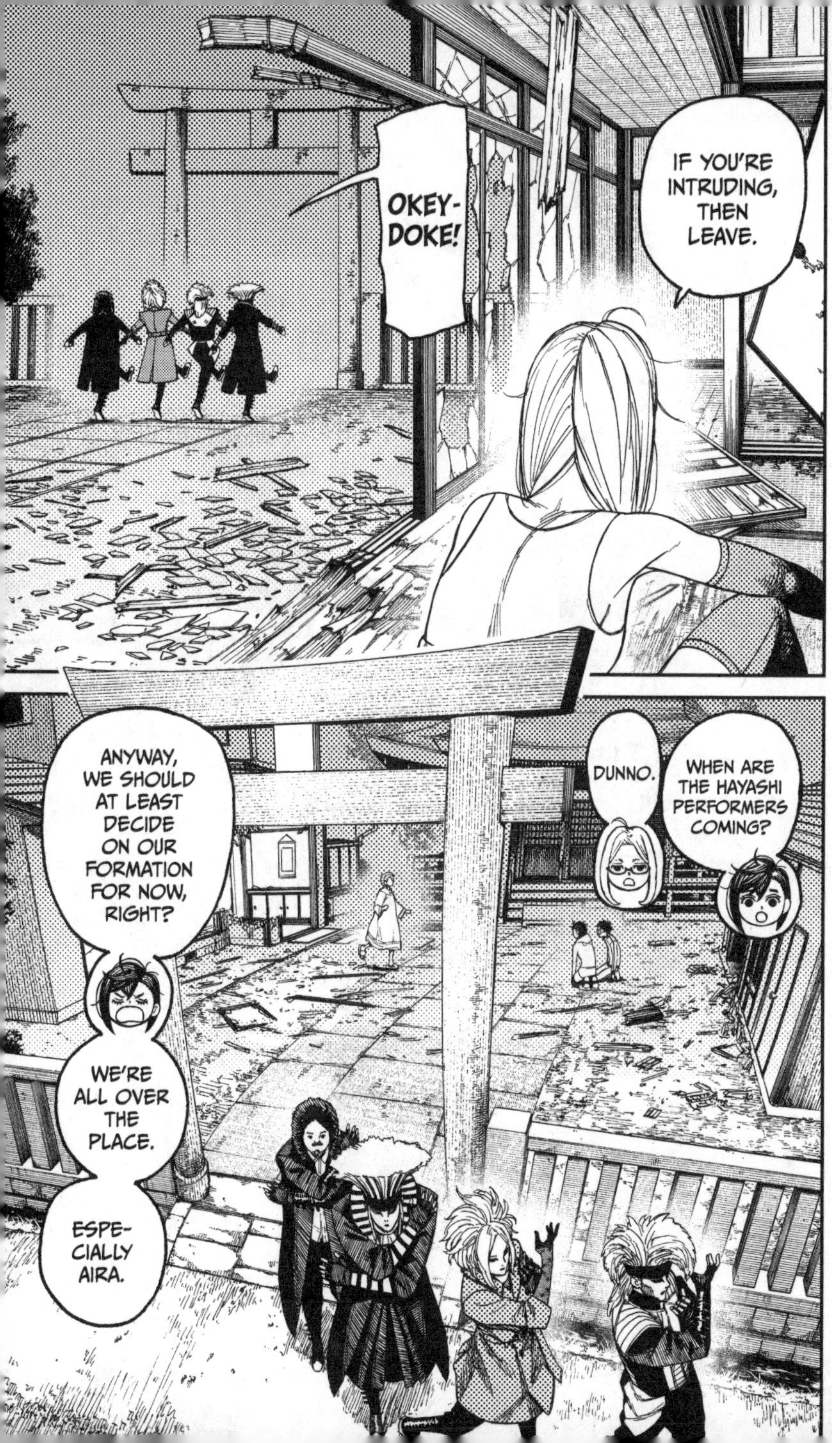
IF YOU'RE INTRUDING, THEN LEAVE.
OKEY-DOKE!
WHEN ARE THE HAYASHI PERFORMERS COMING?
DUNNO.
ANYWAY, WE SHOULD AT LEAST DECIDE ON OUR FORMATION FOR NOW, RIGHT?
WE'RE ALL OVER THE PLACE.
ESPE-CIALLY AIRA.

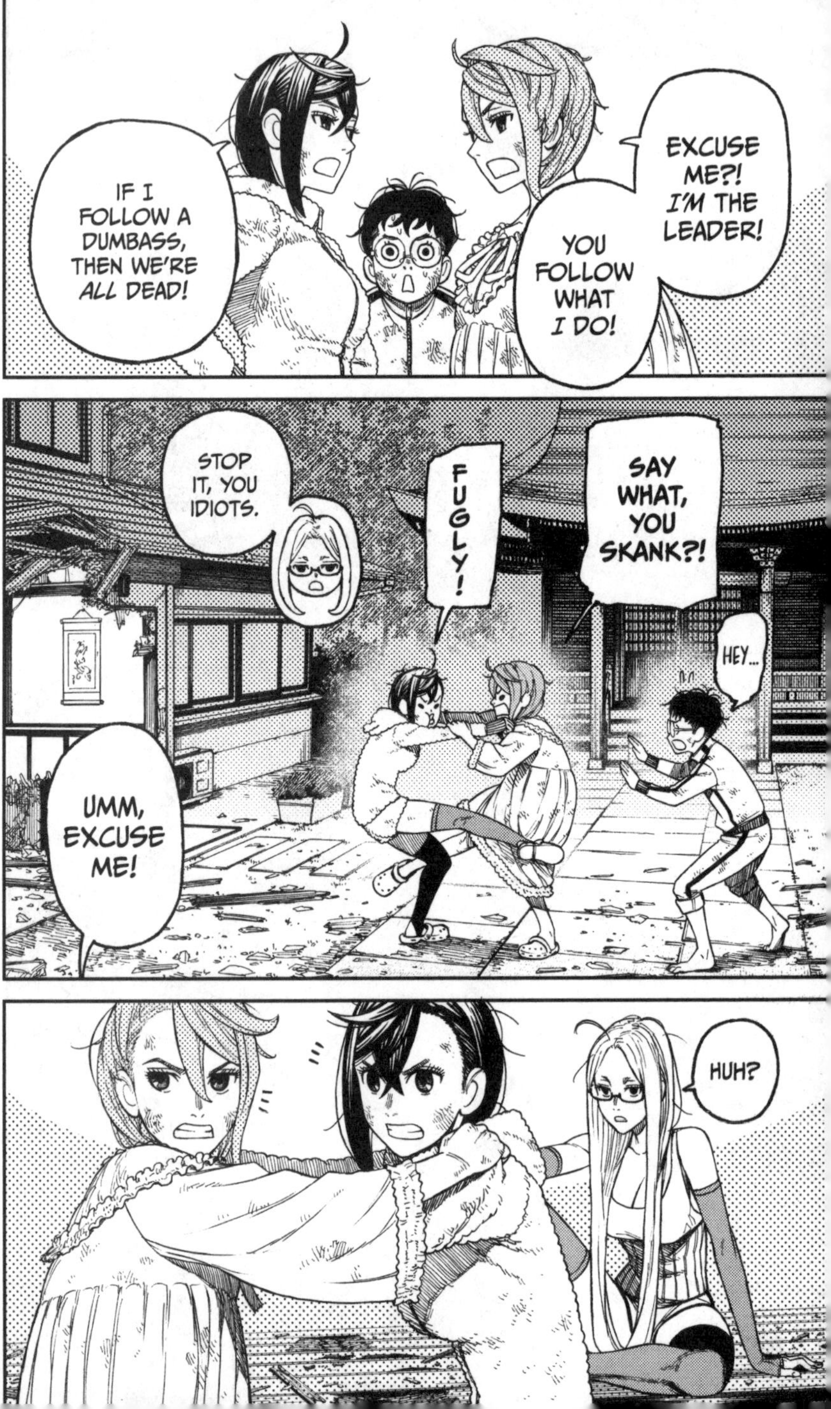
EXCUSE ME?! *I'M* THE LEADER!
YOU FOLLOW WHAT *I* DO!
IF I FOLLOW A DUMBASS, THEN WE'RE *ALL* DEAD!
SAY WHAT, YOU SKANK?!
HEY...
FUGLY!
STOP IT, YOU IDIOTS.
UMM, EXCUSE ME!
HUH?

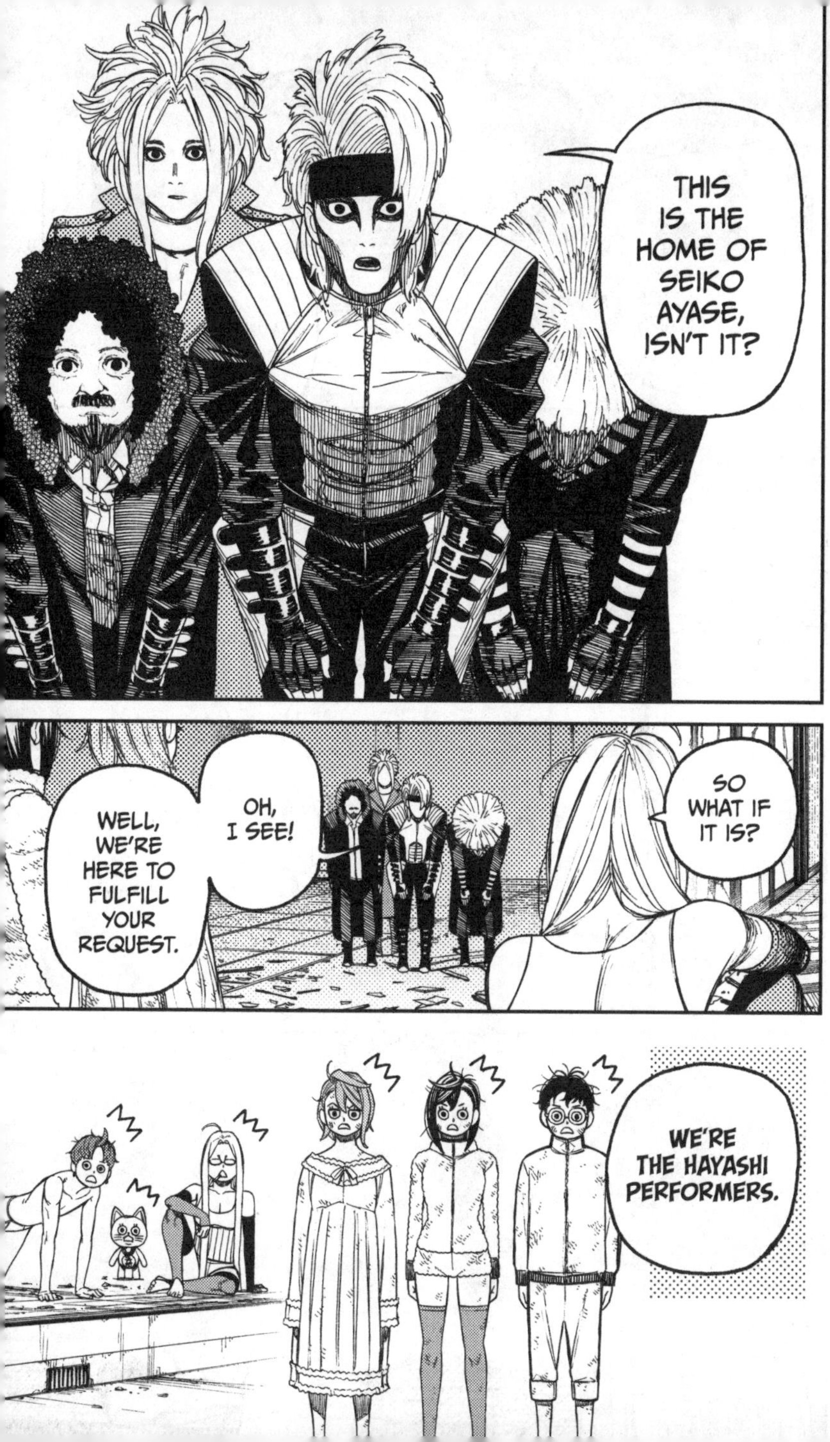
THIS IS THE HOME OF SEIKO AYASE, ISN'T IT?
SO WHAT IF IT IS?
OH, I SEE!
WELL, WE'RE HERE TO FULFILL YOUR REQUEST.
WE'RE THE HAYASHI PERFORMERS.

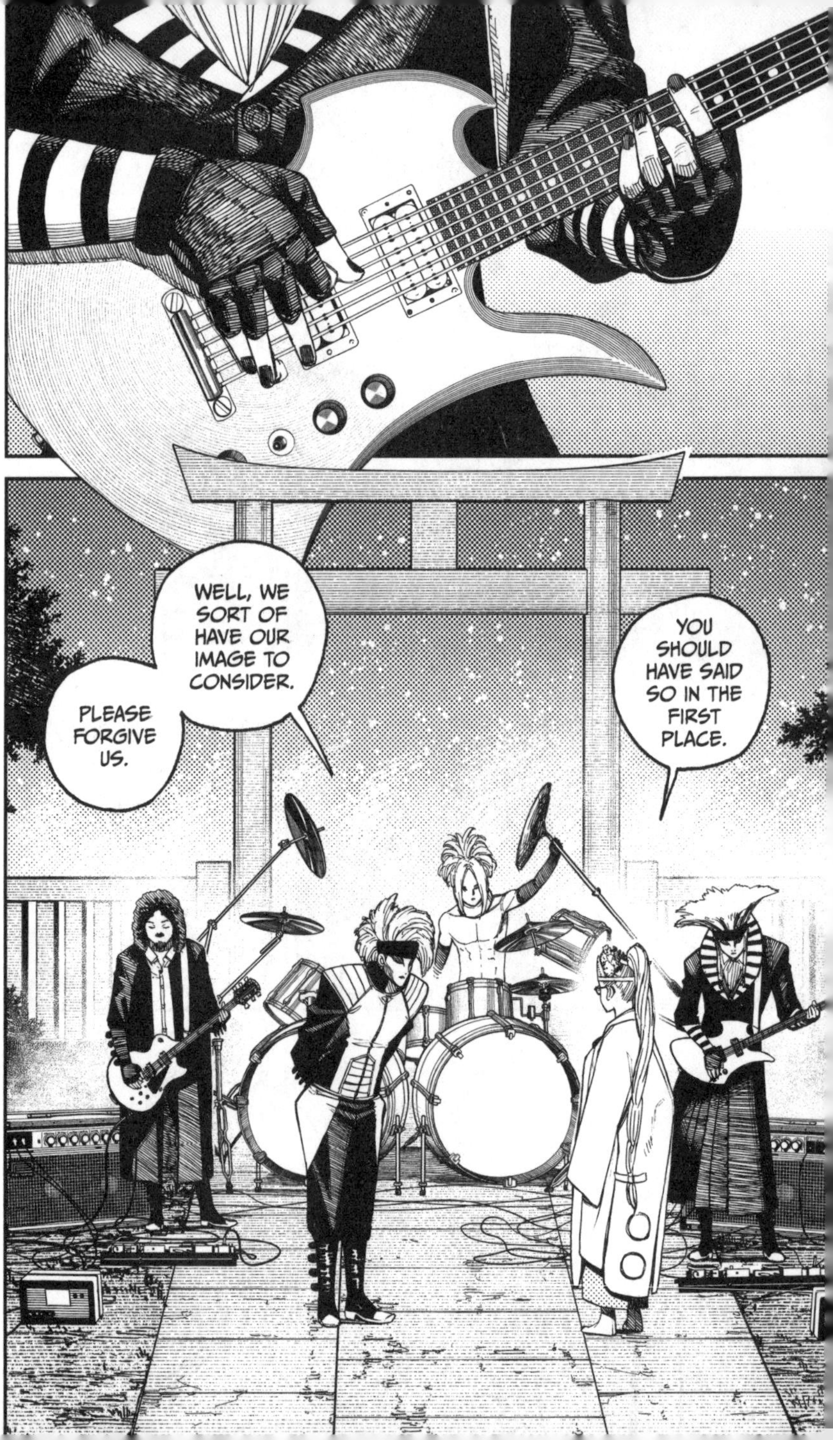
YOU SHOULD HAVE SAID SO IN THE FIRST PLACE.
WELL, WE SORT OF HAVE OUR IMAGE TO CONSIDER.
PLEASE FORGIVE US.

IS THIS A JOKE?

THEY'RE SO COOOL!

WICKED! THEY'RE NOT WHAT I EXPECTED ...

I'M KINDA EXCITED!

BUT THEIR PERFORMANCE IS THE REAL DEAL.

THEY HAVE THE POWER TO MAKE THEIR SOUND REACH EVEN THE REALM OF THE DEAD.

SO THEY'RE SPIRIT MEDIUMS?

NO.

THEY'RE NOT EVEN SPIRIT SENSITIVE.

HUH?

PLUS, THE LESS SPIRIT SENSITIVE THEY ARE...

...THE LESS LIKELY THEY ARE TO BE WON OVER BY EVIL SPIRITS DURING THE EXORCISM.

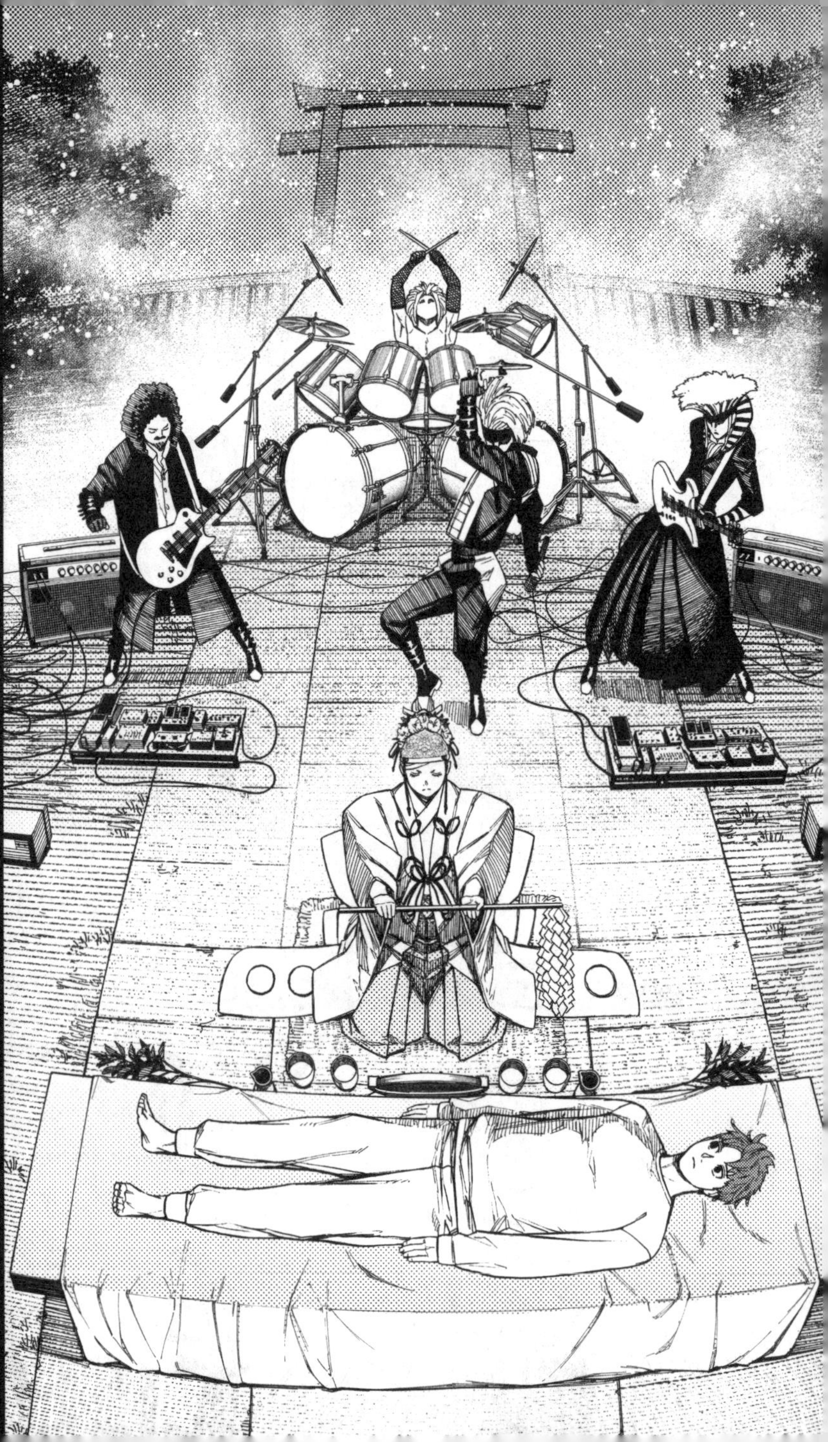

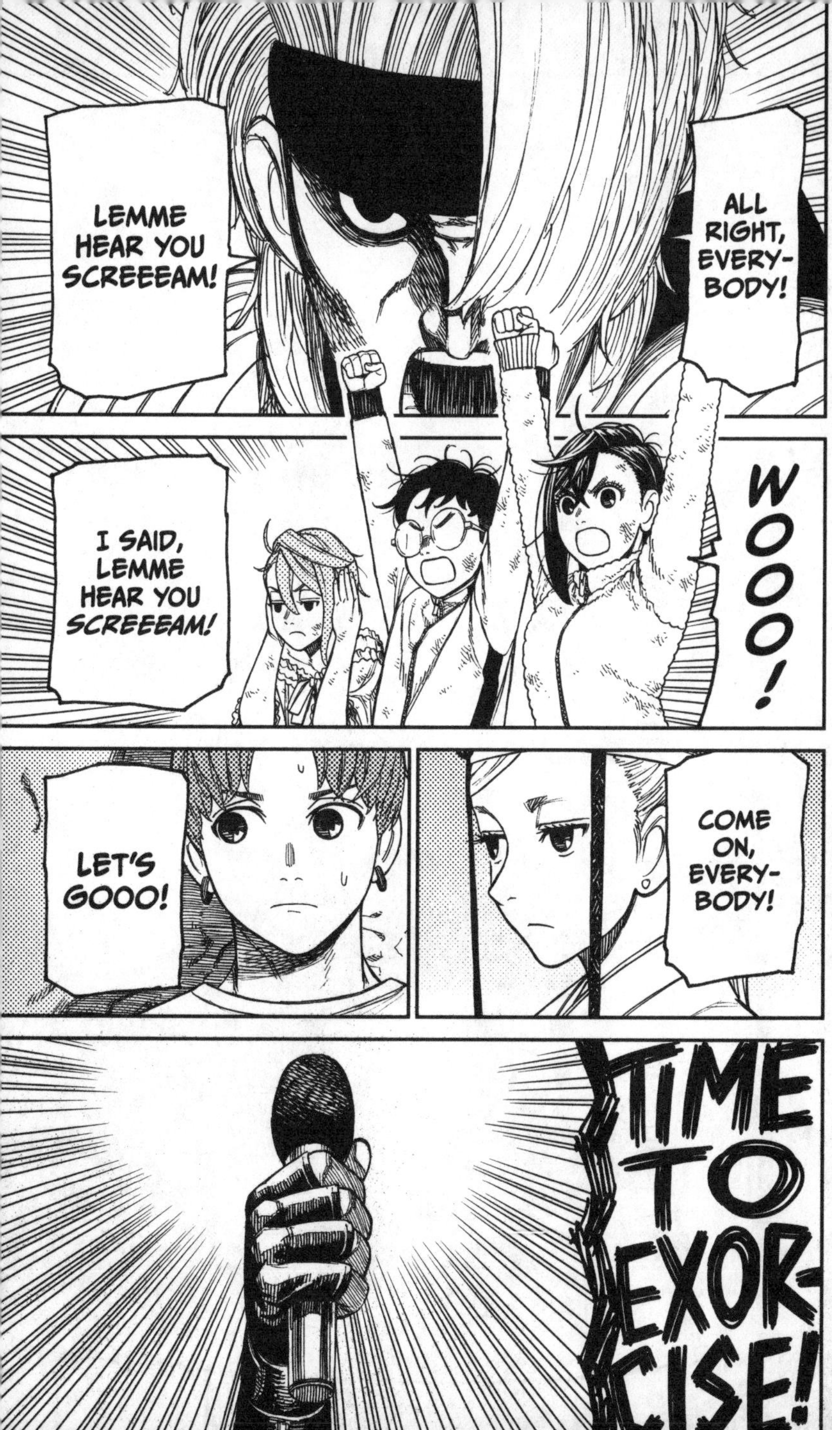
ALL RIGHT, EVERY-BODY!
LEMME HEAR YOU SCREEEAM!
WOOOO!
I SAID, LEMME HEAR YOU SCREEEAM!
COME ON, EVERY-BODY!
LET'S GOOO!
TIME TO EXOR-CISE!

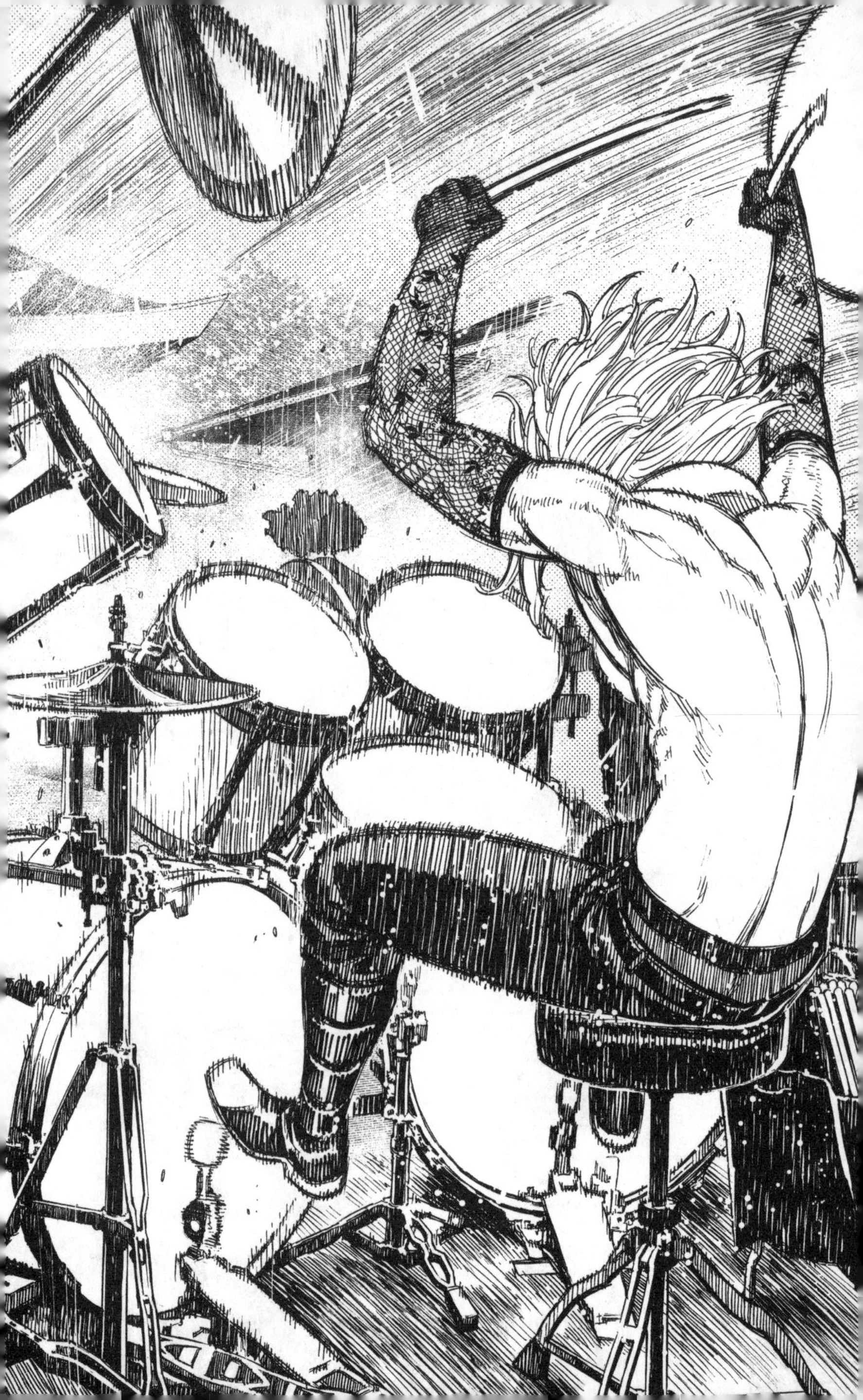

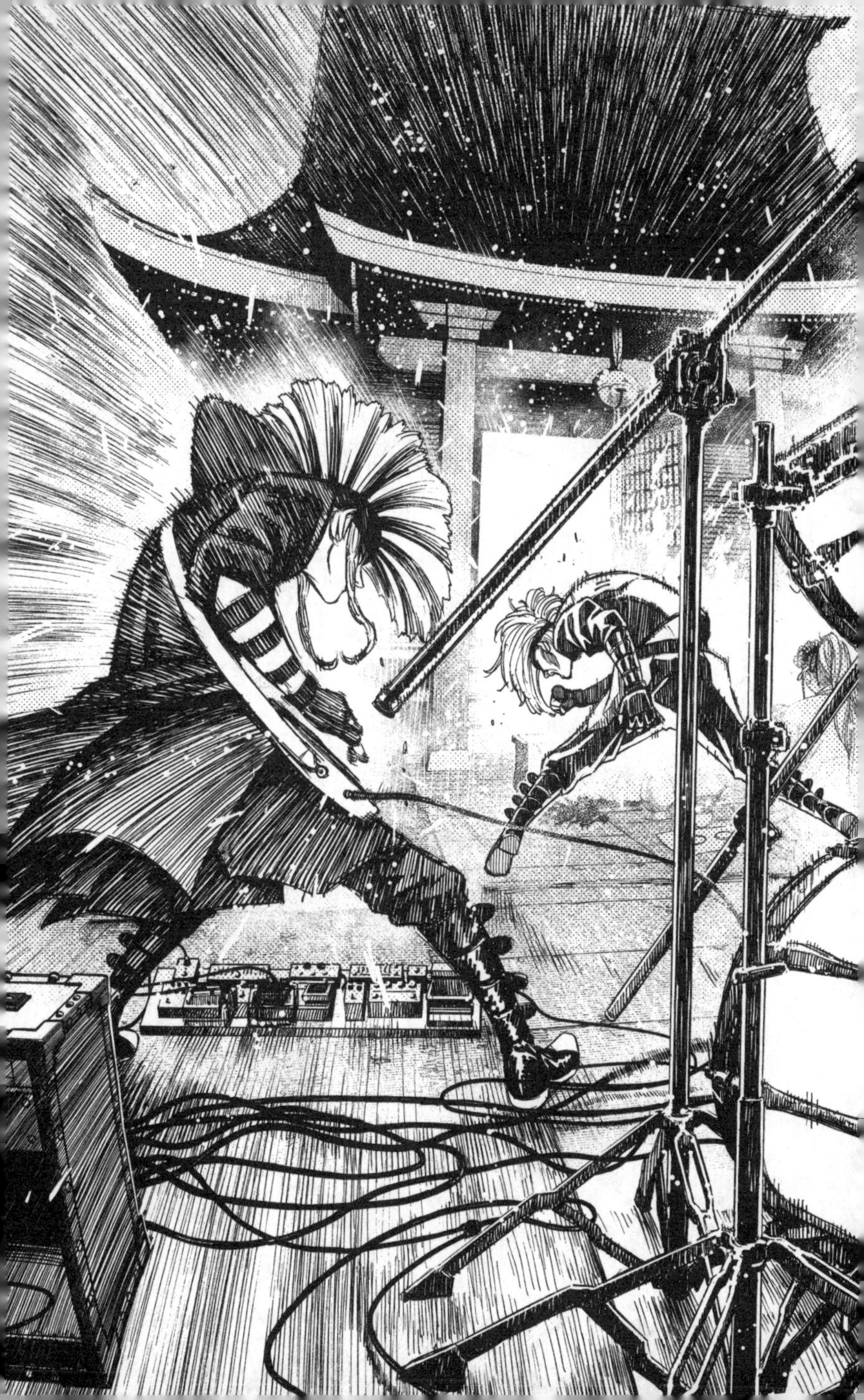

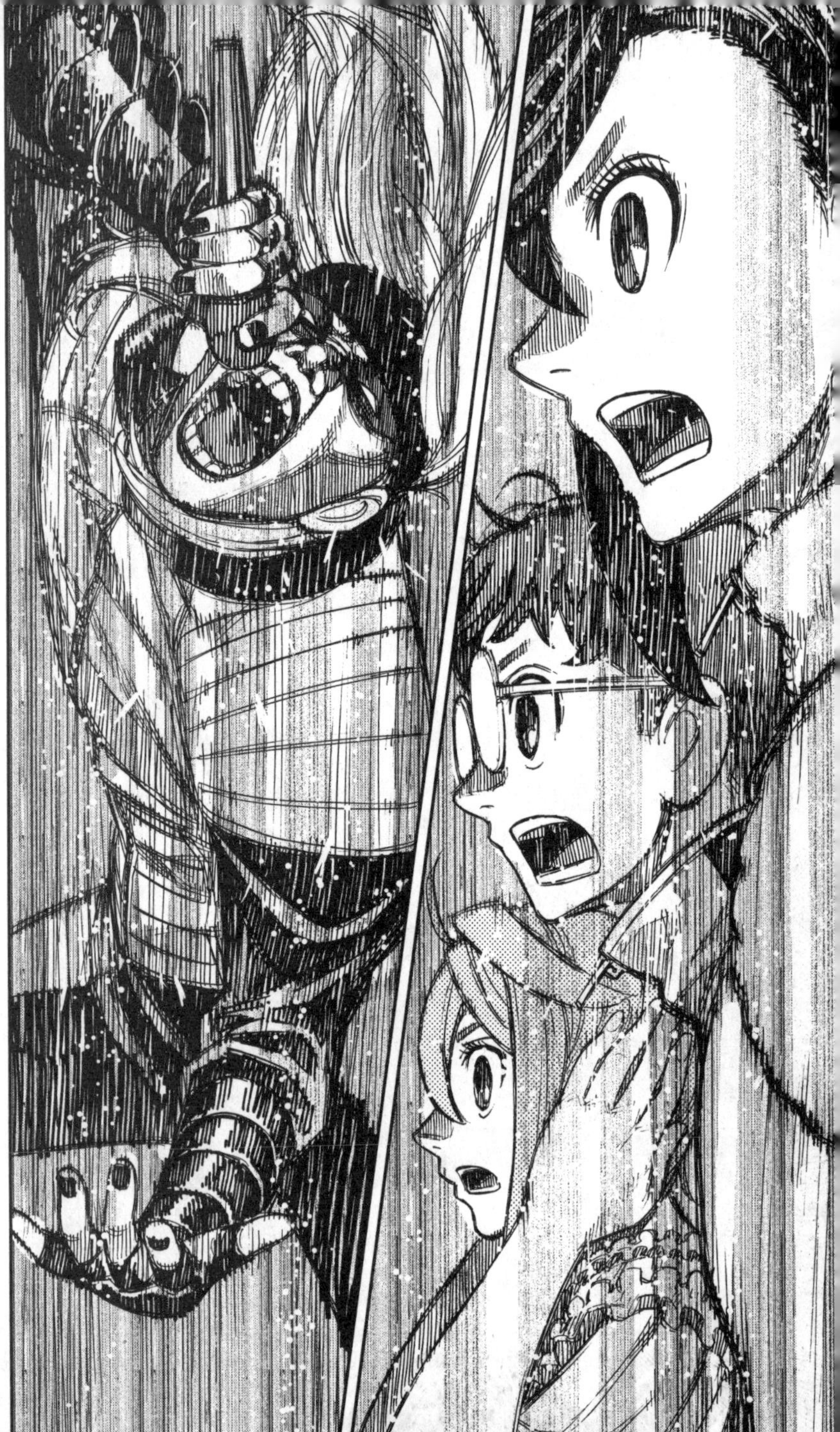

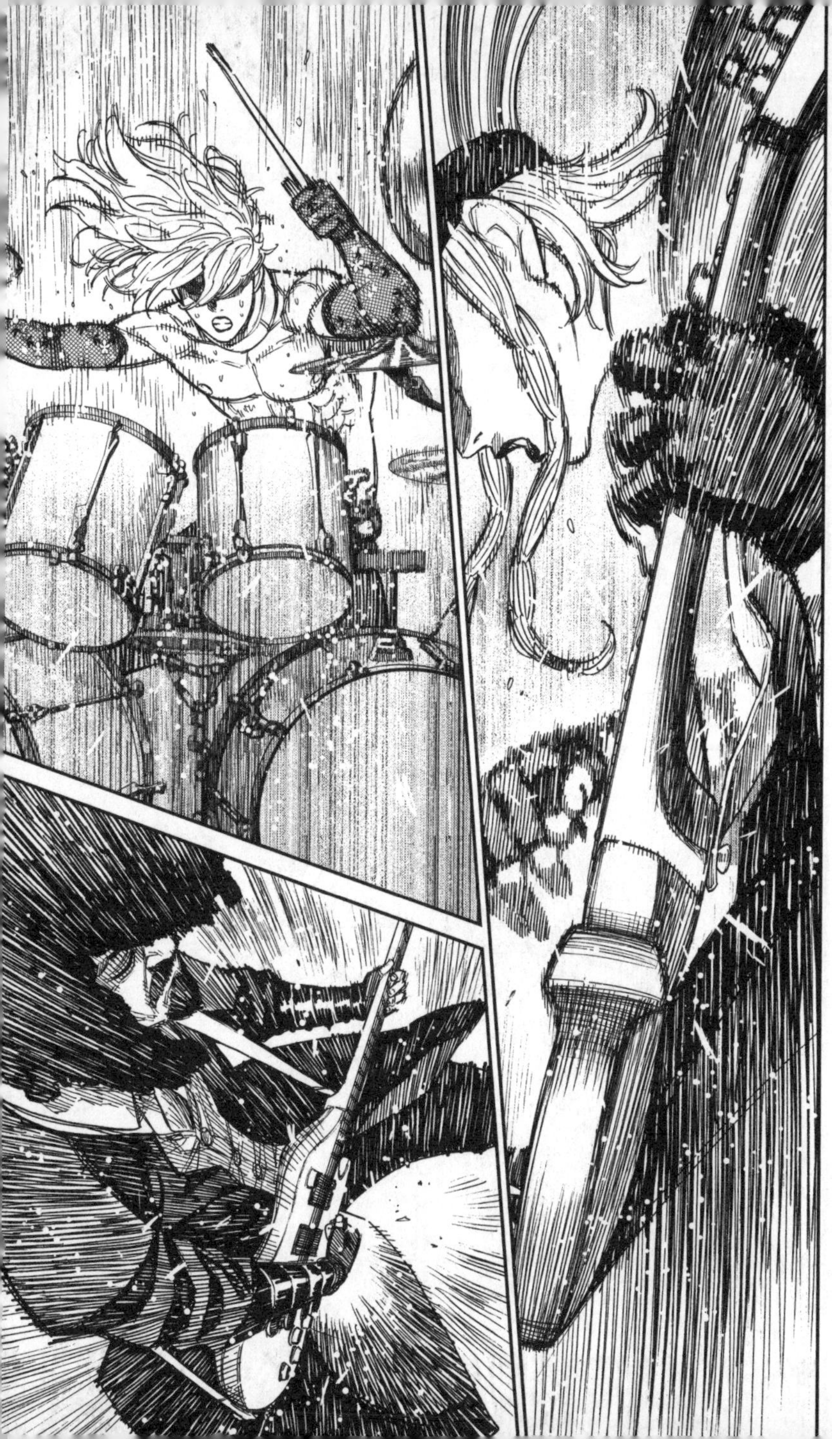

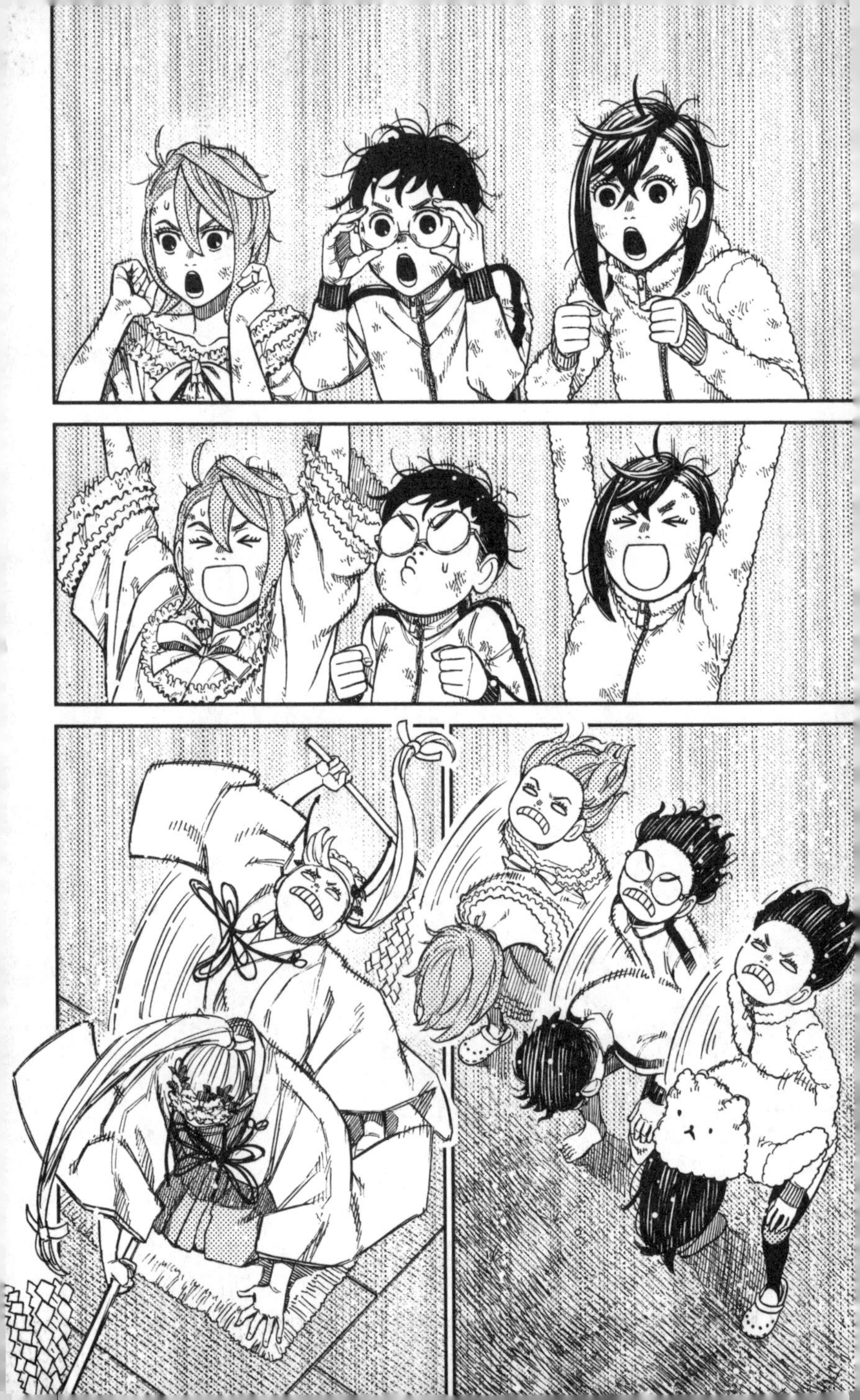

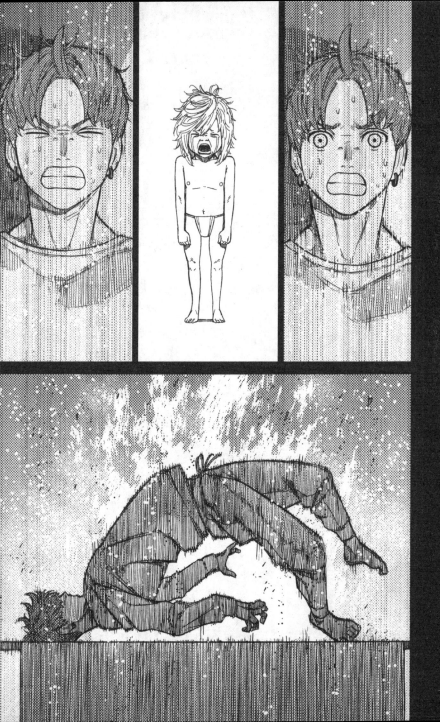

DAN DA DAN

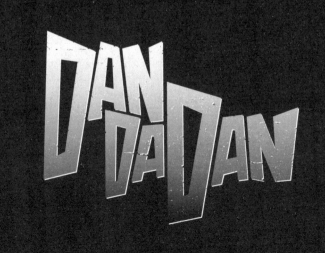

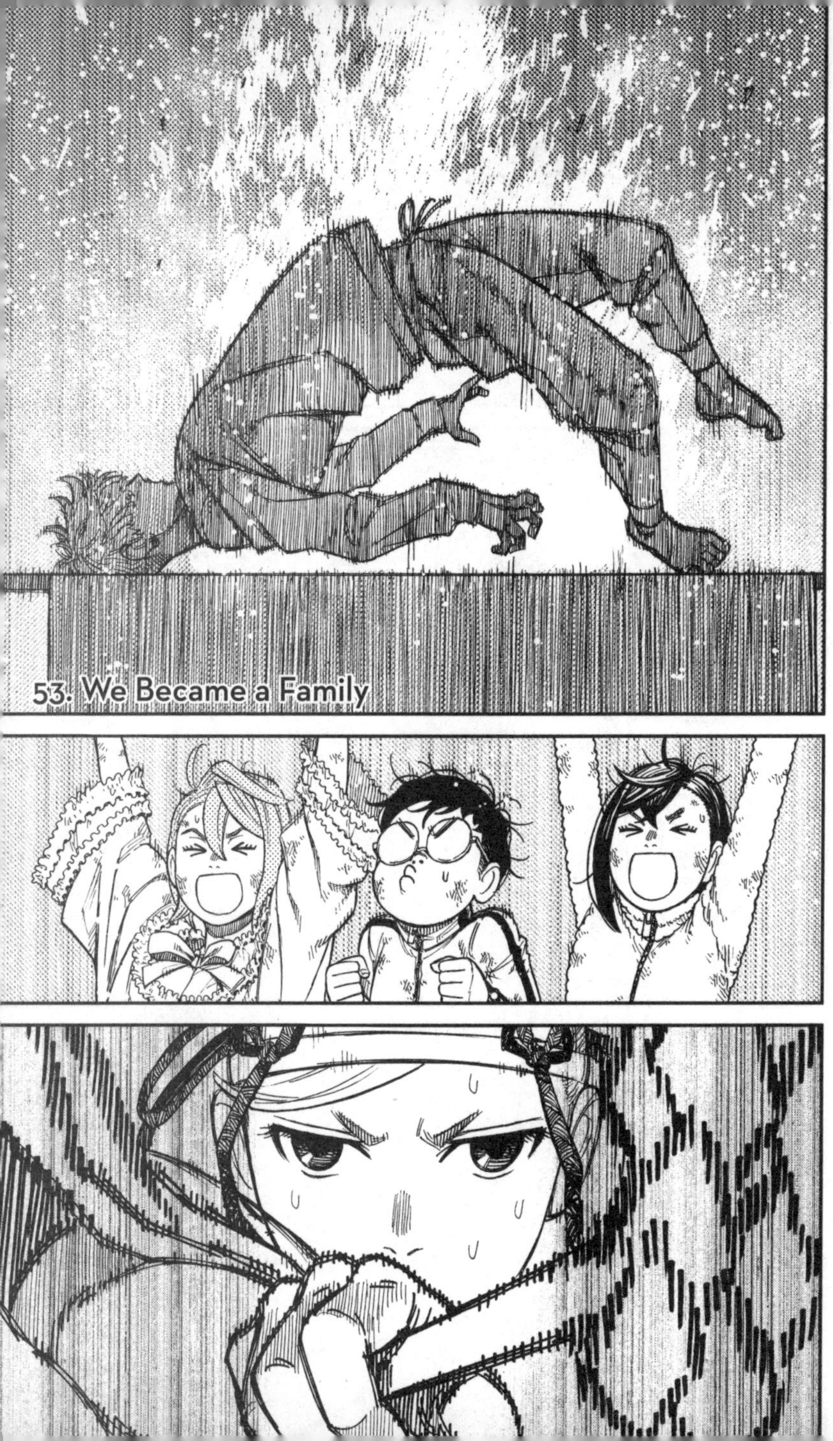
53. We Became a Family

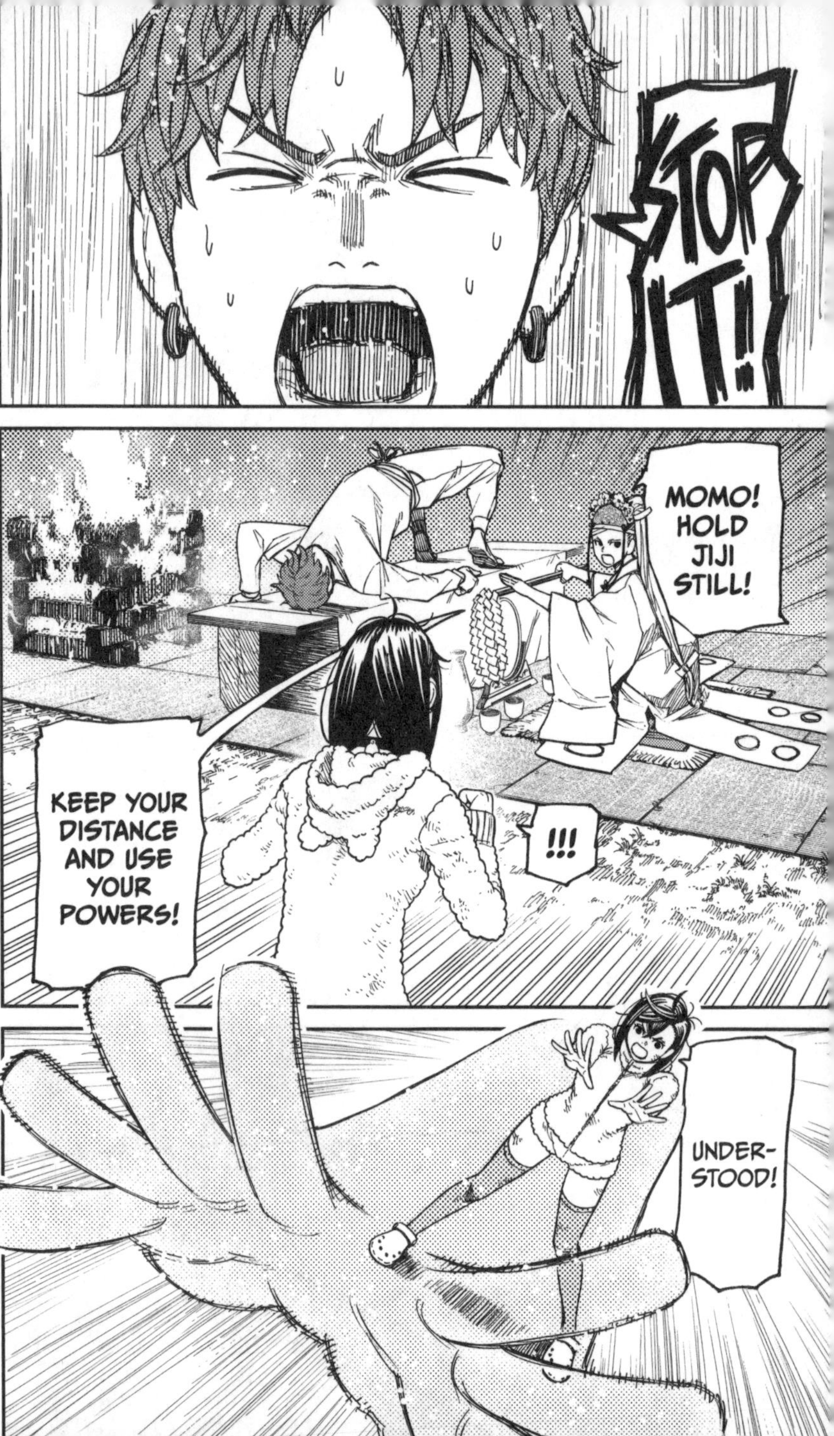
STOP IT!!
MOMO! HOLD JIJI STILL!
KEEP YOUR DISTANCE AND USE YOUR POWERS!
!!!
UNDER-STOOD!

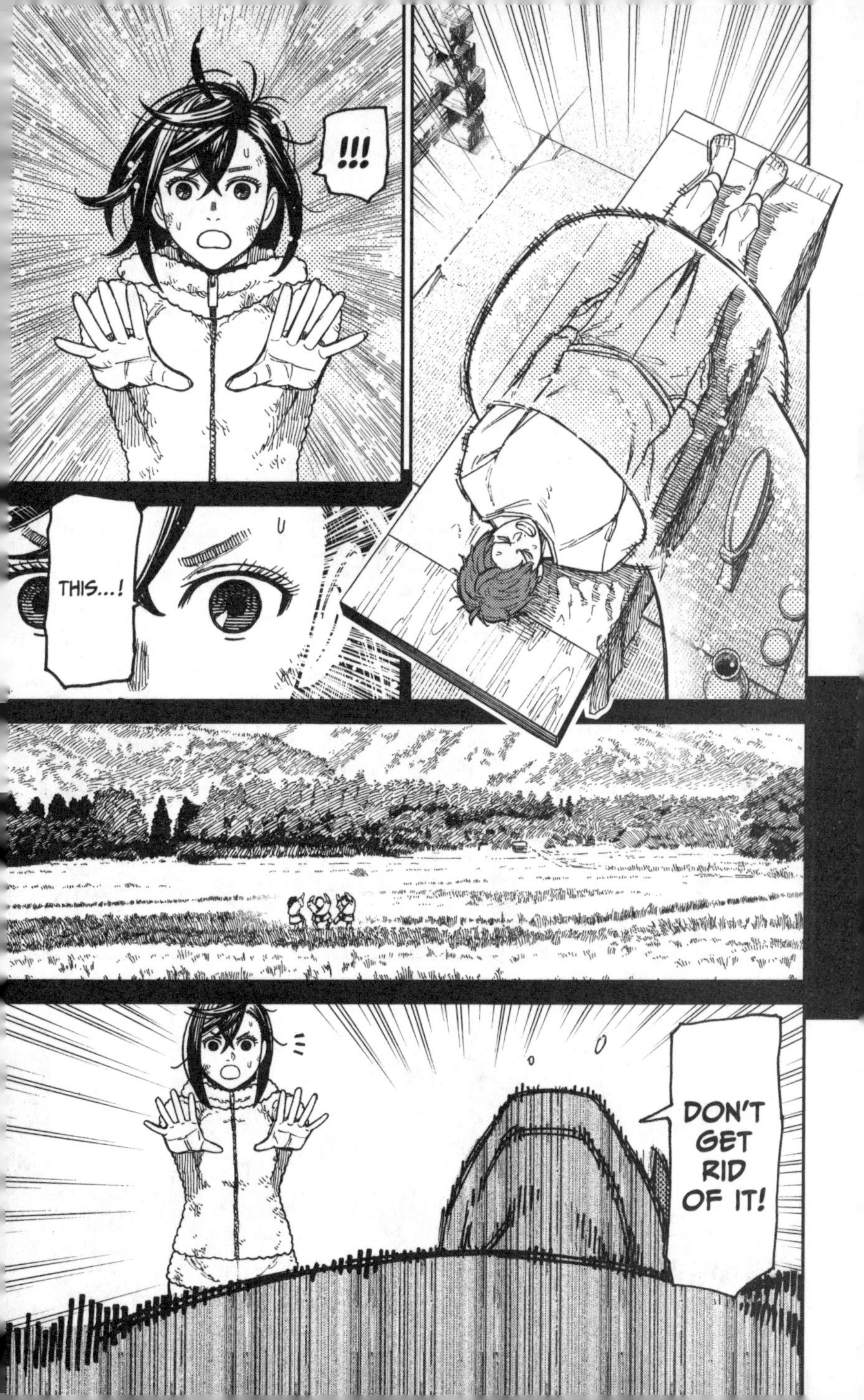
!!!
THIS...!
DON'T GET RID OF IT!

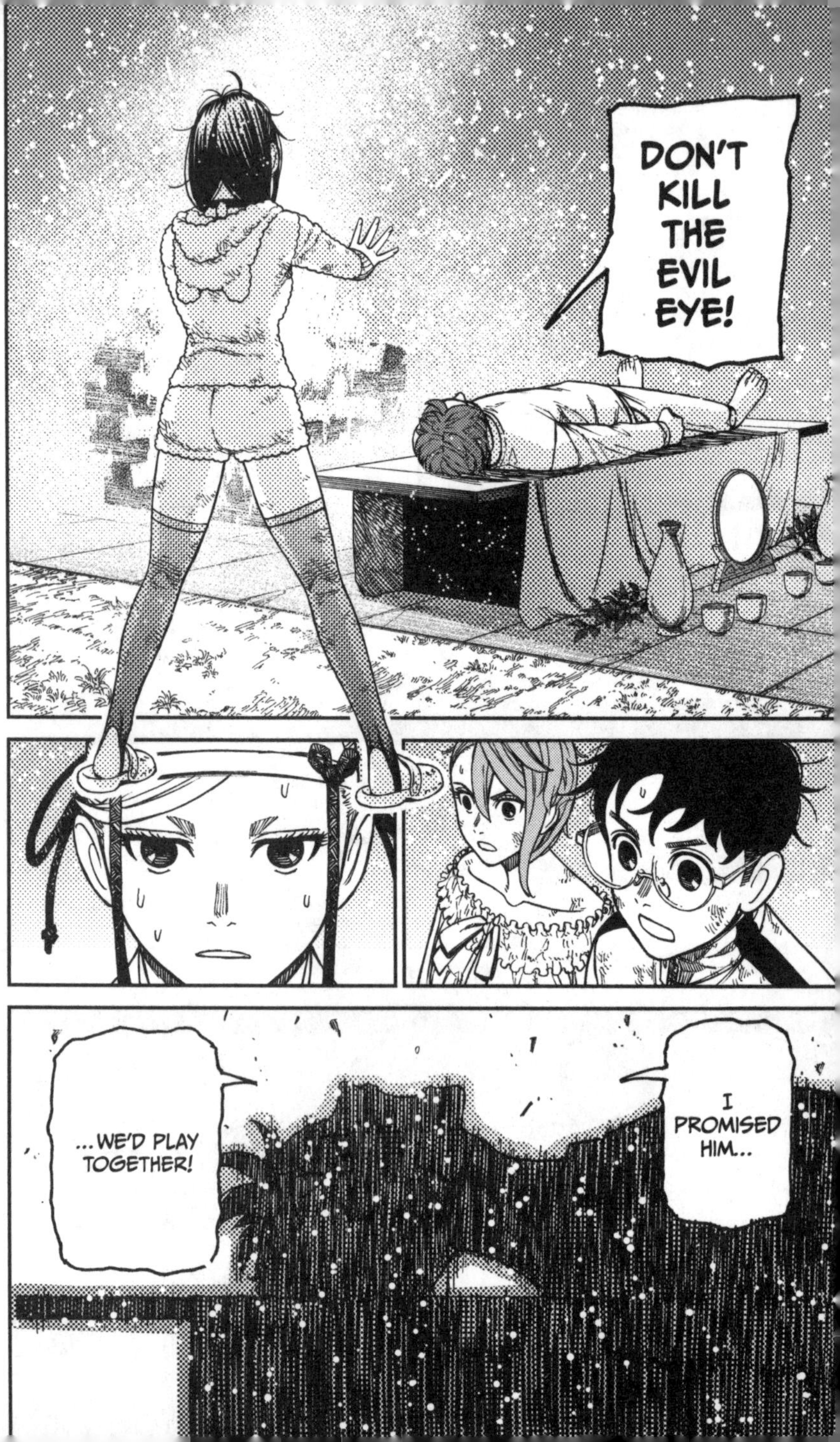
DON'T KILL THE EVIL EYE!
I PROMISED HIM...
...WE'D PLAY TOGETHER!

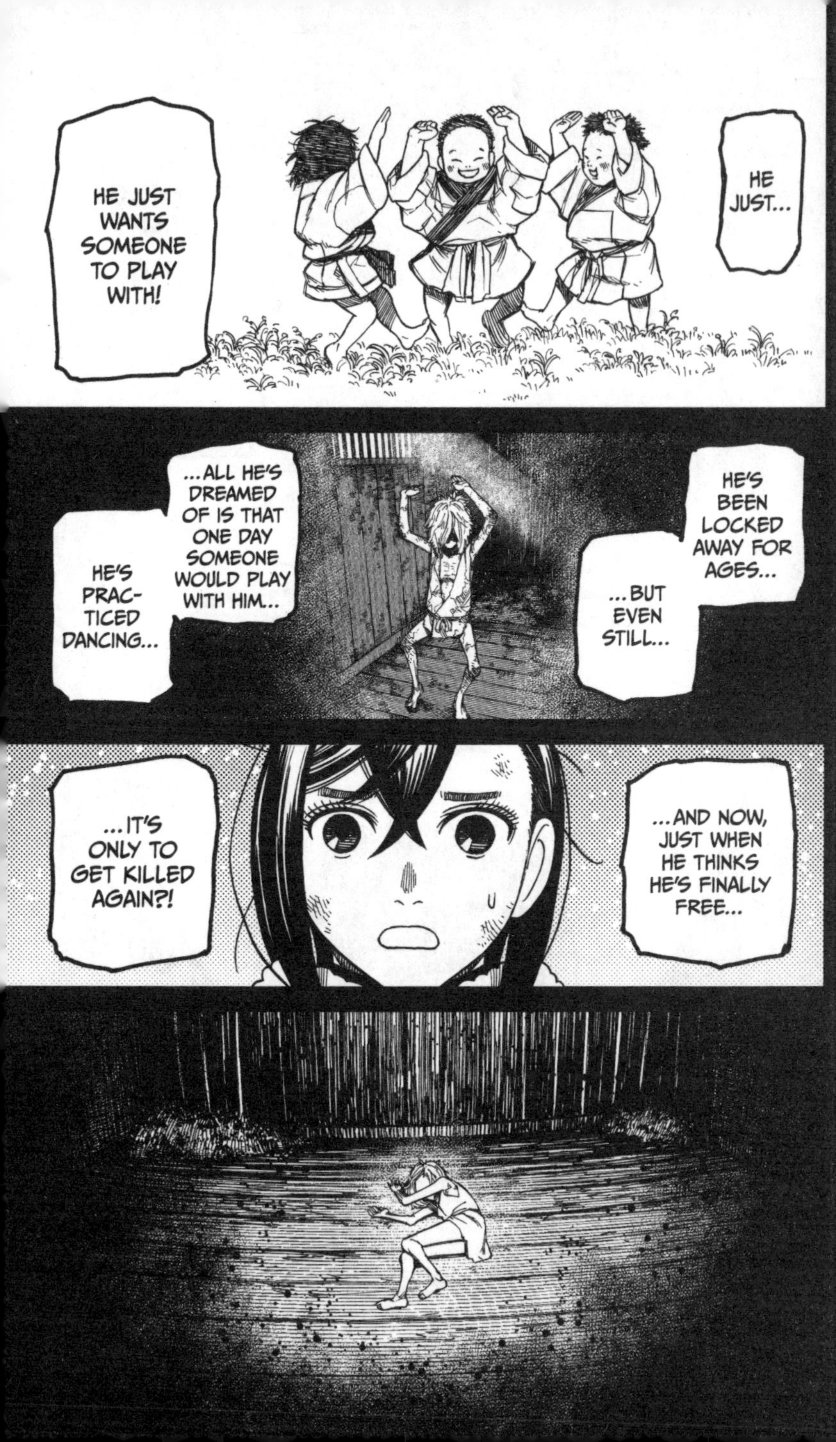
HE JUST...
HE JUST WANTS SOMEONE TO PLAY WITH!
HE'S BEEN LOCKED AWAY FOR AGES...
...BUT EVEN STILL...
HE'S PRAC-TICED DANCING...
...ALL HE'S DREAMED OF IS THAT ONE DAY SOMEONE WOULD PLAY WITH HIM...
...AND NOW, JUST WHEN HE THINKS HE'S FINALLY FREE...
...IT'S ONLY TO GET KILLED AGAIN?!

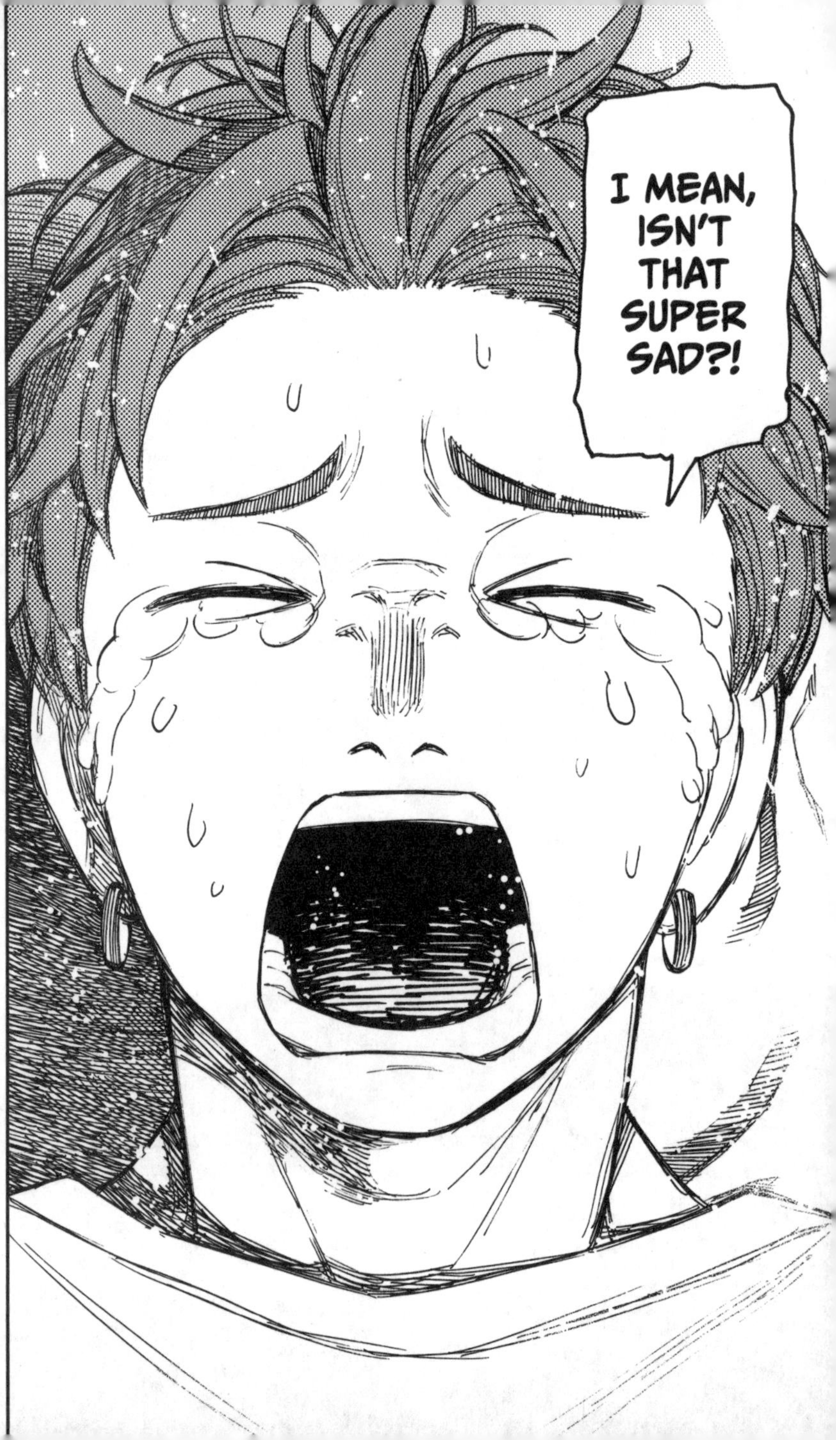
I MEAN, ISN'T THAT SUPER SAD?!

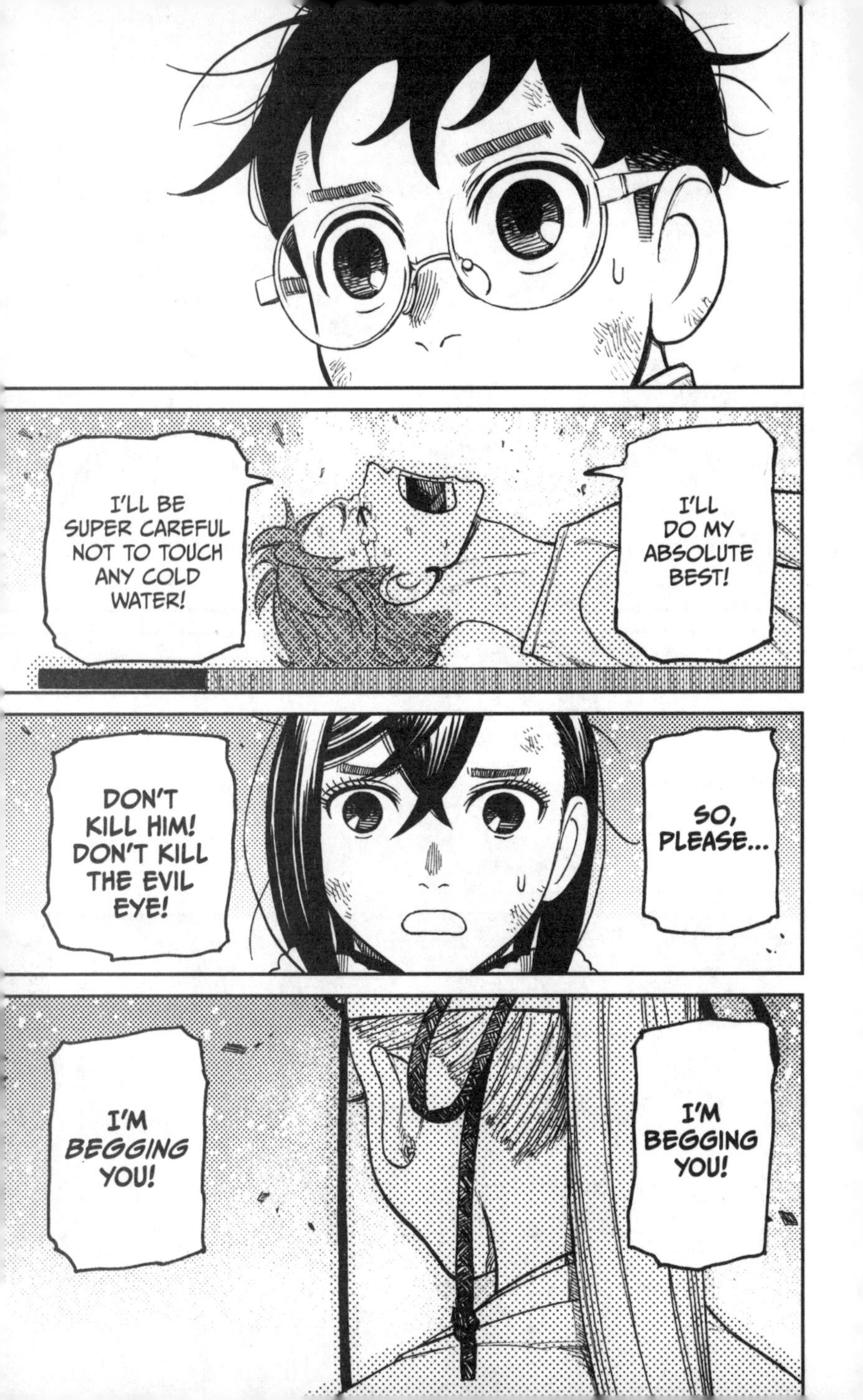
I'LL DO MY ABSOLUTE BEST!
I'LL BE SUPER CAREFUL NOT TO TOUCH ANY COLD WATER!
SO, PLEASE...
DON'T KILL HIM! DON'T KILL THE EVIL EYE!
I'M BEGGING YOU!
I'M BEGGING YOU!

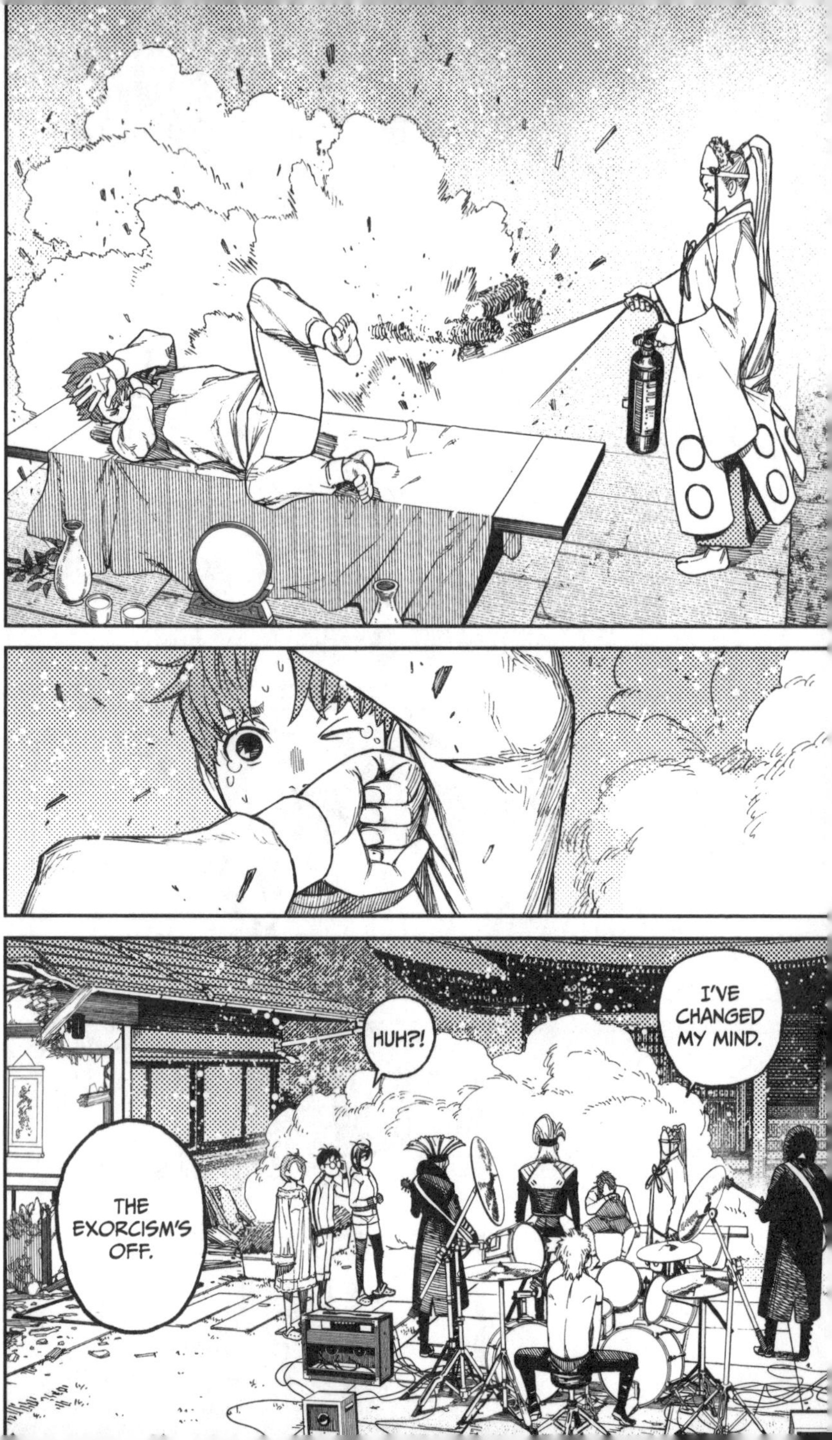
I'VE CHANGED MY MIND.
HUH?!
THE EXORCISM'S OFF.

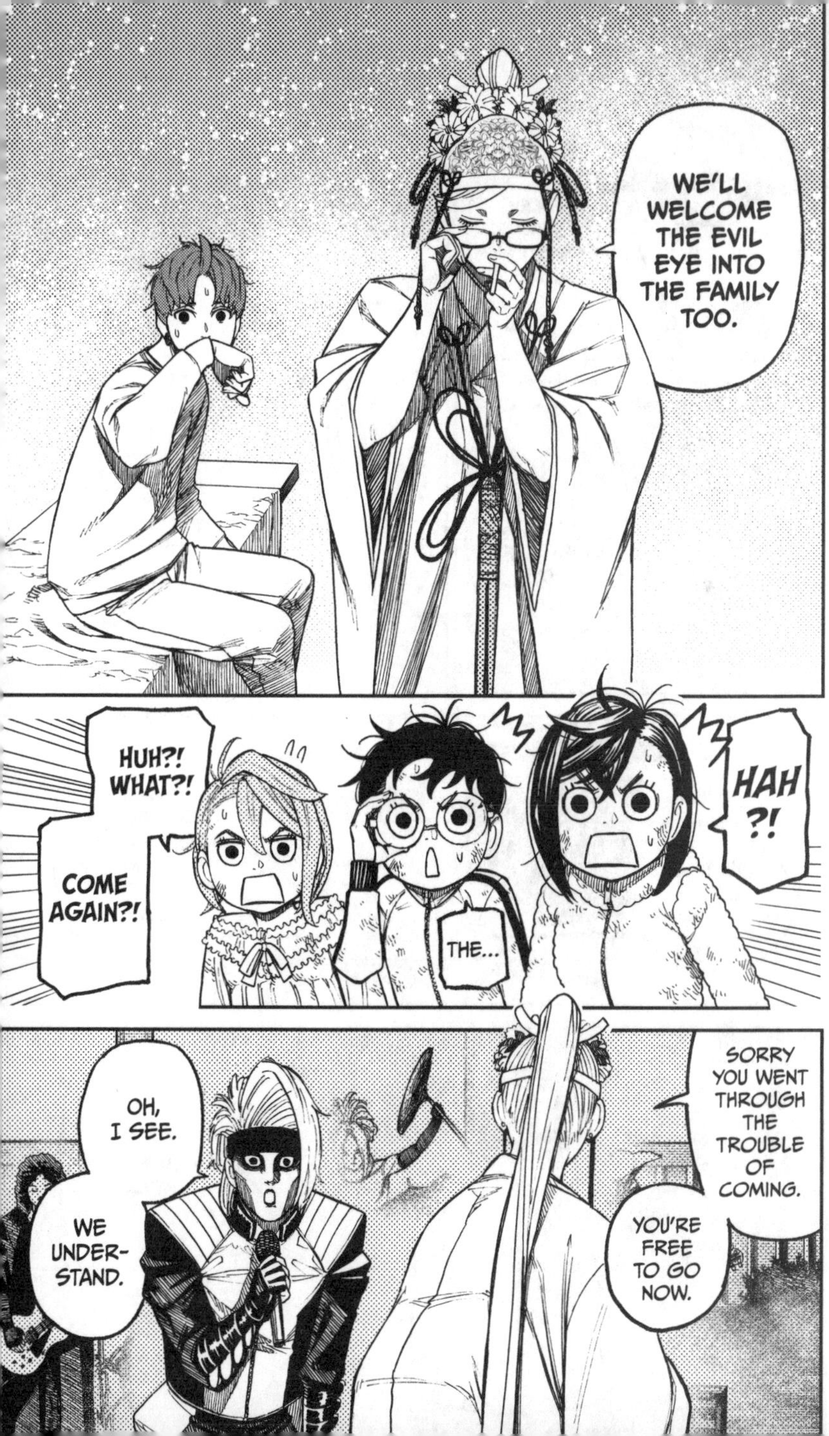
WE'LL WELCOME THE EVIL EYE INTO THE FAMILY TOO.
HAH ?!
THE...
HUH?! WHAT?!
COME AGAIN?!
SORRY YOU WENT THROUGH THE TROUBLE OF COMING.
YOU'RE FREE TO GO NOW.
OH, I SEE.
WE UNDER-STAND.

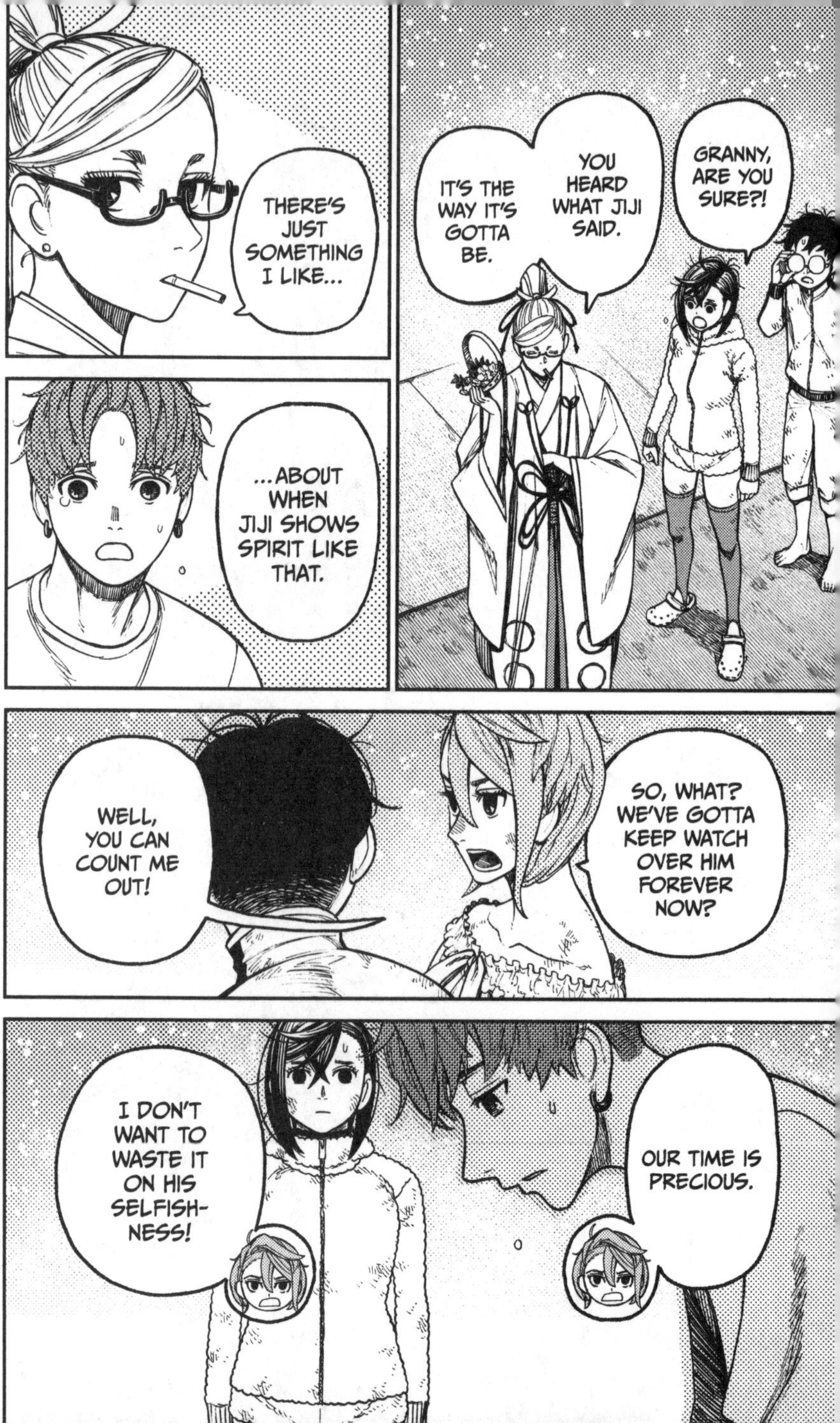
GRANNY, ARE YOU SURE?!
YOU HEARD WHAT JIJI SAID.
IT'S THE WAY IT'S GOTTA BE.
THERE'S JUST SOMETHING I LIKE...
...ABOUT WHEN JIJI SHOWS SPIRIT LIKE THAT.
SO, WHAT? WE'VE GOTTA KEEP WATCH OVER HIM FOREVER NOW?
WELL, YOU CAN COUNT ME OUT!
OUR TIME IS PRECIOUS.
I DON'T WANT TO WASTE IT ON HIS SELFISH-NESS!

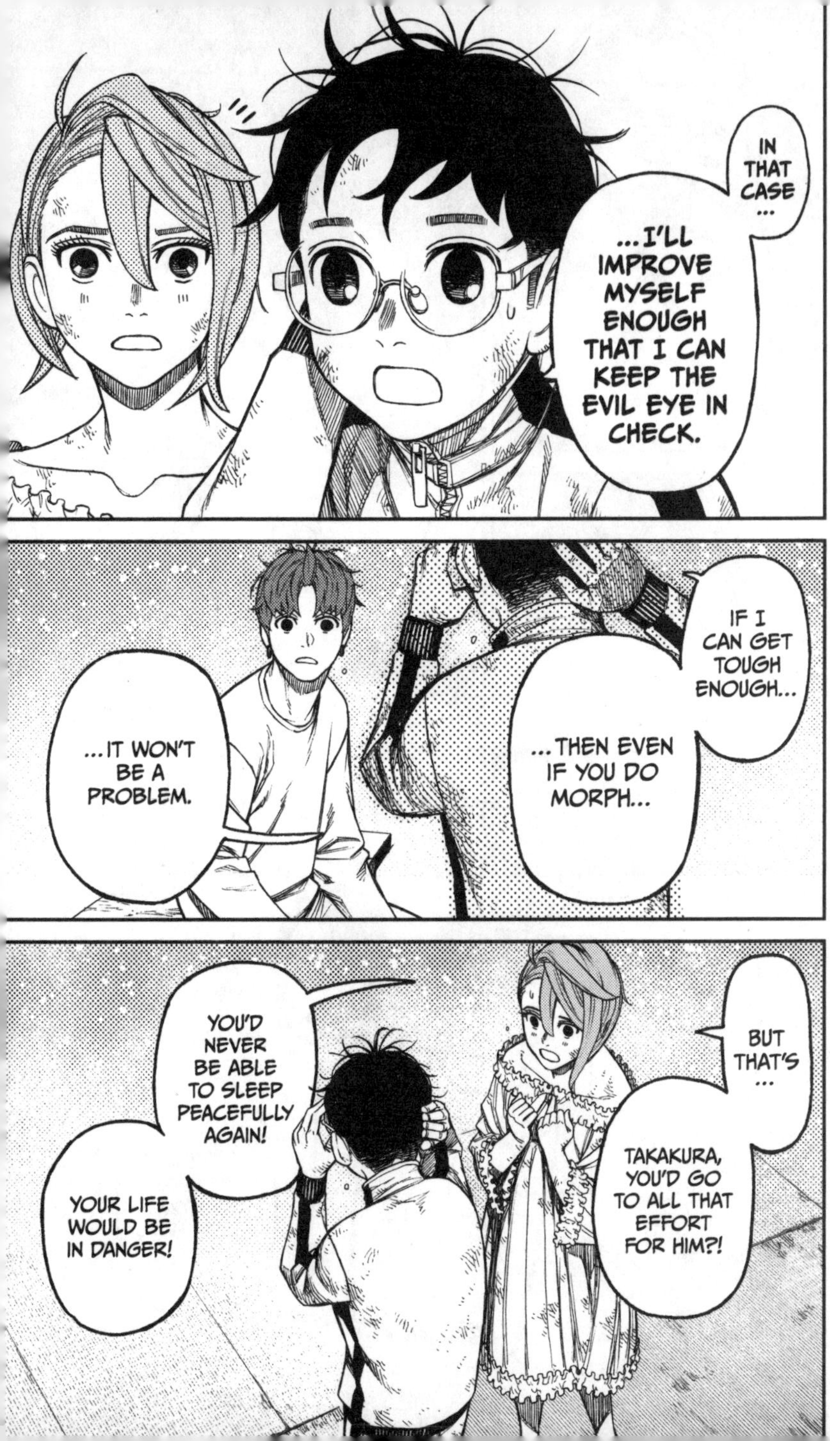
IN THAT CASE...
...I'LL IMPROVE MYSELF ENOUGH THAT I CAN KEEP THE EVIL EYE IN CHECK.
IF I CAN GET TOUGH ENOUGH...
...THEN EVEN IF YOU DO MORPH...
...IT WON'T BE A PROBLEM.
BUT THAT'S...
TAKAKURA, YOU'D GO TO ALL THAT EFFORT FOR HIM?!
YOU'D NEVER BE ABLE TO SLEEP PEACEFULLY AGAIN!
YOUR LIFE WOULD BE IN DANGER!

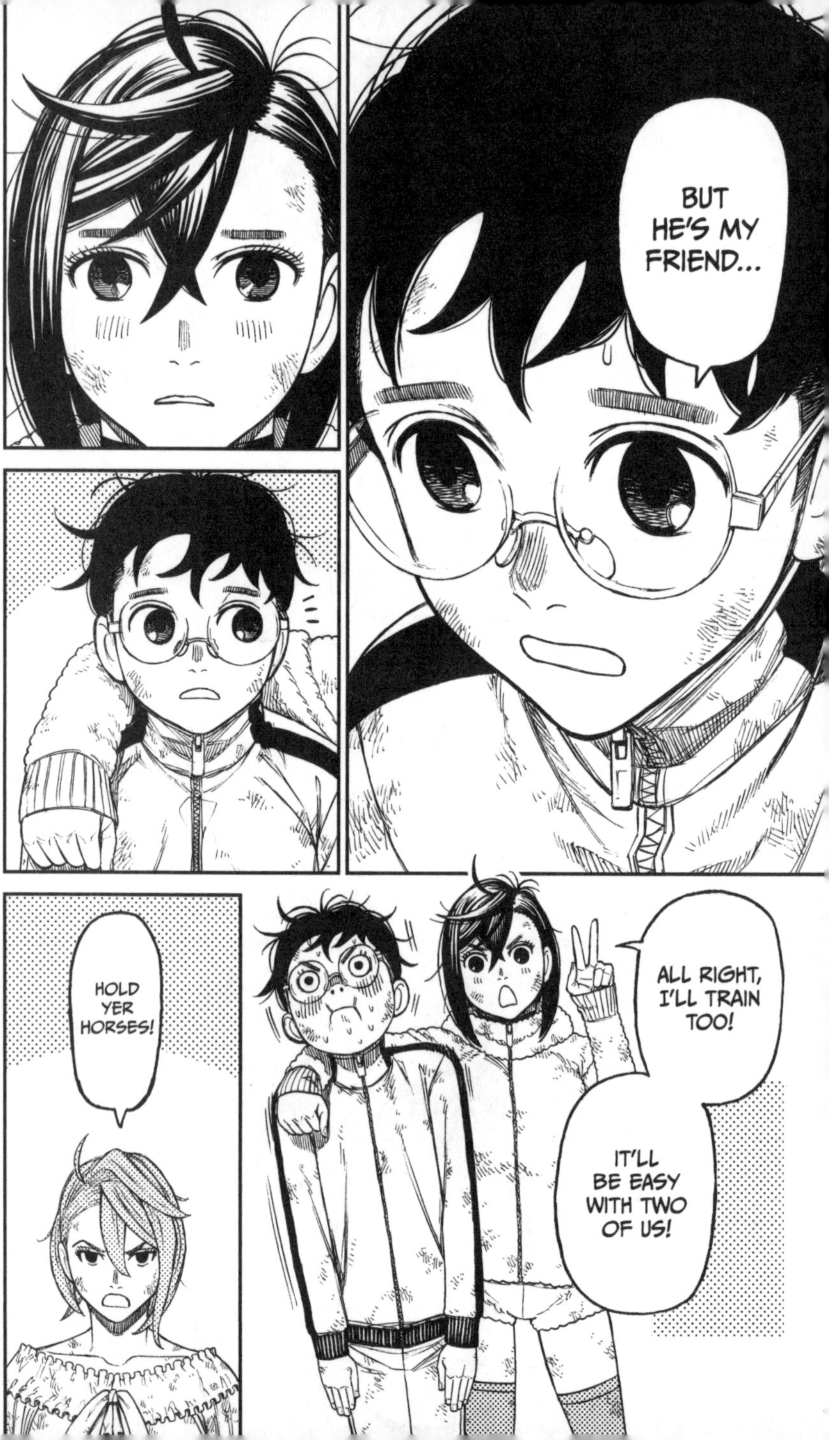
BUT HE'S MY FRIEND...
ALL RIGHT, I'LL TRAIN TOO!
IT'LL BE EASY WITH TWO OF US!
HOLD YER HORSES!

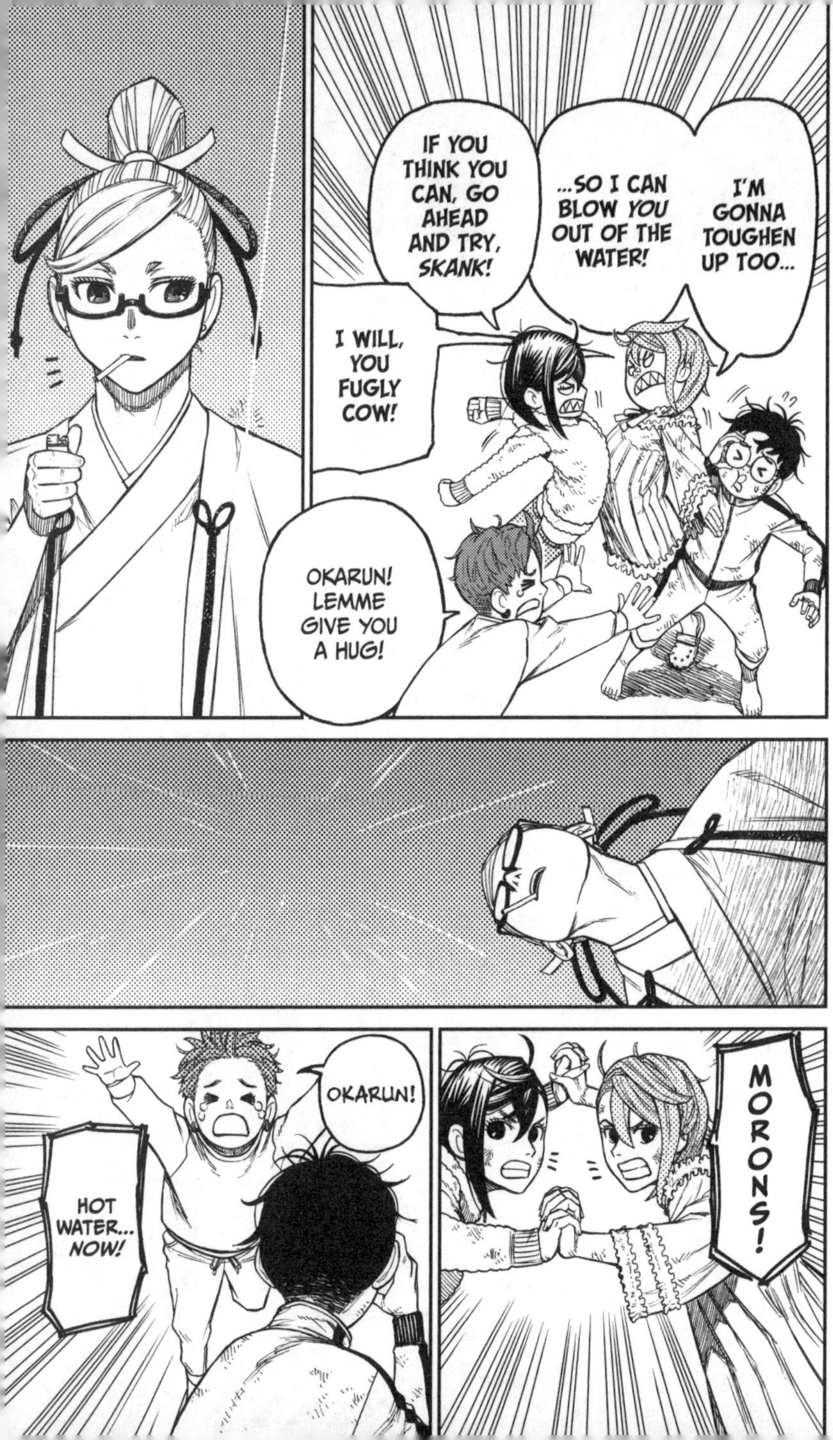
I'M GONNA TOUGHEN UP TOO...
...SO I CAN BLOW YOU OUT OF THE WATER!
IF YOU THINK YOU CAN, GO AHEAD AND TRY, SKANK!
I WILL, YOU FUGLY COW!
OKARUN! LEMME GIVE YOU A HUG!
MORONS!
OKARUN!
HOT WATER... NOW!

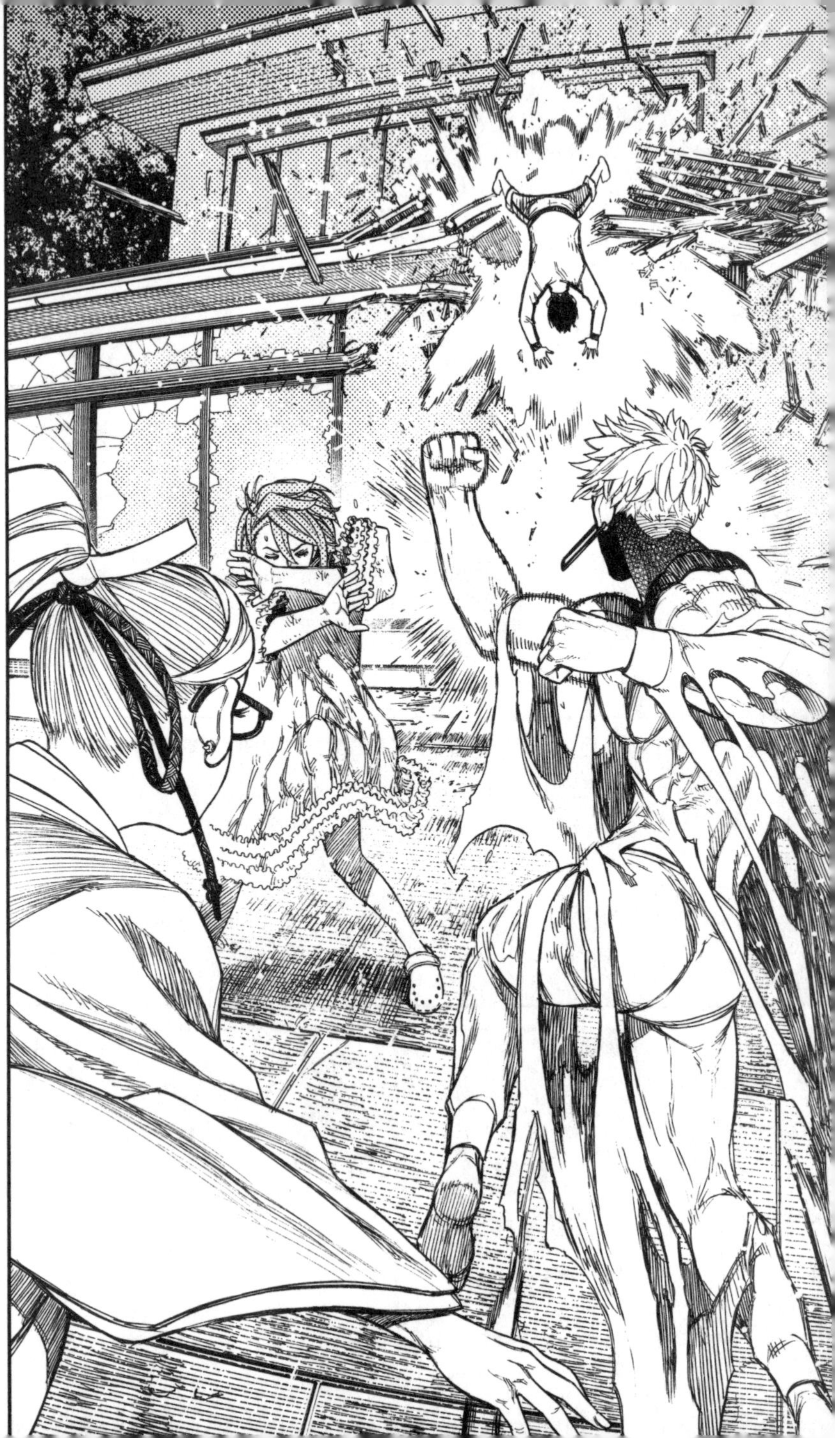

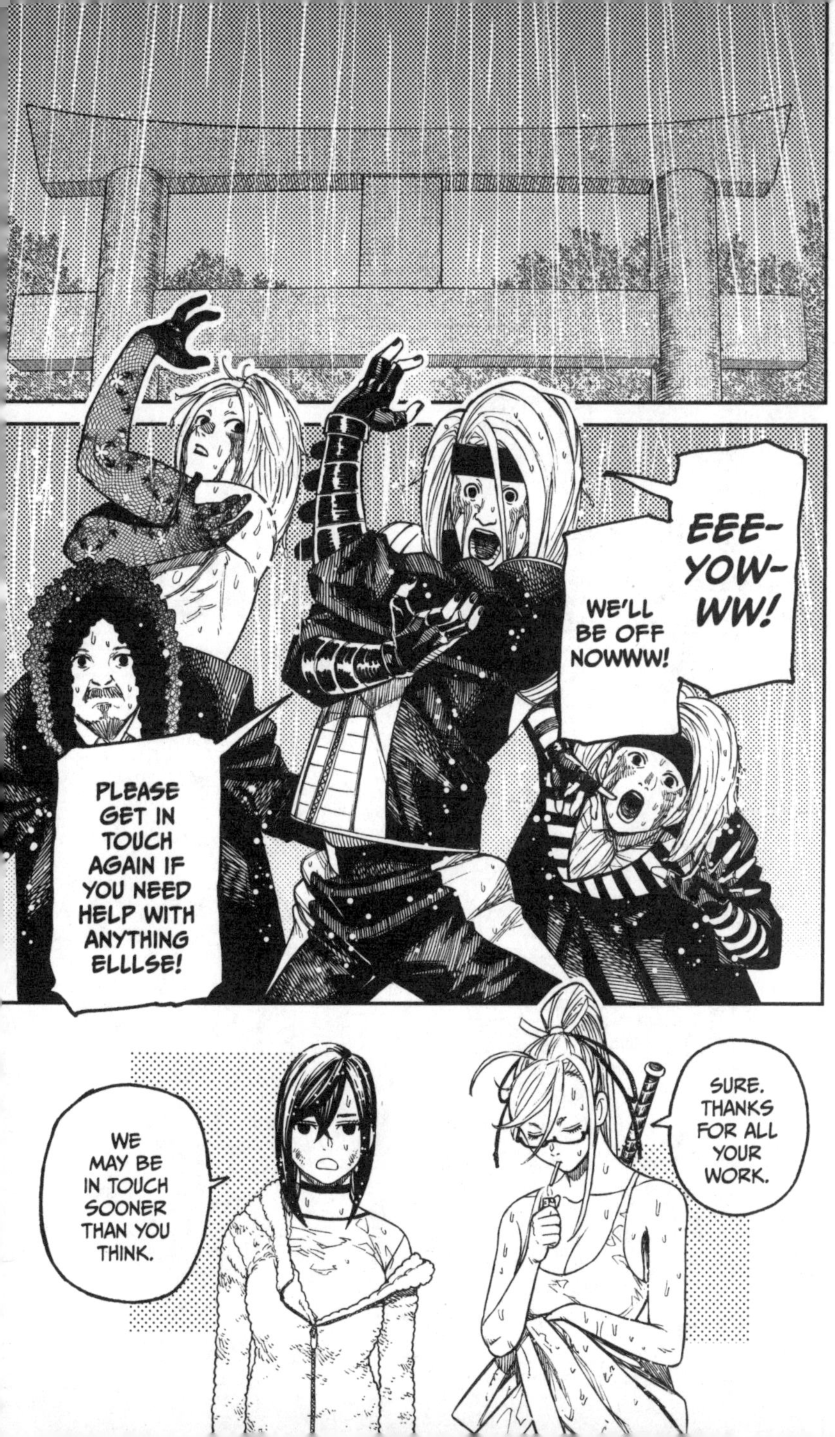
EEE-YOW-WW!
WE'LL BE OFF NOWWW!
PLEASE GET IN TOUCH AGAIN IF YOU NEED HELP WITH ANYTHING ELLLSE!
SURE. THANKS FOR ALL YOUR WORK.
WE MAY BE IN TOUCH SOONER THAN YOU THINK.

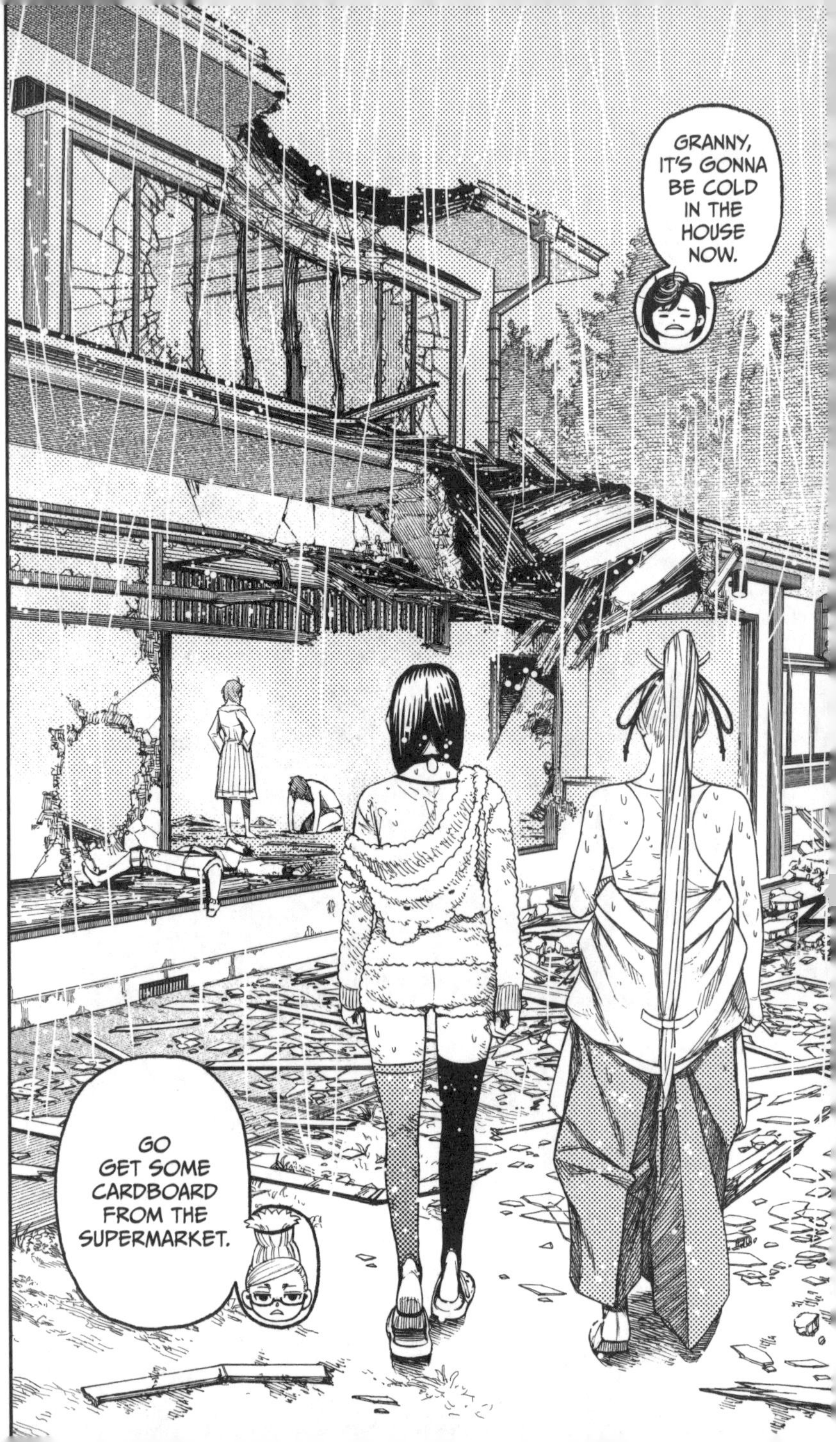
GRANNY, IT'S GONNA BE COLD IN THE HOUSE NOW.
GO GET SOME CARDBOARD FROM THE SUPERMARKET.

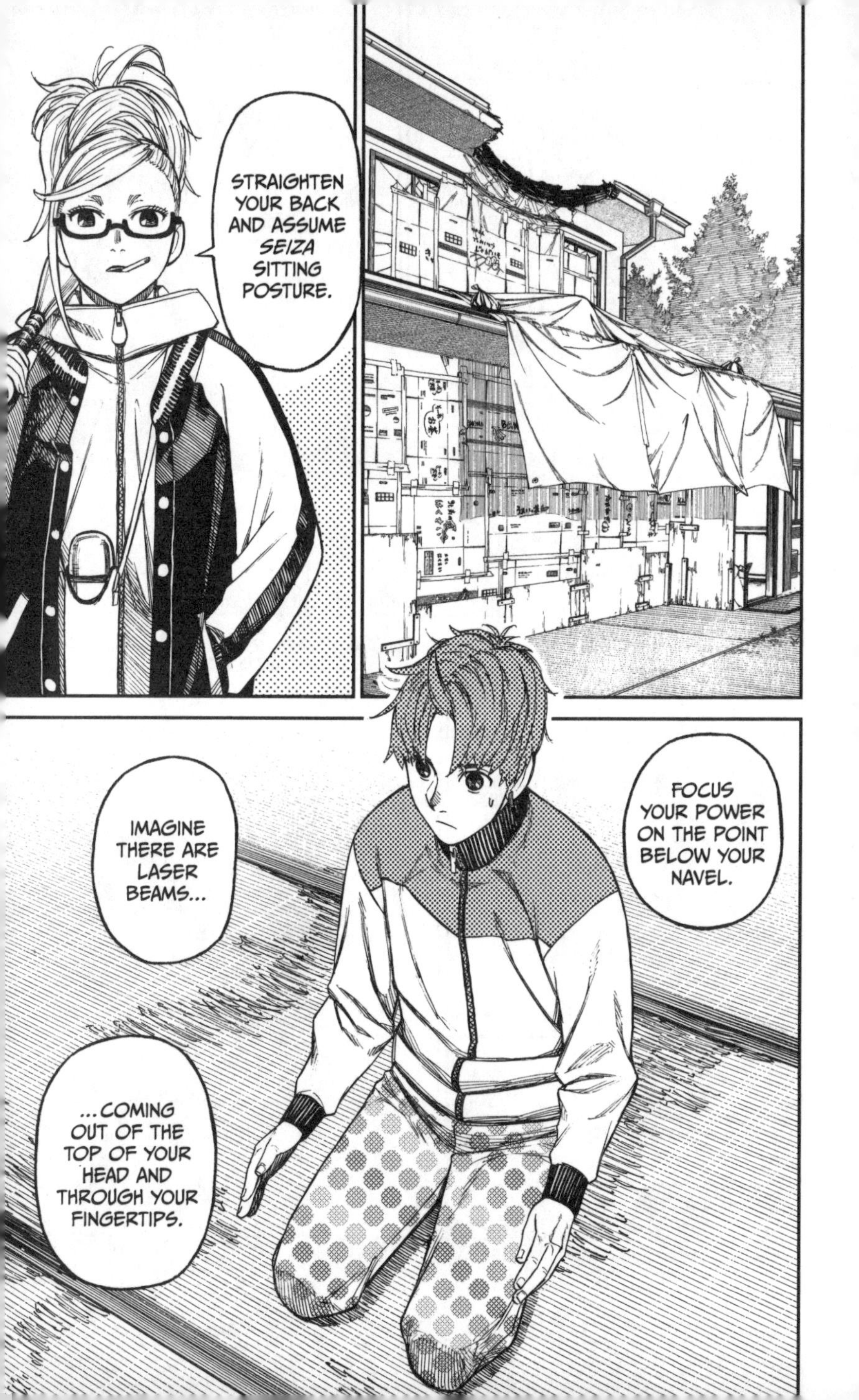
STRAIGHTEN YOUR BACK AND ASSUME *SEIZA* SITTING POSTURE.
FOCUS YOUR POWER ON THE POINT BELOW YOUR NAVEL.
IMAGINE THERE ARE LASER BEAMS...
...COMING OUT OF THE TOP OF YOUR HEAD AND THROUGH YOUR FINGERTIPS.

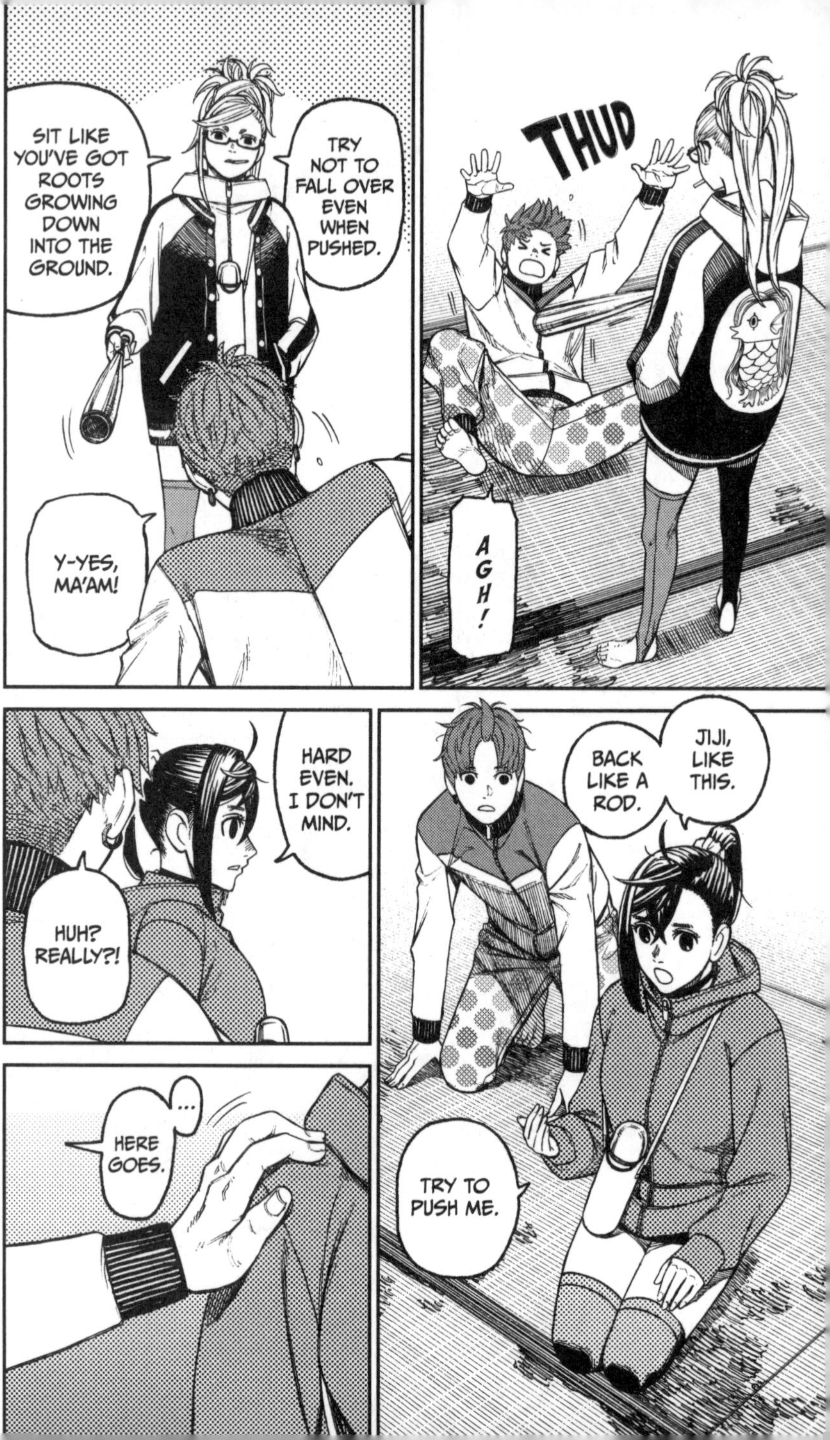
THUD
AGH!
TRY NOT TO FALL OVER EVEN WHEN PUSHED.
SIT LIKE YOU'VE GOT ROOTS GROWING DOWN INTO THE GROUND.
Y-YES, MA'AM!
JIJI, LIKE THIS.
BACK LIKE A ROD.
TRY TO PUSH ME.
HARD EVEN. I DON'T MIND.
HUH? REALLY?!
...
HERE GOES.

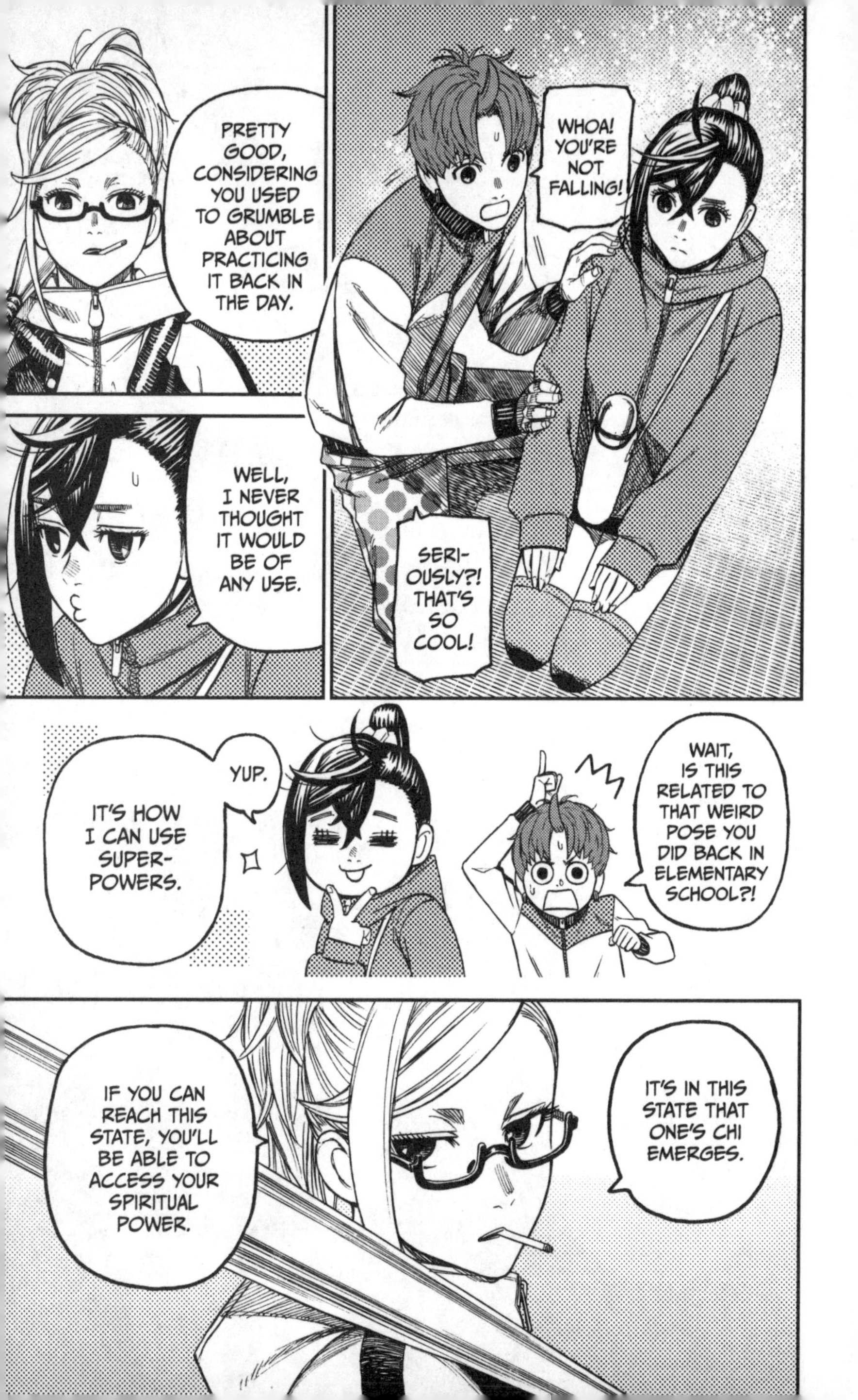
WHOA! YOU'RE NOT FALLING!
SERI-OUSLY?! THAT'S SO COOL!
PRETTY GOOD, CONSIDERING YOU USED TO GRUMBLE ABOUT PRACTICING IT BACK IN THE DAY.
WELL, I NEVER THOUGHT IT WOULD BE OF ANY USE.
WAIT, IS THIS RELATED TO THAT WEIRD POSE YOU DID BACK IN ELEMENTARY SCHOOL?!
YUP.
IT'S HOW I CAN USE SUPER-POWERS.
IT'S IN THIS STATE THAT ONE'S CHI EMERGES.
IF YOU CAN REACH THIS STATE, YOU'LL BE ABLE TO ACCESS YOUR SPIRITUAL POWER.

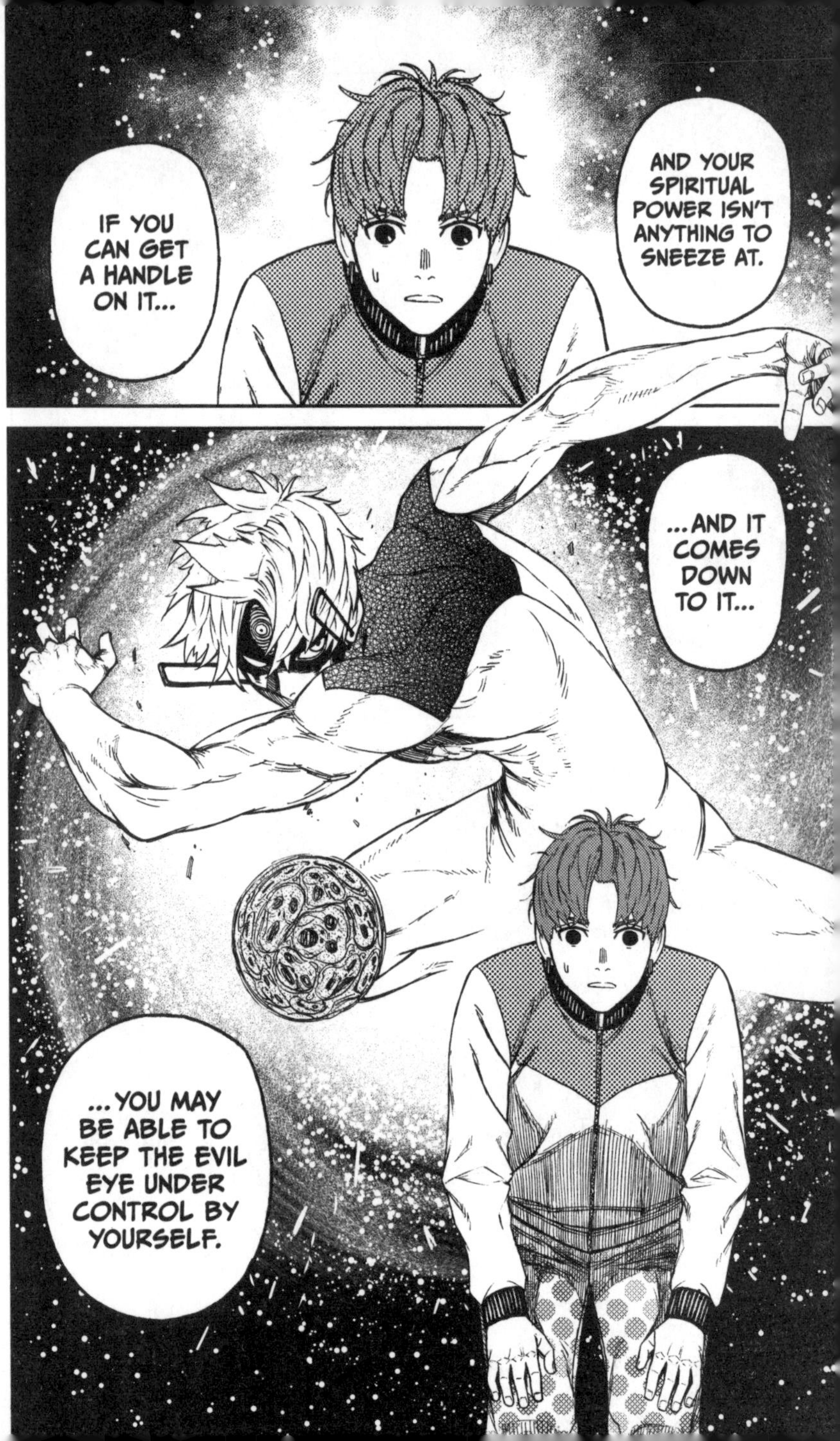
AND YOUR SPIRITUAL POWER ISN'T ANYTHING TO SNEEZE AT.
IF YOU CAN GET A HANDLE ON IT...
...AND IT COMES DOWN TO IT...
...YOU MAY BE ABLE TO KEEP THE EVIL EYE UNDER CONTROL BY YOURSELF.

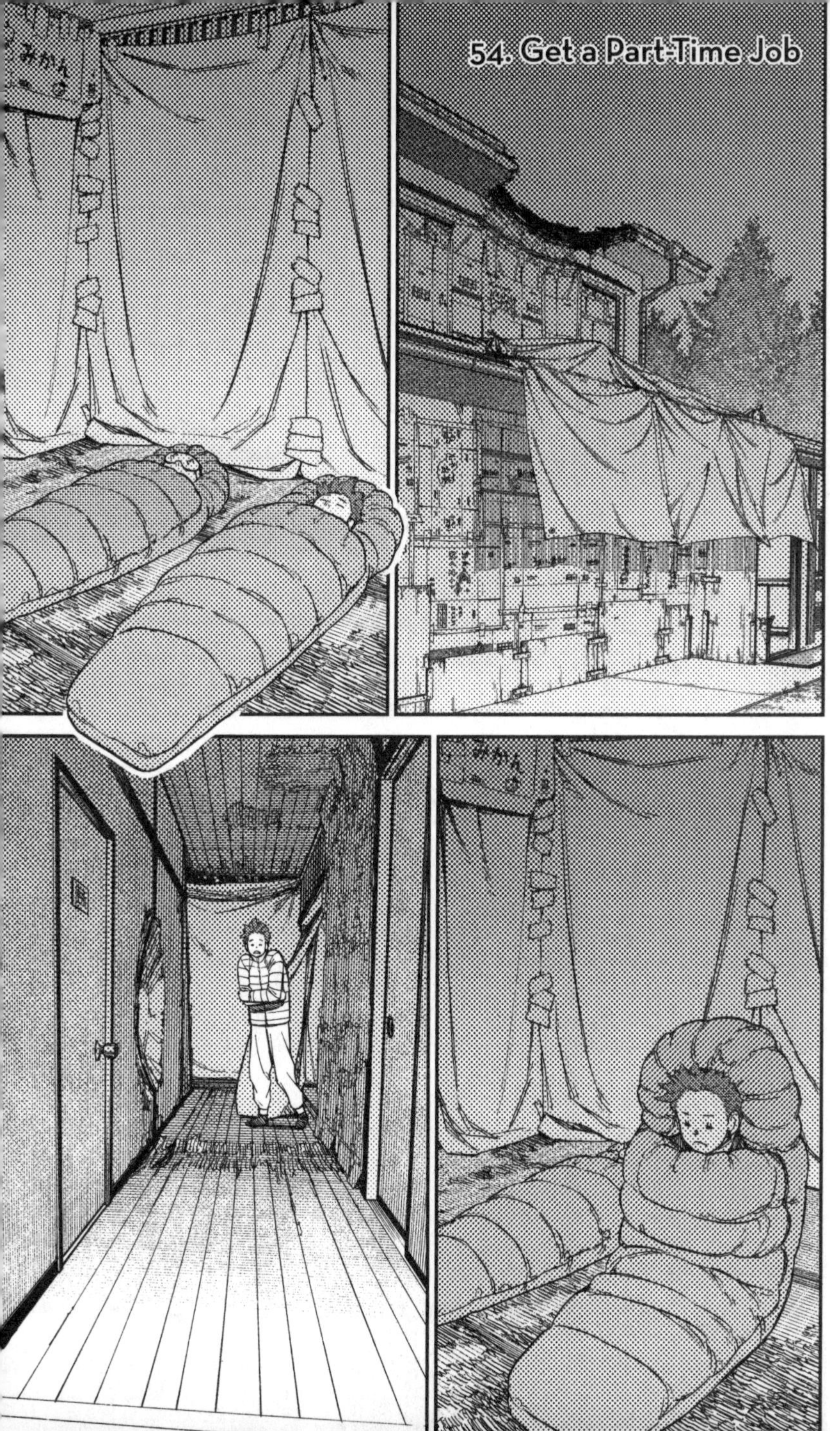
54. Get a Part-Time Job

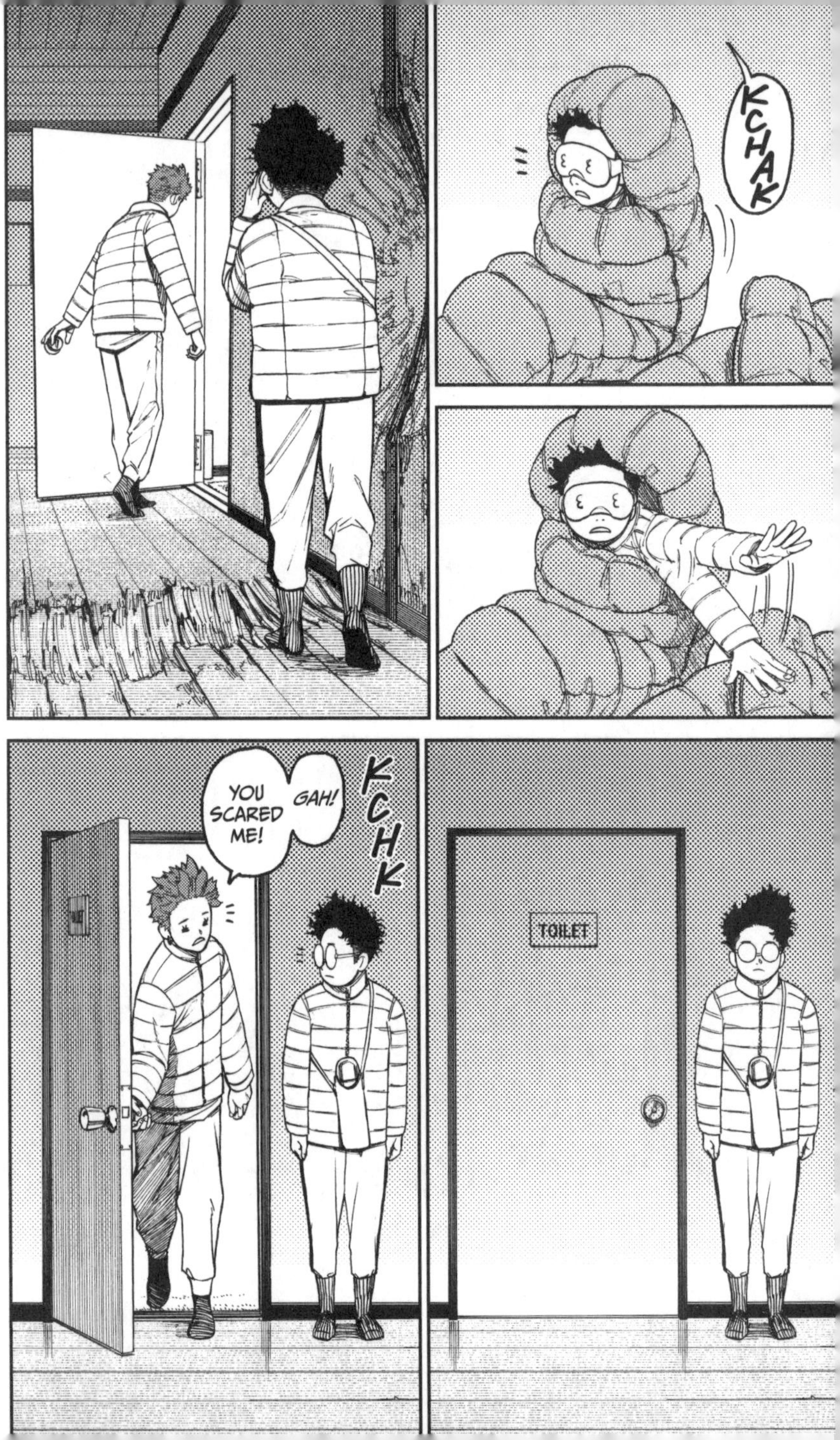
KCHAK
TOILET
KCHK
GAH!
YOU SCARED ME!

THE CARD-BOARD'S COME OFF HERE.

HEY.

SURE.

THANKS, OKARUN.

THERE'S EVENING DEW.

STAY AWAY FROM IT, JIJI.

...I CAUSED A LOT OF TROUBLE FOR MISS AYASE AND THE OTHERS.

WHEN I WAS CURSED BY TURBO GRANNY...

BUT THEY WENT OUT OF THEIR WAY TO SEE I WAS TAKEN CARE OF.

THIS IS ALL MY FAULT. I'M SORRY.

PLEASE DON'T APOLO-GIZE.

WE'RE ALL IN THIS TOGETHER.

WHAT'S THE POINT OF PAYING ME BACK? MORON.

I PROMISED MYSELF I'D PAY BACK...

...THE LIVING EXPENSES AND CLOTHING COSTS, ET CETERA...

BUT THEN...

...SO I DELIVERED NEWSPAPERS AND BROUGHT HER SOME MONEY.

...YOU CAN PAY IT FORWARD BY HELPING SOMEONE ELSE WHO'S IN TROUBLE.

...FOR LOOKING AFTER YOU...

IF YOU'RE FEELING INDEBTED TO ME...

THAT'S WHAT BEING IN THIS TOGETHER REALLY MEANS.

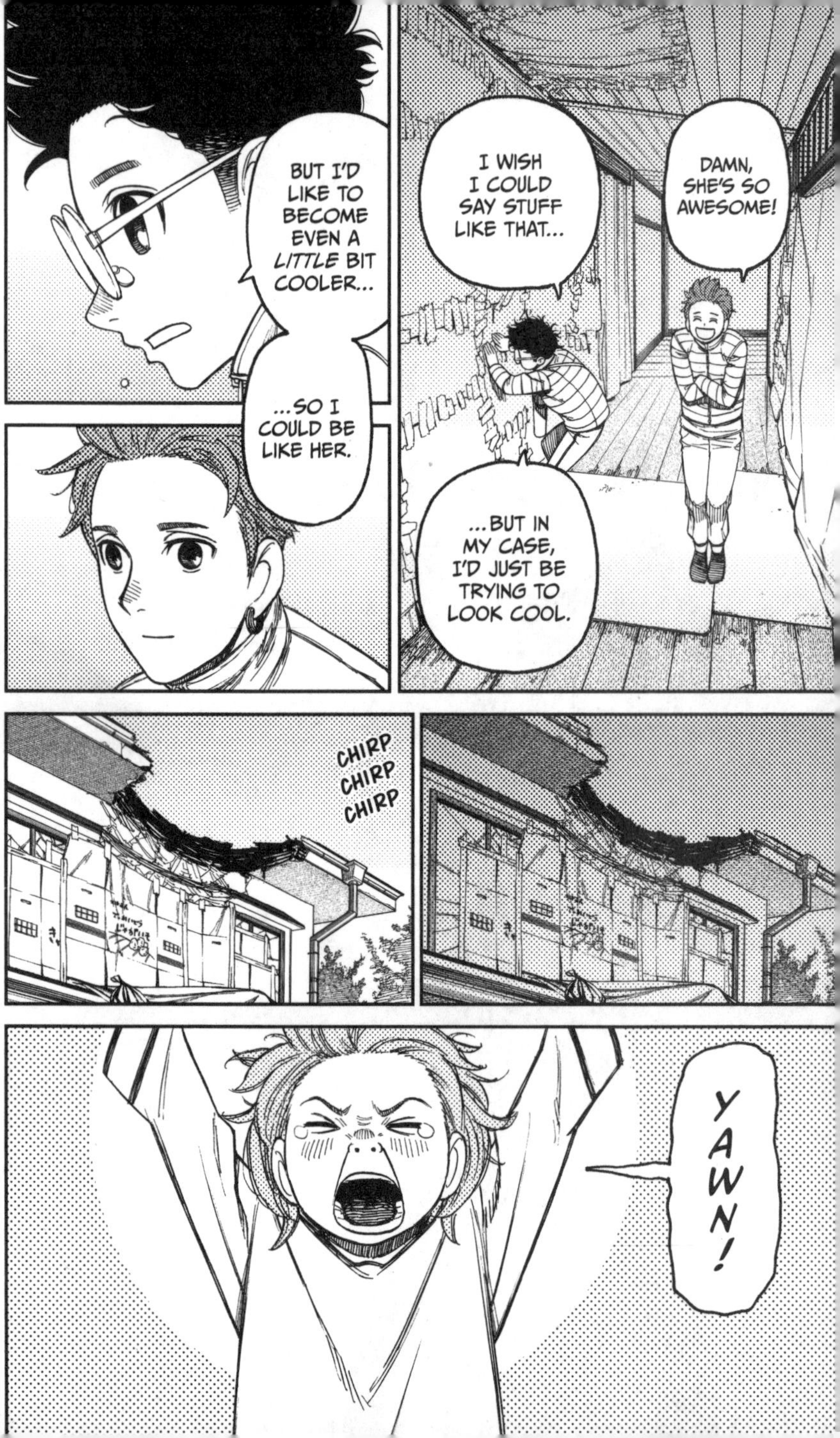
DAMN, SHE'S SO AWESOME!
I WISH I COULD SAY STUFF LIKE THAT...
...BUT IN MY CASE, I'D JUST BE TRYING TO LOOK COOL.
BUT I'D LIKE TO BECOME EVEN A *LITTLE* BIT COOLER...
...SO I COULD BE LIKE HER.
CHIRP CHIRP CHIRP
YAWN!

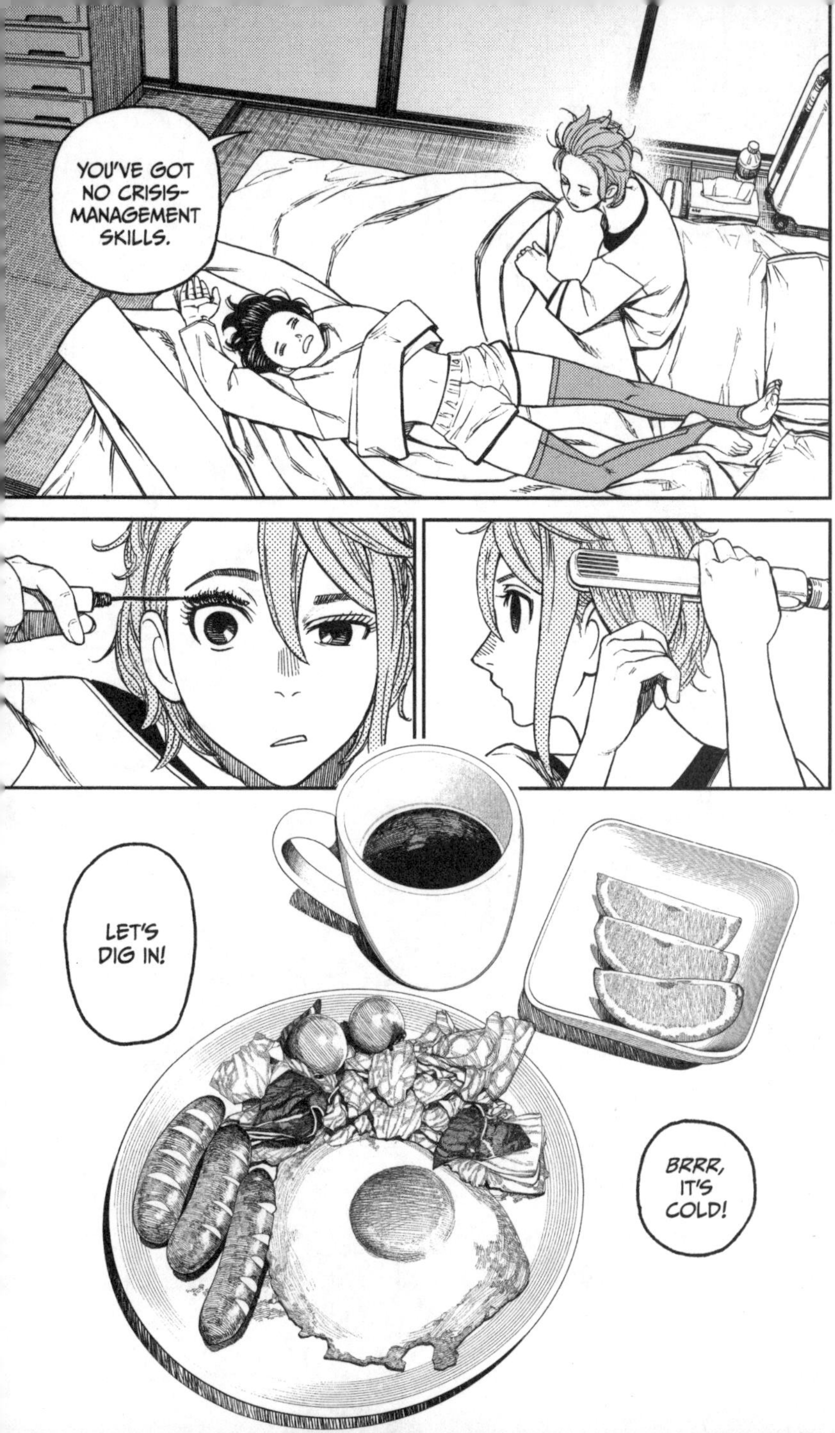
YOU'VE GOT NO CRISIS-MANAGEMENT SKILLS.
BRRR, IT'S COLD!
LET'S DIG IN!

NO, IT WOULD NOT.

SO IF MOMO AND JIJI HAD TEA TOGETHER, WOULD *THAT* BE A DATE?

WOULDN'T YOU CALL THAT A DATE?!

WE'RE JUST GOING TO HAVE SOME TEA!

I DON'T GO ON DATES!

THEN WHAT'S THE DIFF, YOU PIECE O'...?!

MRF MRF MRF!

FINE! DON'T HAVE A SINGLE DROP THEN!

I WON'T!

YOU'LL GET THIRSTY.

I WON'T DRINK A SINGLE DROP OF TEA!

OKARUN! RIGHT HERE, RIGHT HERE!

I WILL NOT!

Moe! Moe! Tri-Beam!
MAID CAFE
MOE! MOE! TRI-BEAM!

OKA-
RUN!

WHUT
THE...

MISS
AYASE!

AAH!

THREE!

HOW
MANY
IN YOUR
PARTY?

WELCOME
BACK,
MASTER!

....!

HEY,
MAID
LADY!

SERVE
THIS CUS-
TOMER!

EXCUSE ME. THAT MAID'S GOT A BAD ATTITUDE.

FINE. WELC'M.

THIS WAY.

MISS AYASE! BE MORE COURTE-OUS!

AND SPEAK CLEARLY!

YES, MA'AM...

WELCOME TO OUR ESTAB-LISHMENT, YOU SACK OF SHIT.

MISS AYASE! HOW COULD YOU?!

YOU'RE SUPPOSED TO SAY, "WELCOME BACK"!

SORRY! IT SLIPPED OUT!

I THINK I'LL HAVE THE TEA.

HMM. LET'S SEE...

PURE APPLE JUICE.

MAY WE TAKE YOUR ORDER?

MISS AYASE'S MAKING ALL THIS EFFORT...

BUT I DO! I WANT SOME-THING!

HUH ?!

YOU DIDN'T NEED ANYTHING TO DRINK, RIGHT, OKARUN?

BUT YOU SAID BEFORE YOU DIDN'T NEED ANYTHING TO DRINK, TURD!

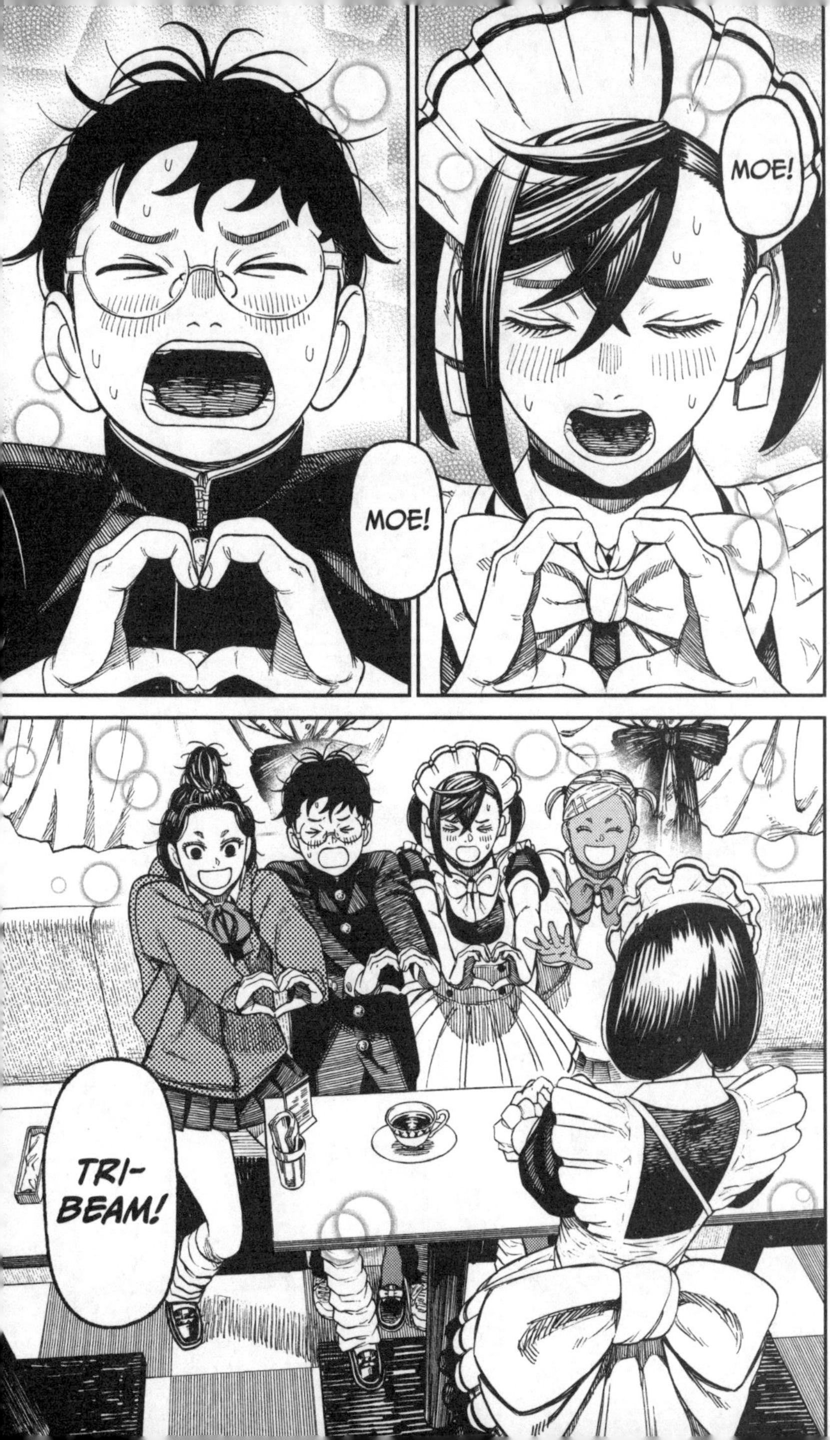
MOE!
MOE!
TRI-BEAM!

DAN DA DAN

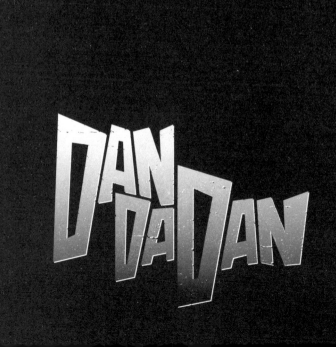

YOU BASTARDS! YOU'LL REGRET THIS, DAMN YOU!

I TOOK SOME ADORABLE PHOTOS OF YOU, MOMO!

NICE WORK YOU'RE DOING THERE!

WHO CARES?! YOU'RE A MAID!

YOU'RE SO CUTE!

YOU TOLD ME THE JOB WAS AT A RESTAURANT!

DID YOU JUST COME HERE TO MAKE FUN OF ME?!

55. Moe! Moe! Tri-beam!

WHAT'S UP?

OKARUN, LET'S GO.

ACTUALLY, I'M GOING TO STAY...

GIVE IT YOUR ALL!

SEE YA. THANKS FOR YOUR SERVICE.

SHOO!

SHOO!

LEAVE! GO!

YOU'RE ON THE ROAD TO RENOVATING!

OKARUN, YOU GOTTA GET OUTTA HERE ASAP.

JIJI WILL BE WAITING FOR YOU.

HMMM?

HAVE FUN!

SORRY FOR BARGING INTO YOUR PLACE OF WORK.

YOU SHOULD BE!

DON'T EVER COME HERE AGAIN!

MISS AYASE, WHAT TIME ARE YOU HERE TILL?

GEEZ, IT'S COLD!

UH... TEN.

HUH?!

THEN I'LL STAY HERE UNTIL YOU'RE DONE.

ALL RIGHT.

IT'S DANGEROUS FOR A GIRL TO GO HOME...

...ALONE AT NIGHT.

AND IT'S FREEZING. YOU'LL CATCH A COLD!

NO. I TOLD YOU TO LEAVE.

TAKE CARE.

OKAY, THEN...

I'LL BE FINE.

I'M TOUGH.

NUH-UH!

I... SEE...

HUH. GUESS I'LL HEAD HOME, THEN.

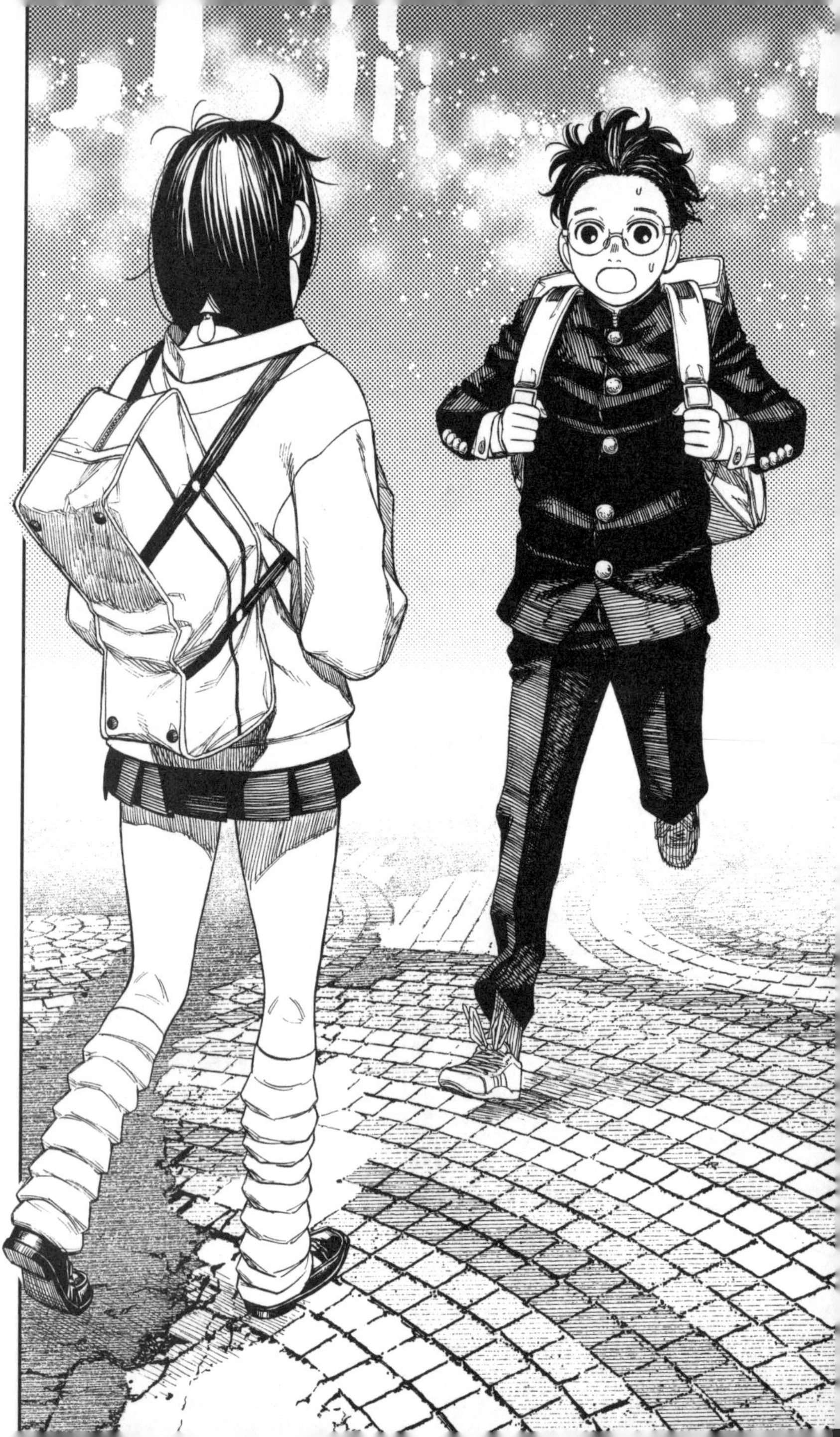

ALL DONE WITH WORK?!

HUFF HUFF

HUH?! WAIT. YOU DIDN'T GO HOME?!

HUFF HUFF

MISS AYASE!

NOW LET'S GET HOME QUICKLY!

I CAN'T VERY WELL LEAVE A GIRL BY HERSELF AT THIS HOUR!

BRR, IT SURE IS COLD!

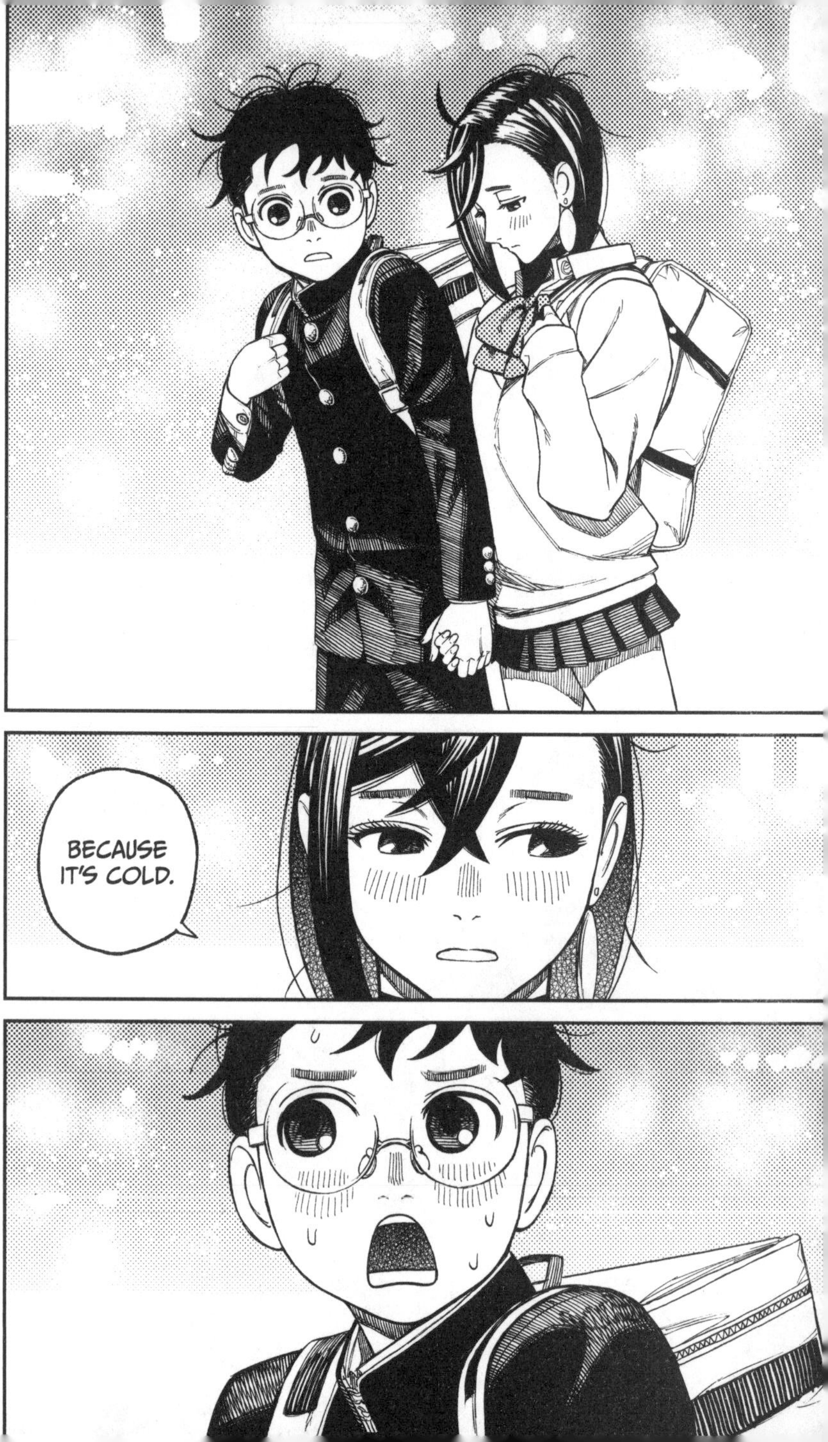
BECAUSE IT'S COLD.

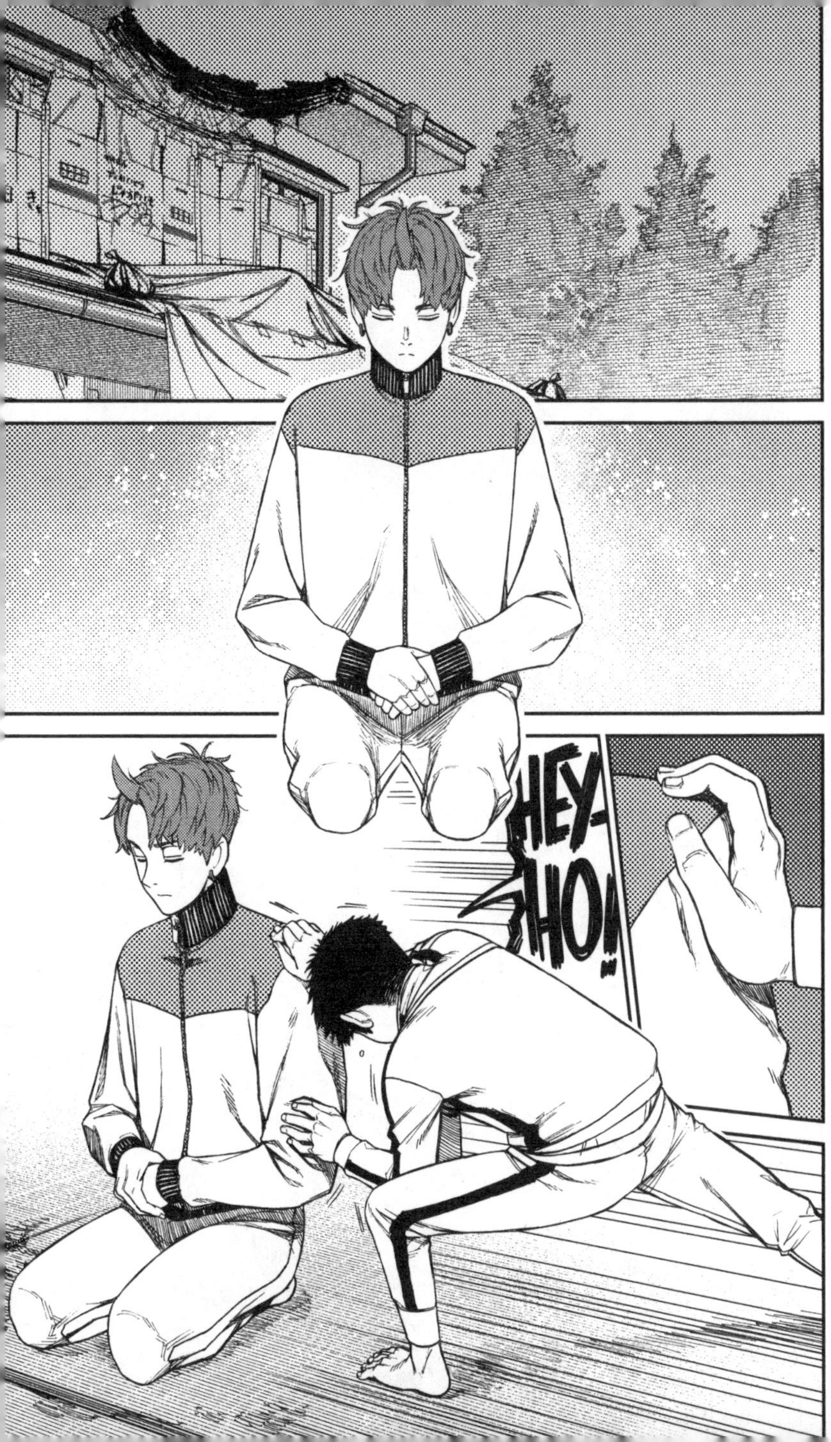
HEY-HO!!

IT'LL BE OKAY.

BELIEVE IN YOUR- SELF.

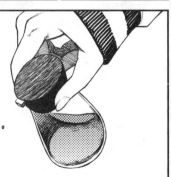

OKAY. HERE WE GO.

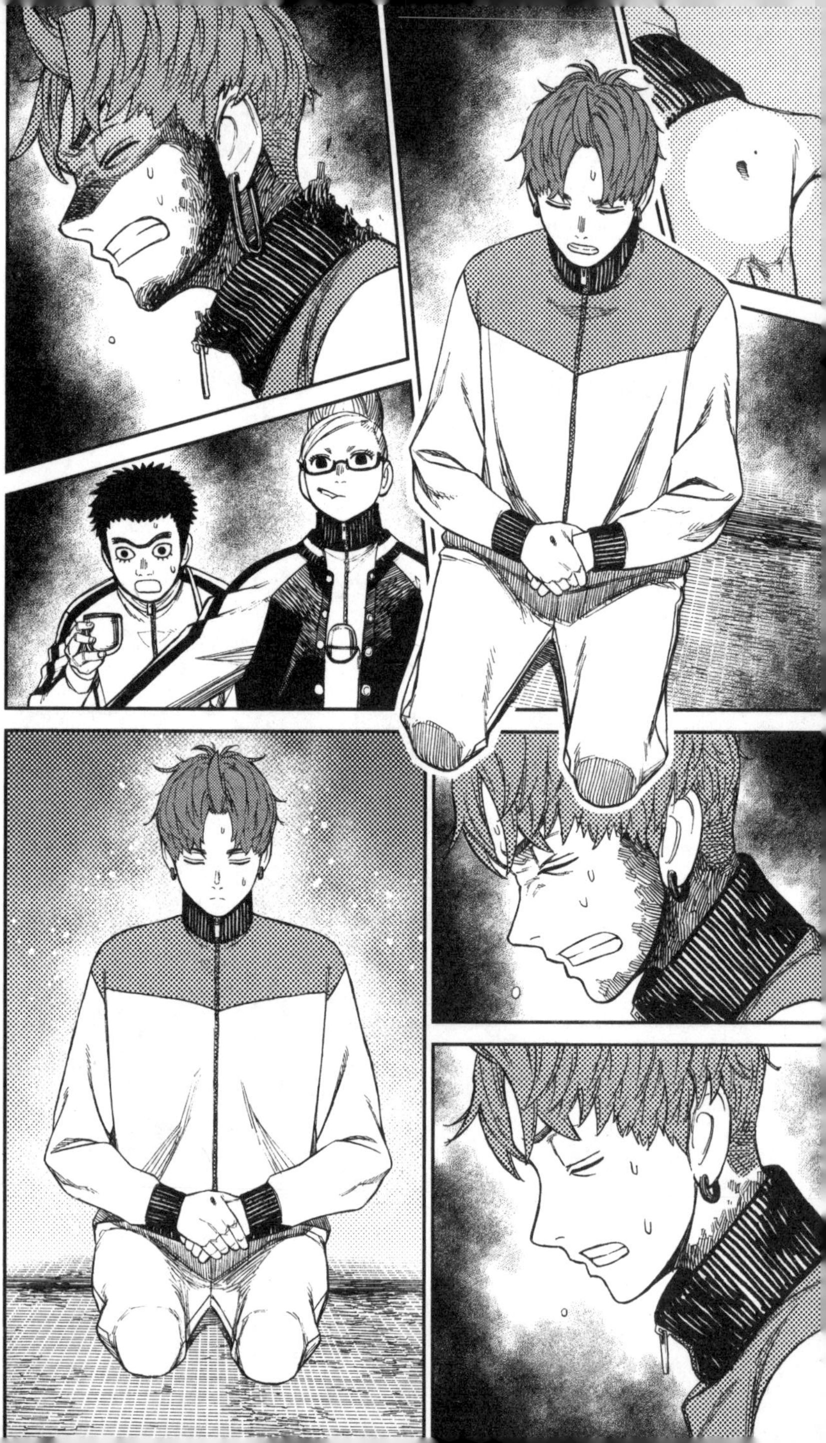

THAT TOTALLY DRAINED ALL MY STRENGTH!

YIKES!

AMAZING! IS SUCH A THING EVEN POSSIBLE?!

THAT WAS CLOSE!

YOU'RE A REAL PRODIGY, YOU KNOW.

UN-REAL.

...BUT COLD ONES ARE STILL OUT.

YOU MAY BE ABLE TO HANDLE ROOM TEMPERATURE LIQUIDS...

DON'T DROP YOUR GUARD.

IT SEEMS YOU'LL BE ABLE TO RETURN TO NORMAL LIFE.

AT LEAST IT'S GOOD TO KNOW YOU'RE CAPABLE OF SUPPRESSING IT.

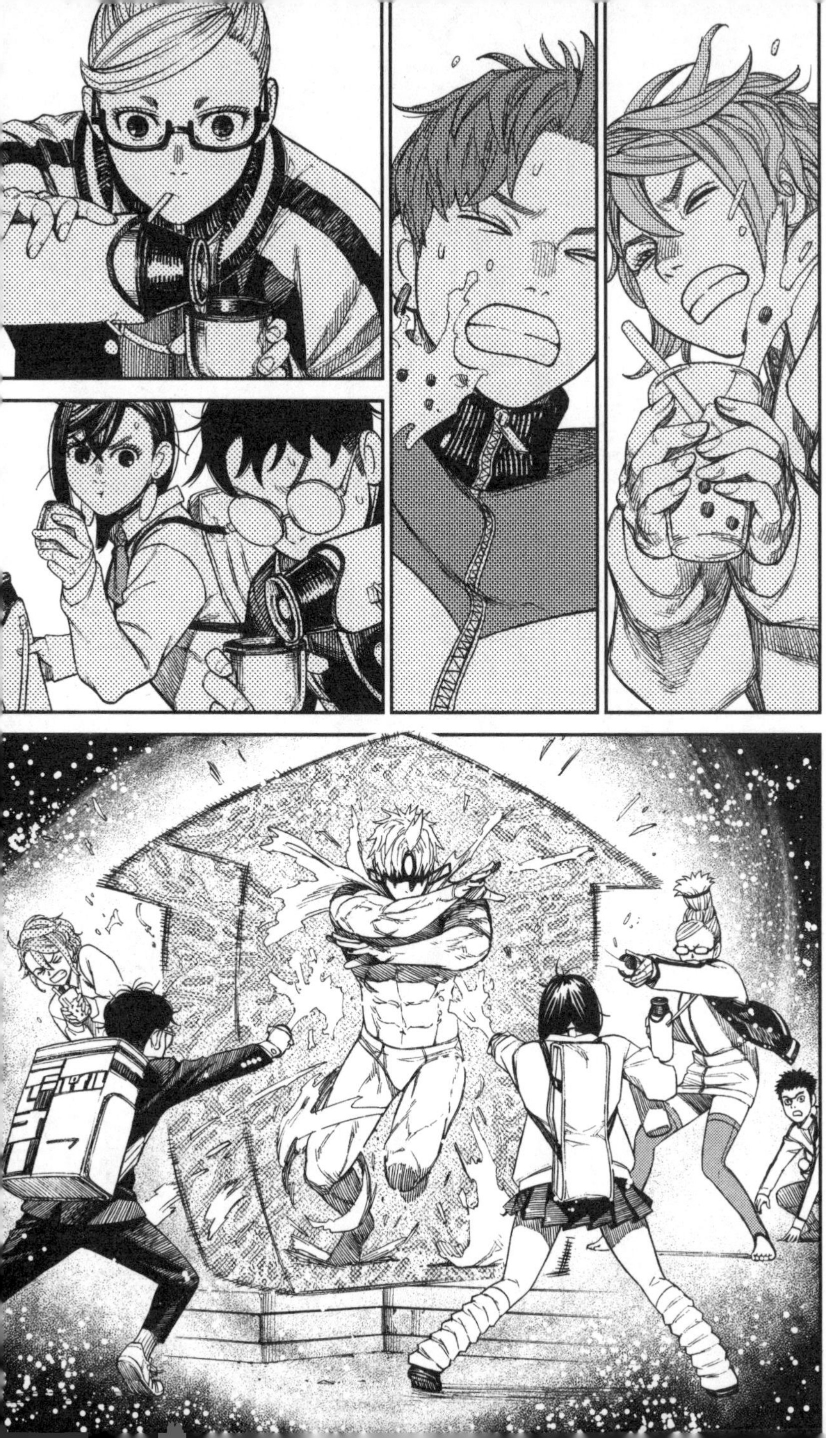

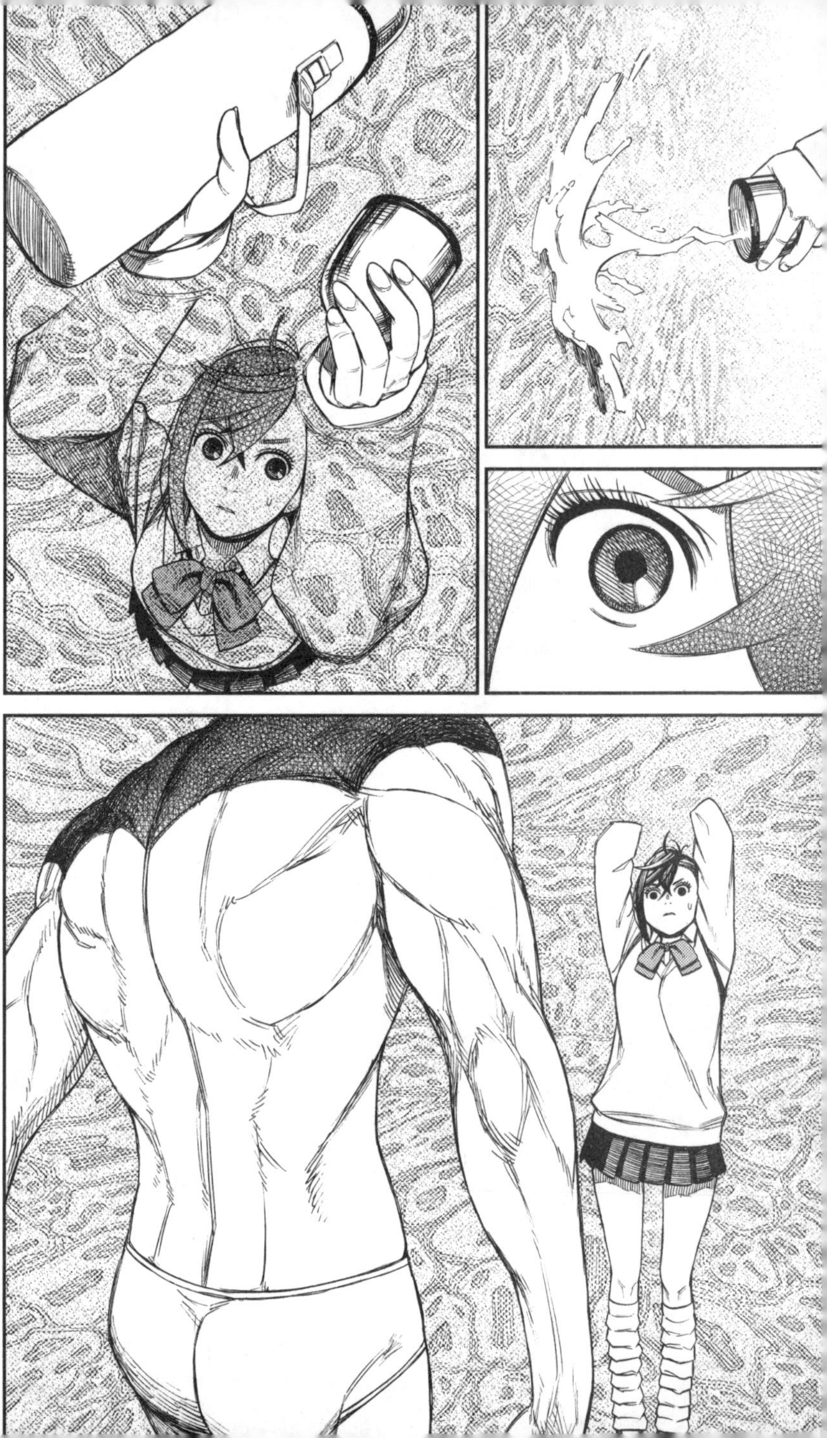

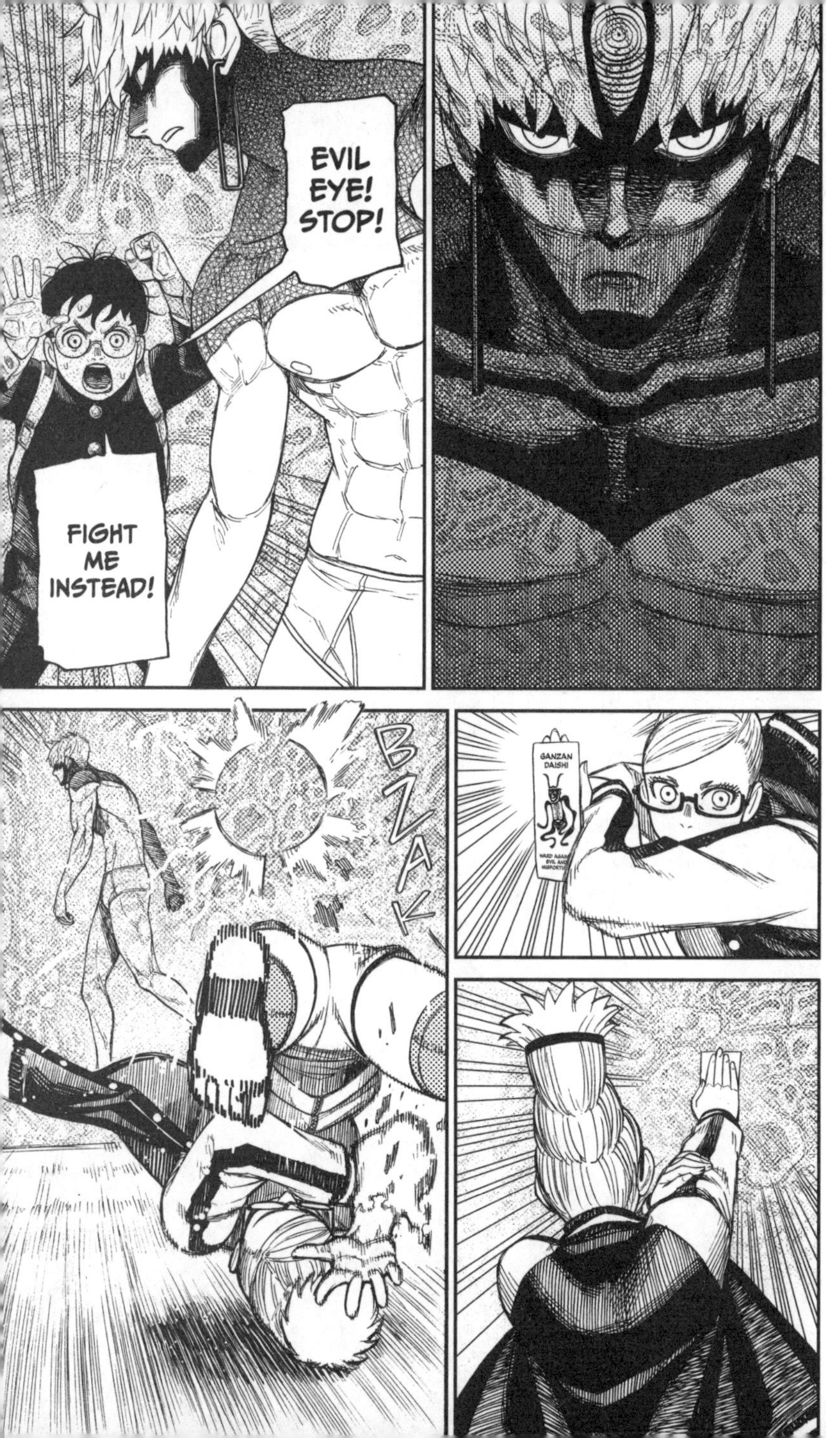
EVIL EYE! STOP!
FIGHT ME INSTEAD!
GANZAN DAISHI
BZAK

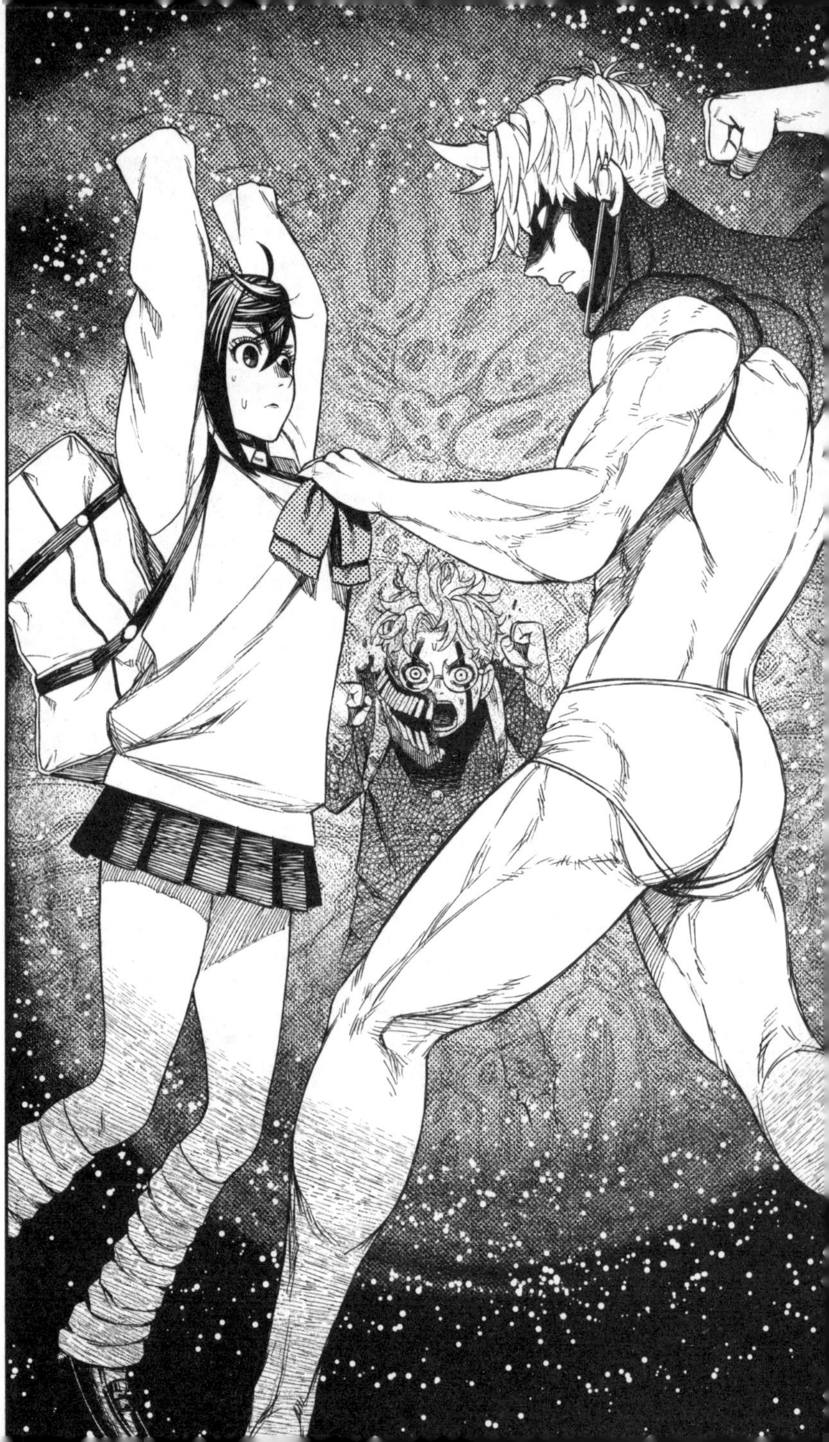

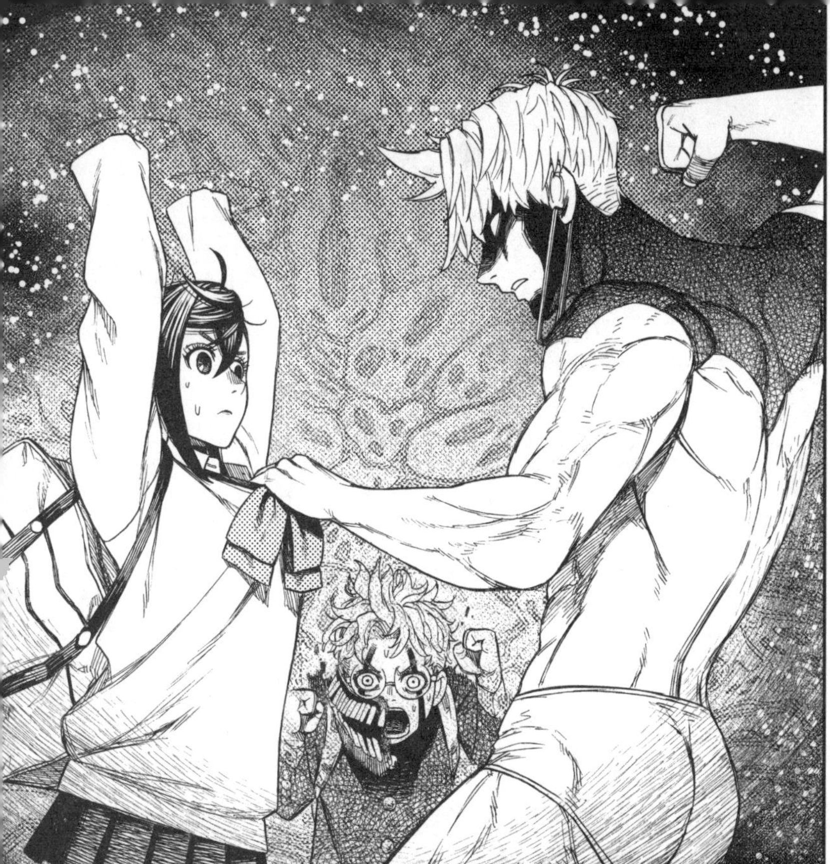
56. Feeling Kinda Gloomy
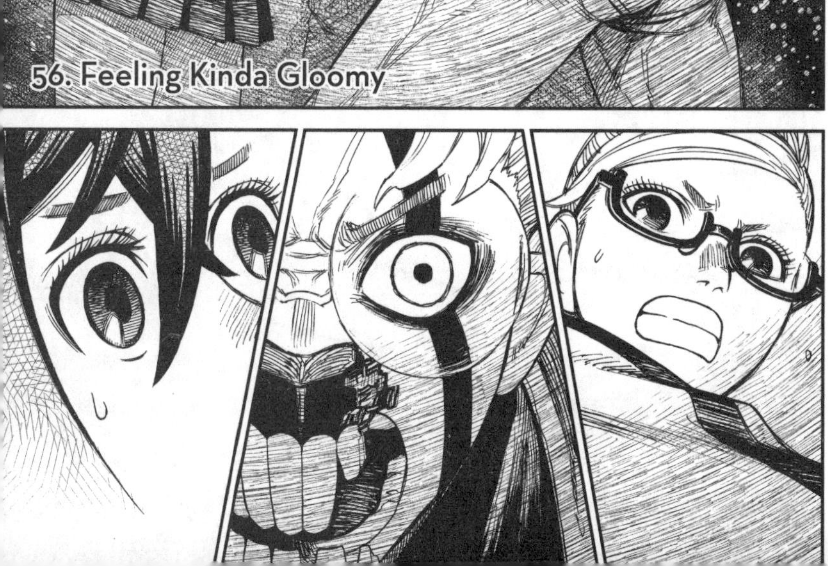

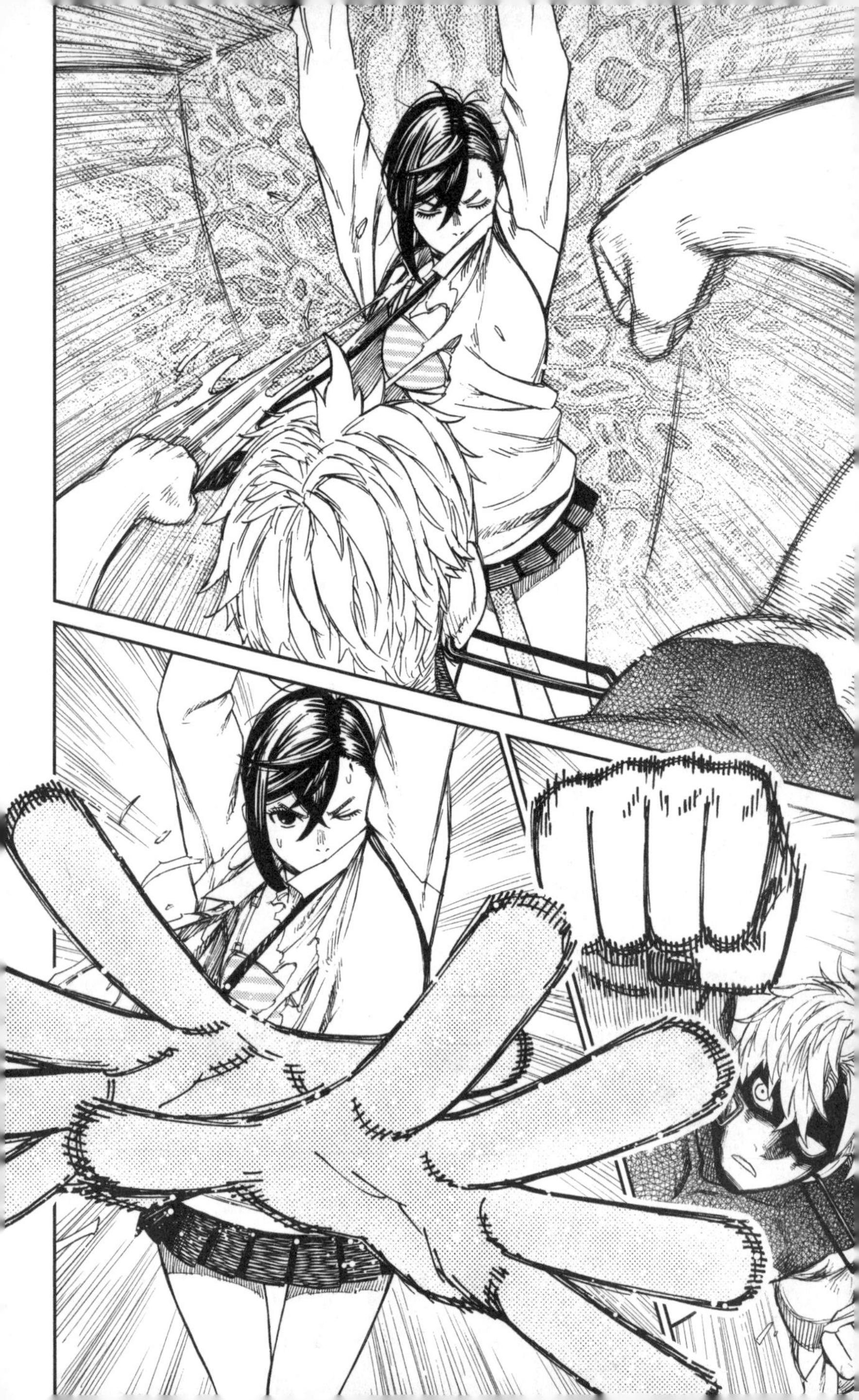

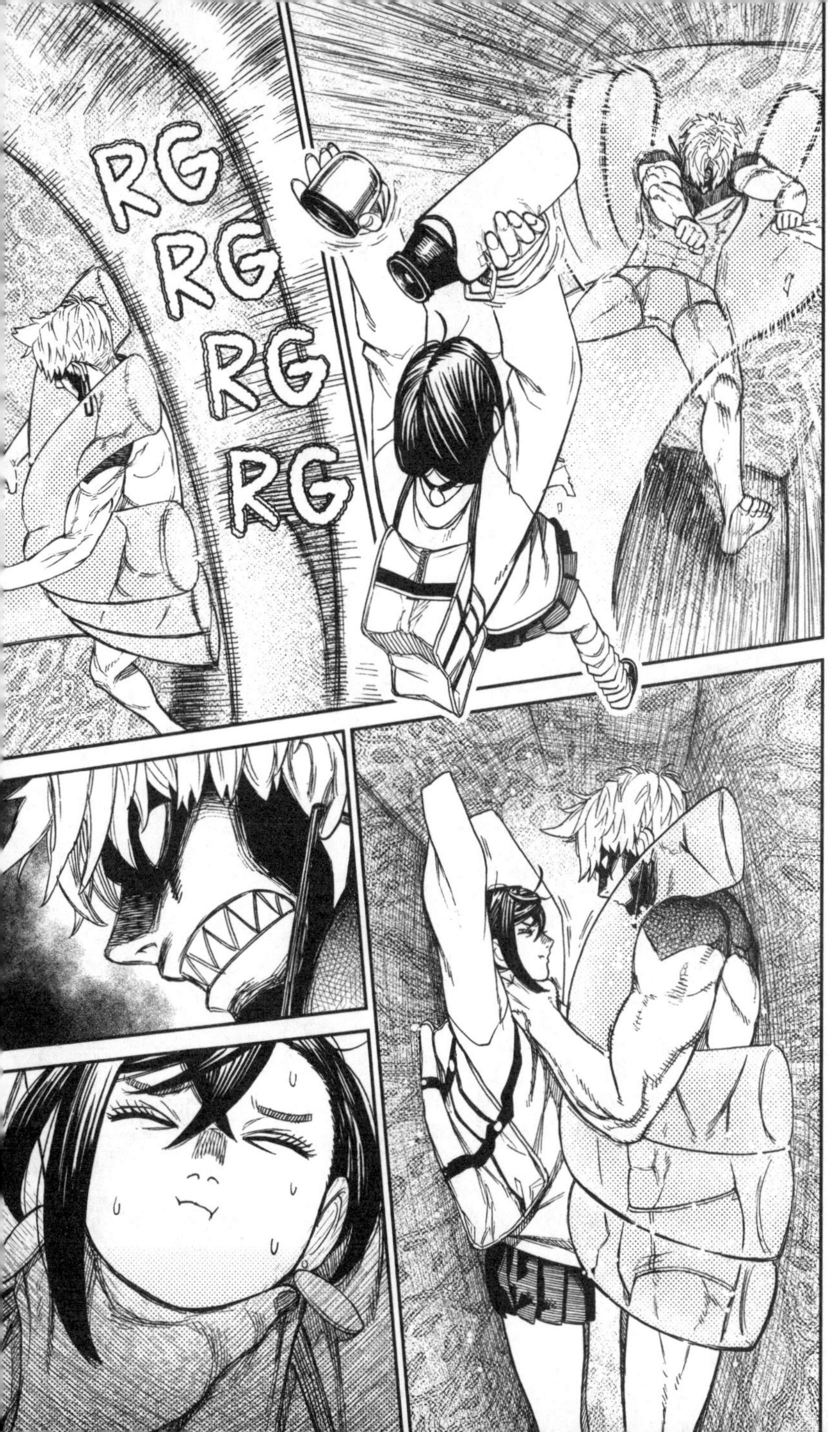
RG
RG
RG
RG

I'LL HAVE SOME OF THIS HOT WATER, IF I MAY.

THAT WAS CLOSE!

THANK GOD I DIDN'T SWALLOW IT!

I... CAN'T BELIEVE I DID THAT!

MOMO! I'M SO SORRY!

IT'S OKAY! IT'S OKAY!

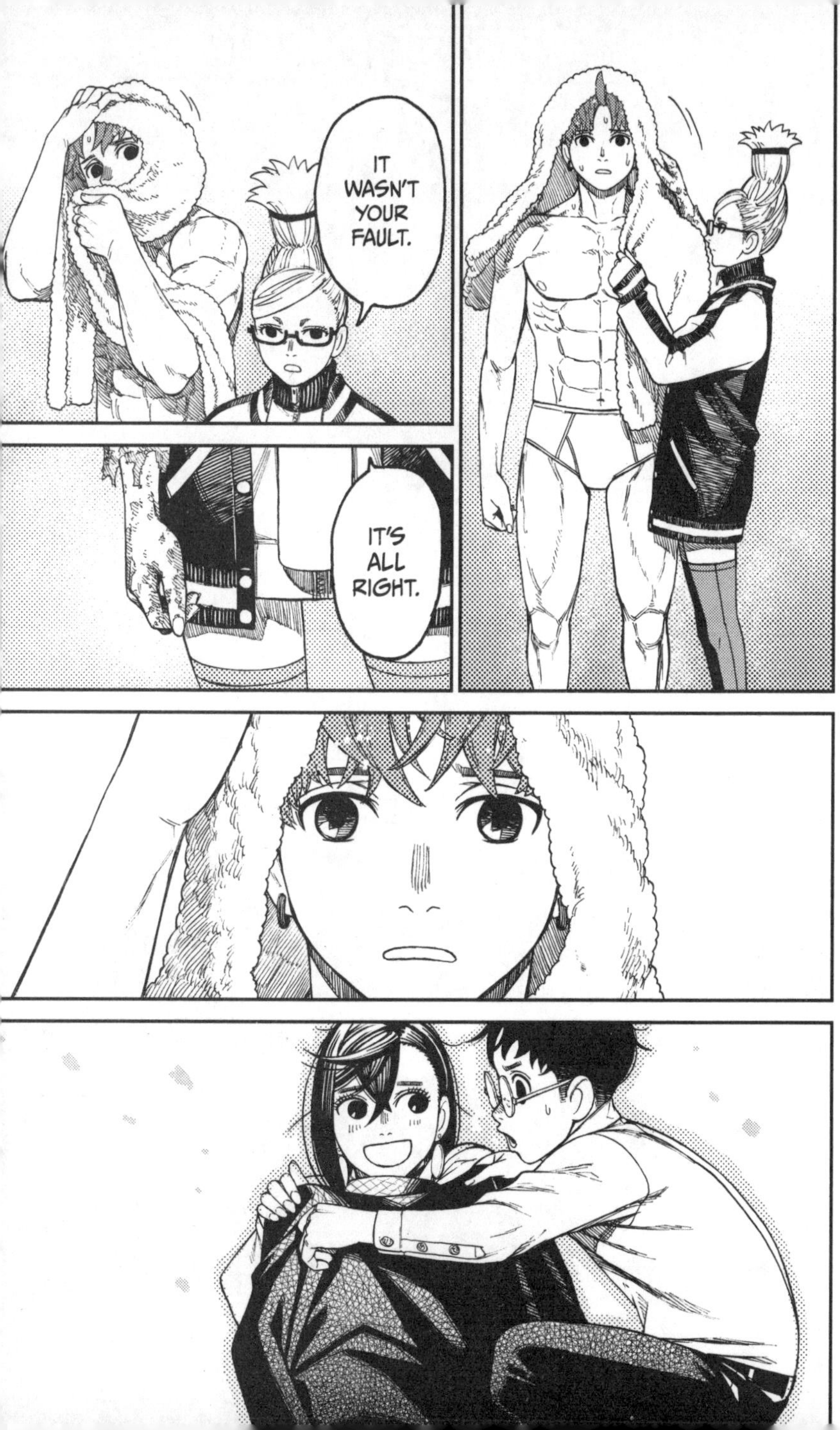
IT WASN'T YOUR FAULT.
IT'S ALL RIGHT.

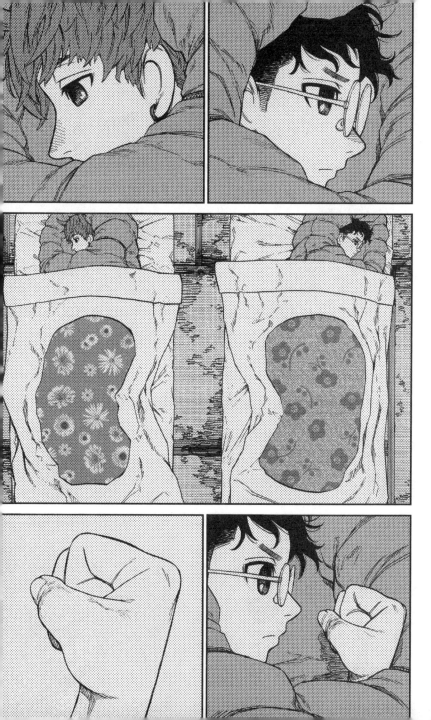

UH, IF I HELP, WILL YOU MAKE ME YOUR APPRENTICE?

THERE'S NO TIME TO BE PUTTING YOUR FEET UP.

EH?!

ANYWAY, COULD YOU TAKE THESE BAGS OVER THERE?

NO WAY.

WHY NOT ?!

WEEZ WEEZ

I WON'T... LOSE HEART!

NOT ME...

TOMOR-ROW, I'LL GET HIM TO TEACH ME TO PUNCH FOR SURE...

I'M BACK!

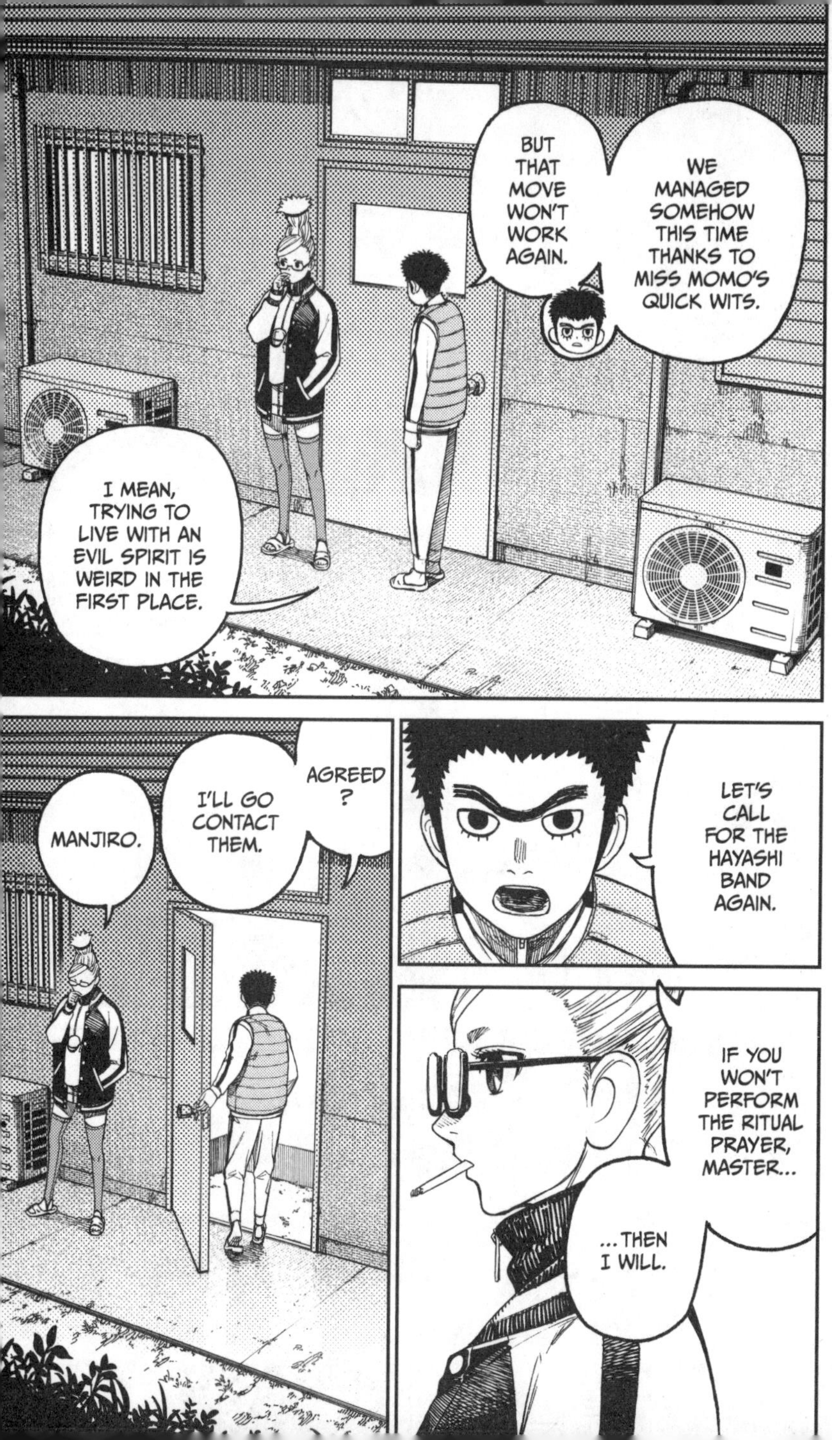
WE MANAGED SOMEHOW THIS TIME THANKS TO MISS MOMO'S QUICK WITS.
BUT THAT MOVE WON'T WORK AGAIN.
I MEAN, TRYING TO LIVE WITH AN EVIL SPIRIT IS WEIRD IN THE FIRST PLACE.
LET'S CALL FOR THE HAYASHI BAND AGAIN.
AGREED?
I'LL GO CONTACT THEM.
MANJIRO.
IF YOU WON'T PERFORM THE RITUAL PRAYER, MASTER...
...THEN I WILL.

IT'S A BITTER PILL.

IT'S ALSO AN ADULT'S RESPONSIBILITY...

...TO SHOW THEM REALITY.

LOOK, I ADMIRE JIJI'S SPIRIT TOO.

BUT WHAT CAN'T BE DONE CAN'T BE DONE.

AS AN ADULT, YOU WISH YOU COULD SHOULDER ALL YOUR KIDS' BURDENS YOURSELF...

...AND TELL THEM...

...TO DO WHATEVER THEY WANT.

HOW SAD...

EMPLOY A SNAPPING MOTION AND...

WHAT DANCE IS *THAT*?

LISTEN, YOU. WHY'RE YOU TRYING TO LEARN TO PUNCH?

PFFT!

CLUMSY SON OF A...

I'M NOT DANCING!

LEAVE ME ALONE!

BECAUSE I WANT TO TOUGHEN UP, OBVIOUSLY!

SOMEONE OUT THERE YOU WANNA MURDERIZE?

AND THEN WHAT?

I'M PISSED OFF.

ALL THE TIME.

...AND SEND HIM FLYING.

I WANT TO OVER-POWER THE EVIL EYE...

IT'S THE SAME.

...TO THROW A PUNCH SO I CAN BECOME STRONG.

I WANT TO LEARN...

OR DO YOU WANNA BECOME STRONG?

SO DO YOU WANNA LEARN HOW TO THROW A PUNCH?

NO. THEY'RE DIFFERENT THINGS.

THE EVIL EYE IS LEVELS ABOVE YOU IN POWER AND TECHNIQUE.

JUST BECAUSE YOU CAN THROW A PUNCH DOESN'T MEAN YOU'LL BE STRONG.

WHAT?!

SO THEN WHAT AM I SUPPOSED TO DO?!

HE CAN EVEN KEEP UP WITH MY POWER.

HIS SPEED'S CONSIDERABLE TOO.

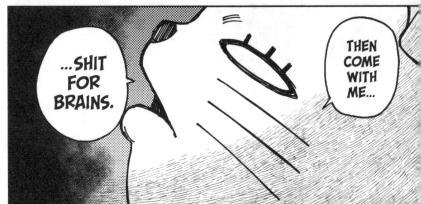

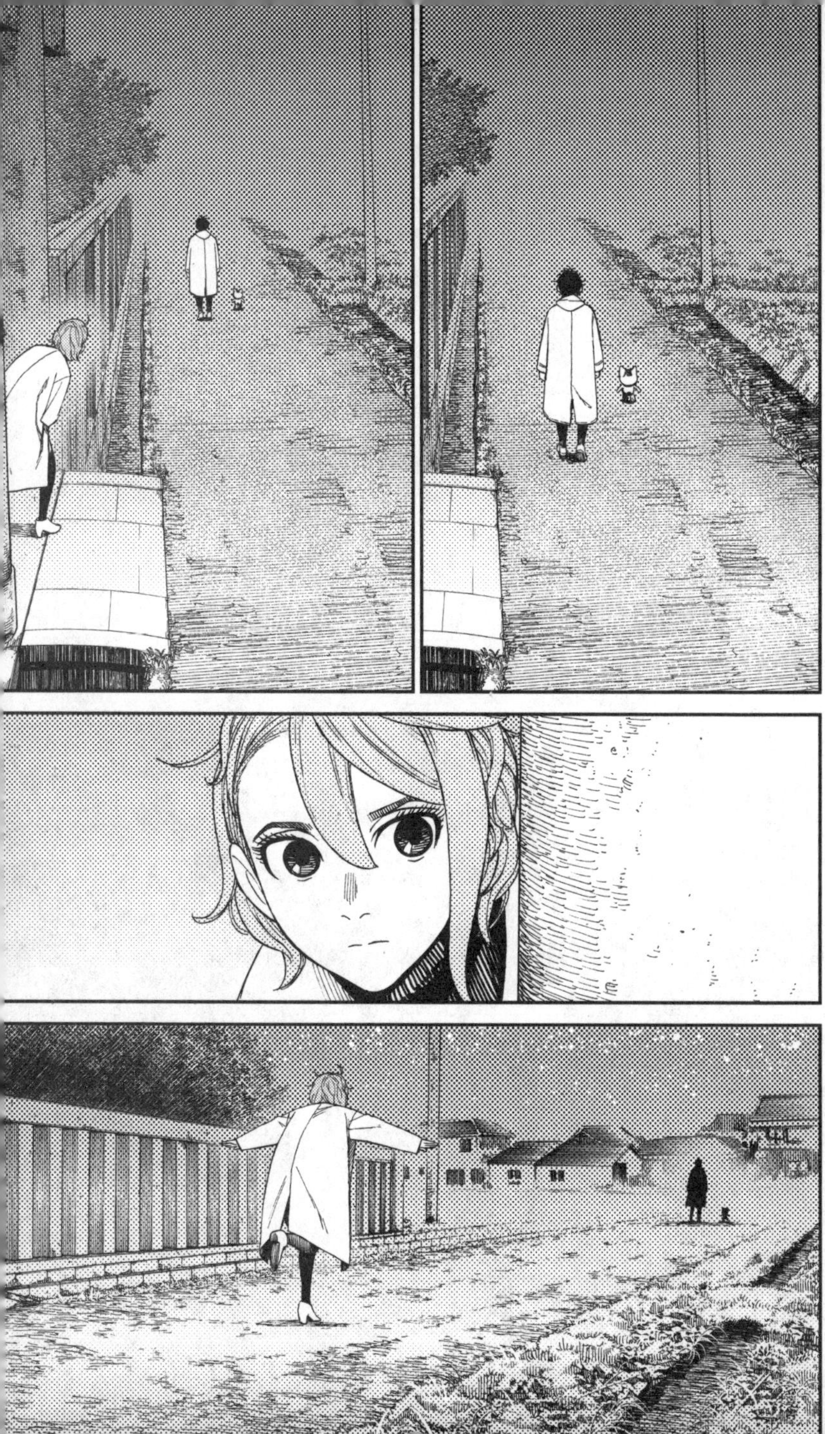

DAN DA DAN

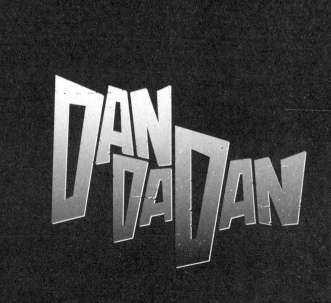

...AND YET SO WEAK AT IT! I HATE IT!

THERE YOU GO, CAPABLE OF USING MY POWERS...

COME WITH ME. AND I WANT 110 PERCENT TOO.

I'M JUST GONNA HAVE T' TOUGHEN YOU UP.

IF SOMEONE GETS MAD, JUST THINK ABOUT RAMEN OR SOMETHING.

THIS IS BAD! IF WE GET CAUGHT, THEY'LL BE MAD!

YOU WANT ME TO GO IN THERE?!

DON'T SWEAT IT.

COME ON. GO IN.

I DON'T WANT ANYONE MAD IN THE FIRST PLACE!

57. Scary Dudes at School

THAT IS YOUR COMBAT RHYTHM.

LOOK AT THAT DUMMY JUMP.

HEY!

WHAT'RE YOU TRYING TO DO HERE?!

AND THIS...

...IS THE EVIL EYE'S RHYTHM.

RHYTHM?

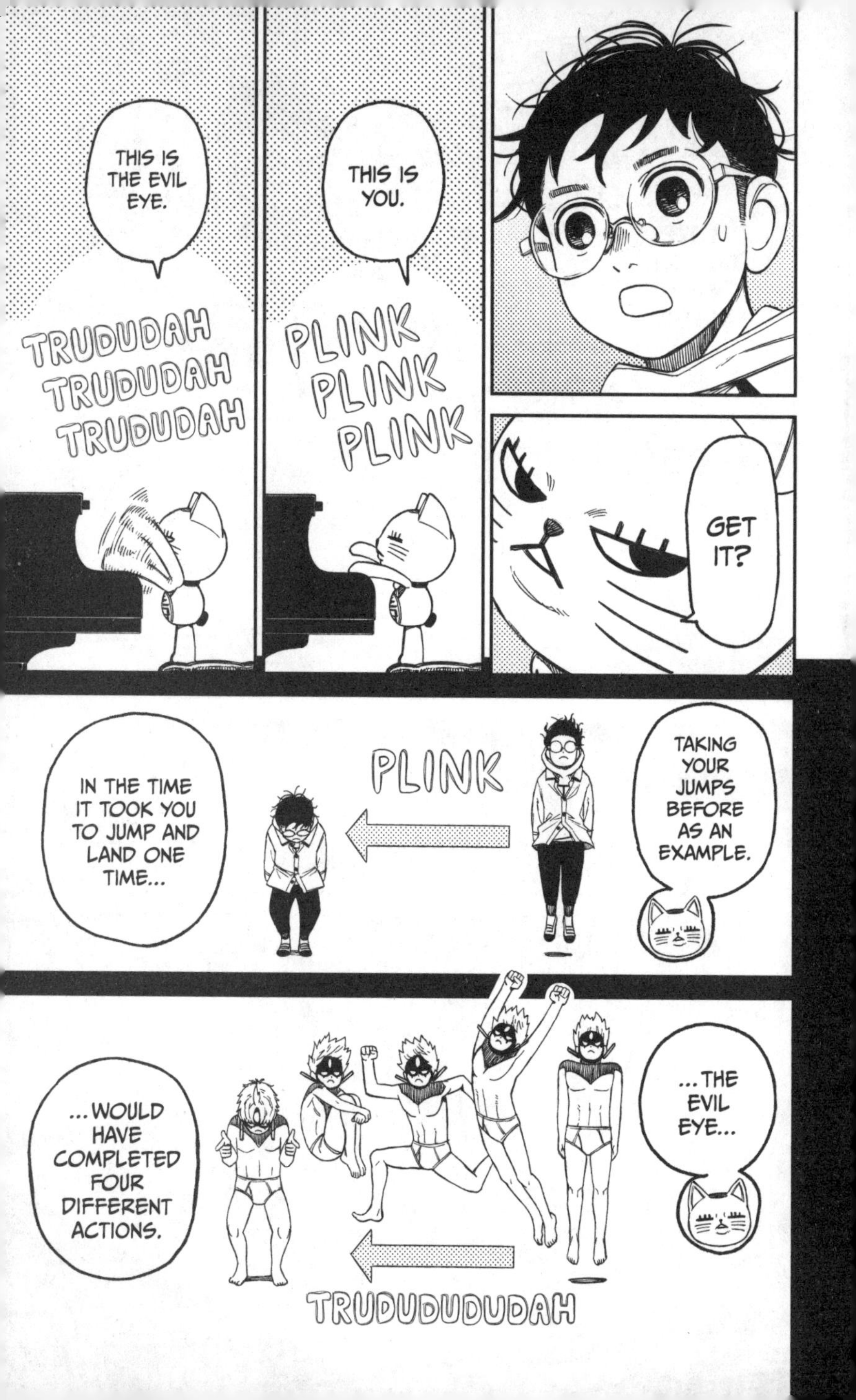
GET IT?
THIS IS YOU.
PLINK PLINK PLINK
THIS IS THE EVIL EYE.
TRUDUDAH TRUDUDAH TRUDUDAH
TAKING YOUR JUMPS BEFORE AS AN EXAMPLE.
PLINK
IN THE TIME IT TOOK YOU TO JUMP AND LAND ONE TIME...
...THE EVIL EYE...
...WOULD HAVE COMPLETED FOUR DIFFERENT ACTIONS.
TRUDUDUDUDAH

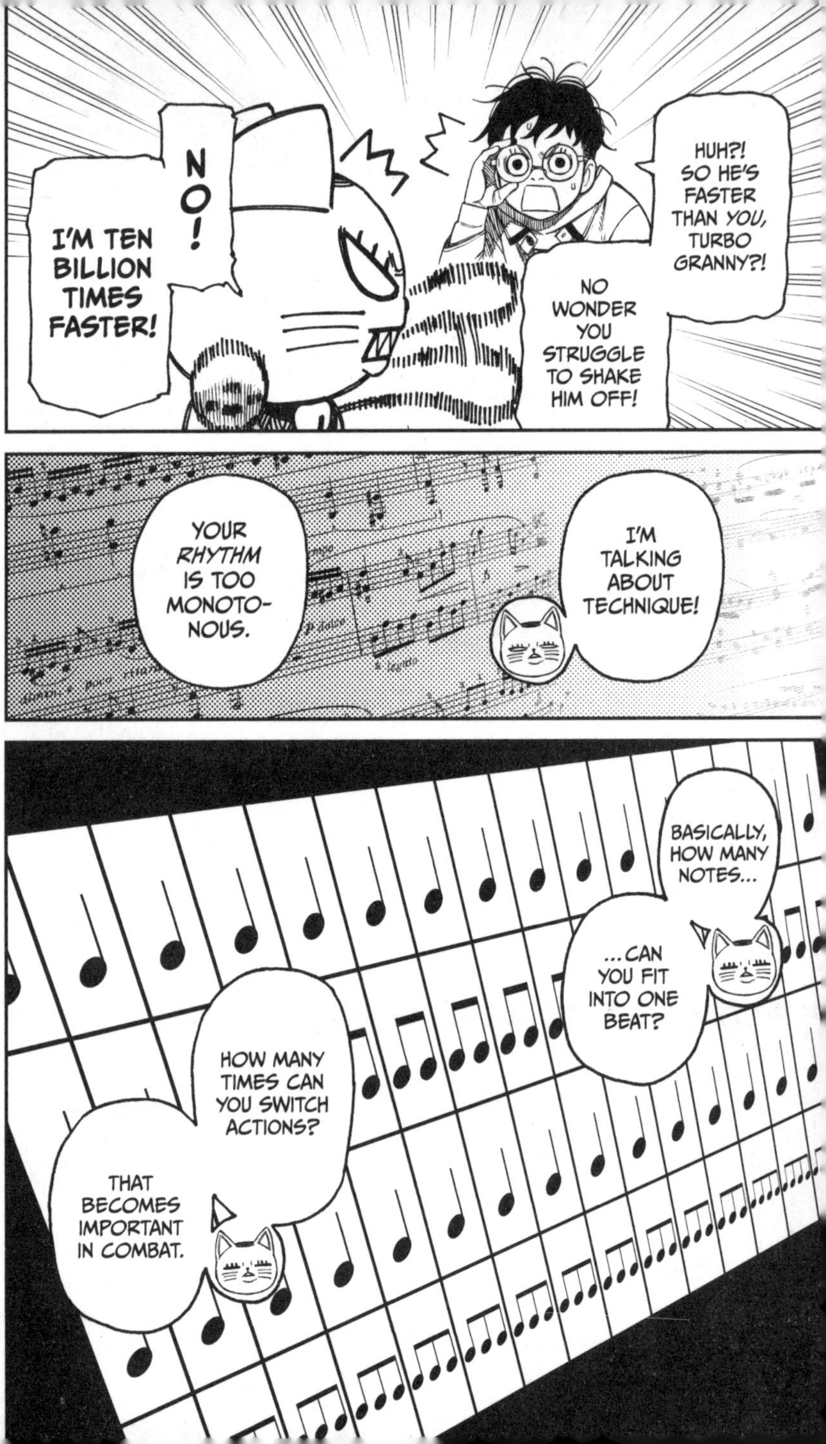
HUH?! SO HE'S FASTER THAN *YOU*, TURBO GRANNY?!
NO WONDER YOU STRUGGLE TO SHAKE HIM OFF!
NO!
I'M TEN BILLION TIMES FASTER!
I'M TALKING ABOUT TECHNIQUE!
YOUR *RHYTHM* IS TOO MONOTONOUS.
BASICALLY, HOW MANY NOTES...
...CAN YOU FIT INTO ONE BEAT?
HOW MANY TIMES CAN YOU SWITCH ACTIONS?
THAT BECOMES IMPORTANT IN COMBAT.

WHERE'S IT COMING FROM?!

THAT NOISE!

AN OR-CHES-TRA?!

HERE?! WHAT'S HERE?!

IT'S SO LOUD, I CAN'T HEAR Y—

THEY'RE HERE.

WHOOO'S MAKING THAT NOISE?!

I CAN HEEEAR SOME IMPURE SOUNNNDS.

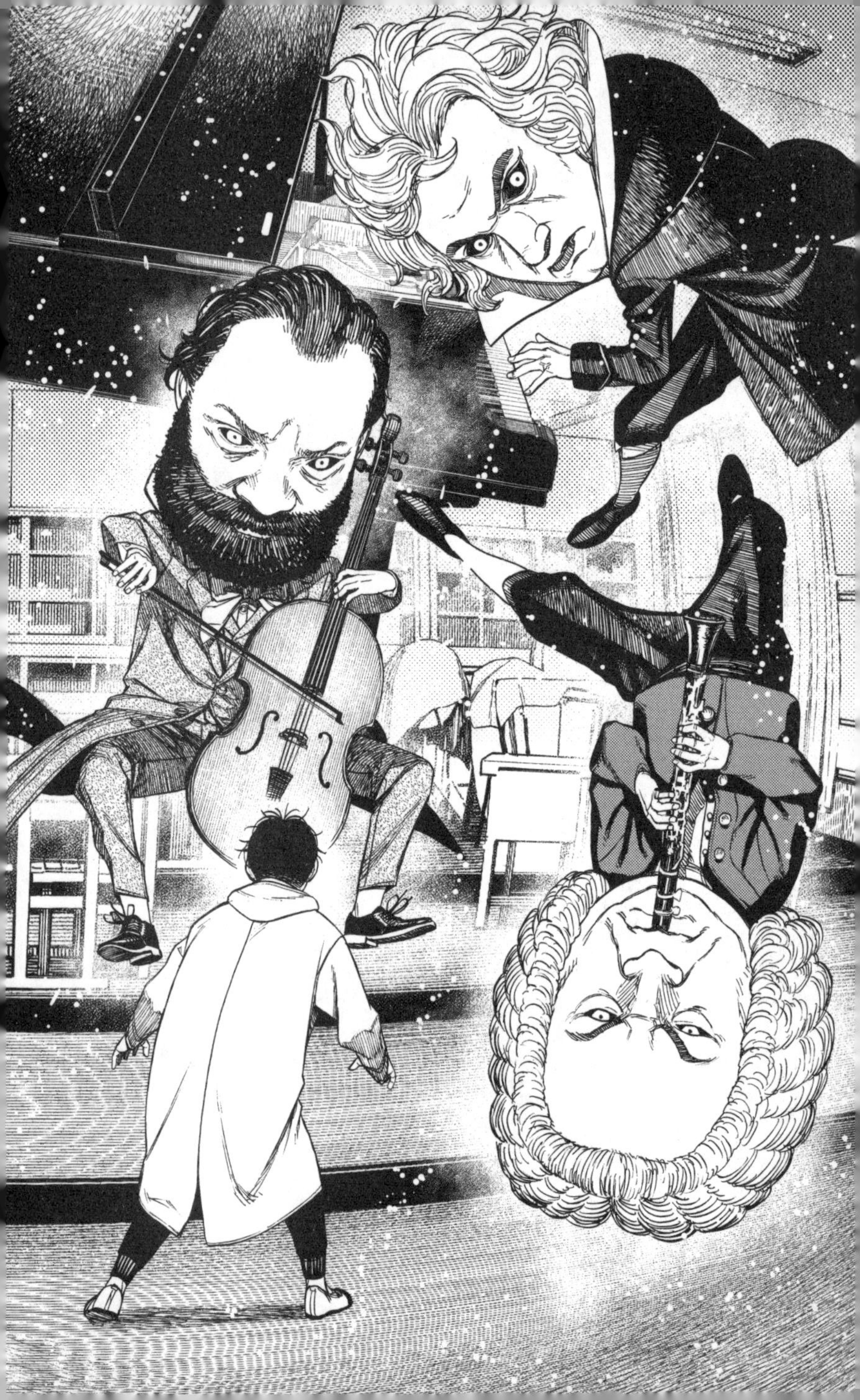

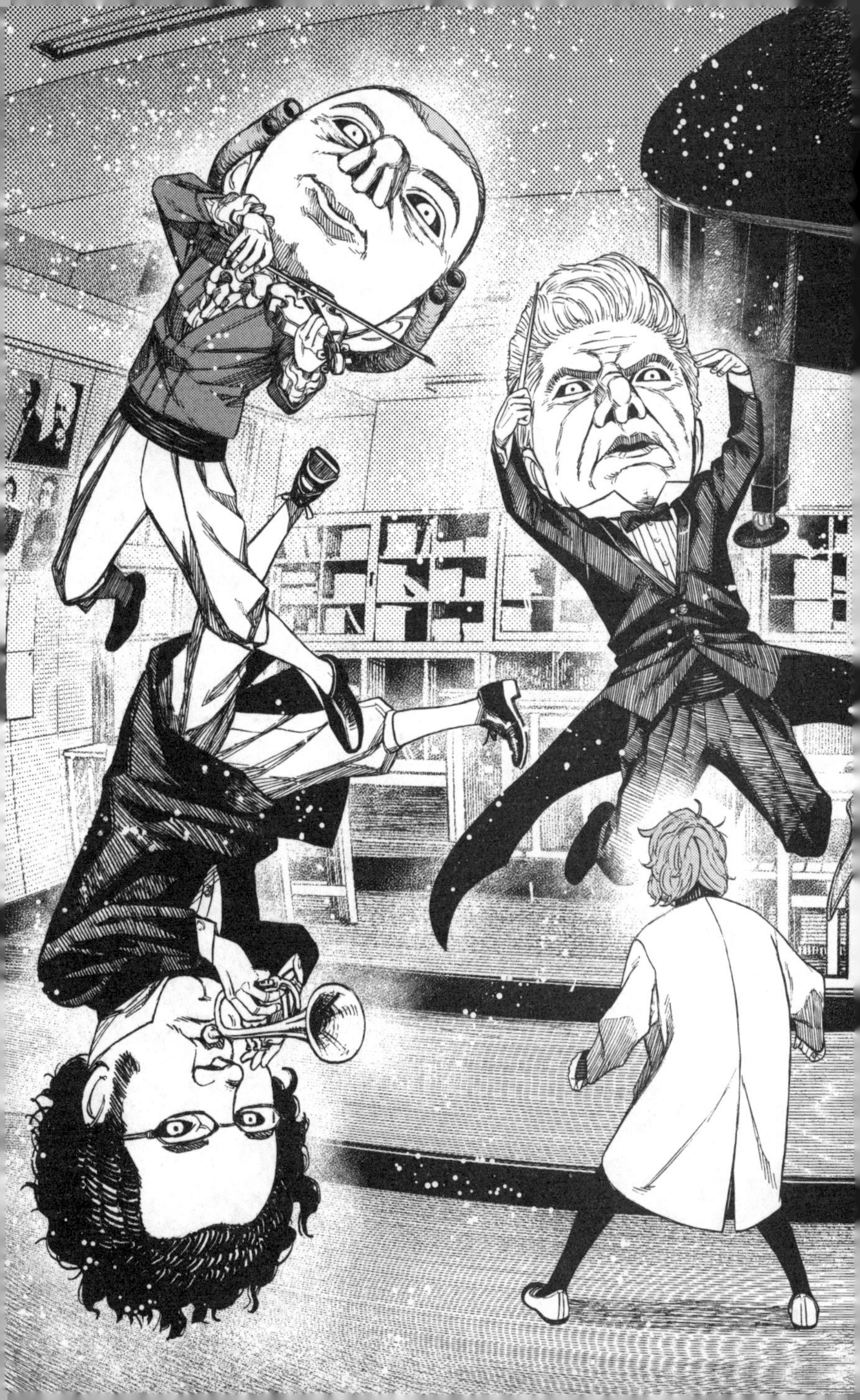

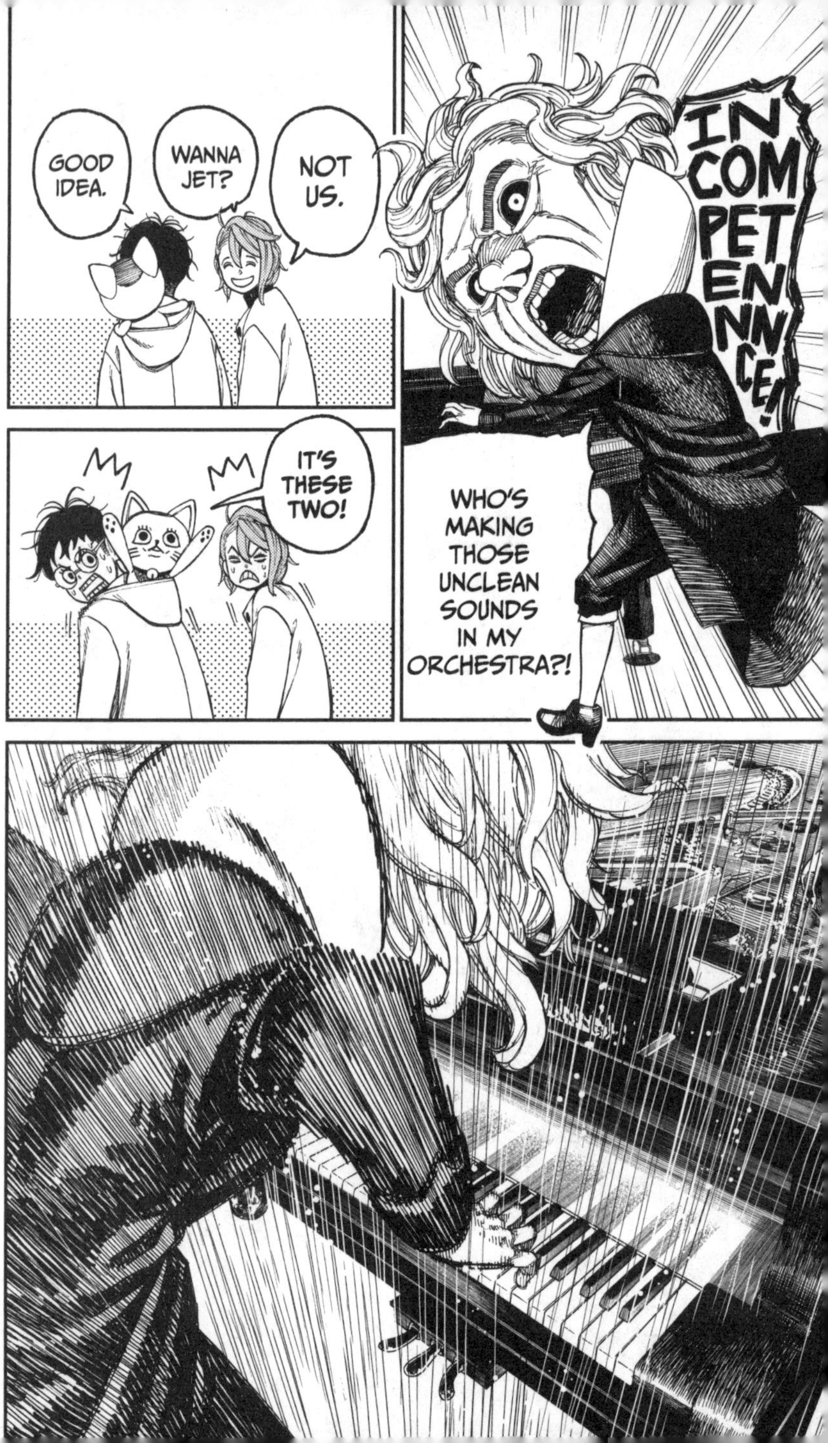
INCOMPETENNCE!
WHO'S MAKING THOSE UNCLEAN SOUNDS IN MY ORCHESTRA?!
NOT US.
WANNA JET?
GOOD IDEA.
IT'S THESE TWO!

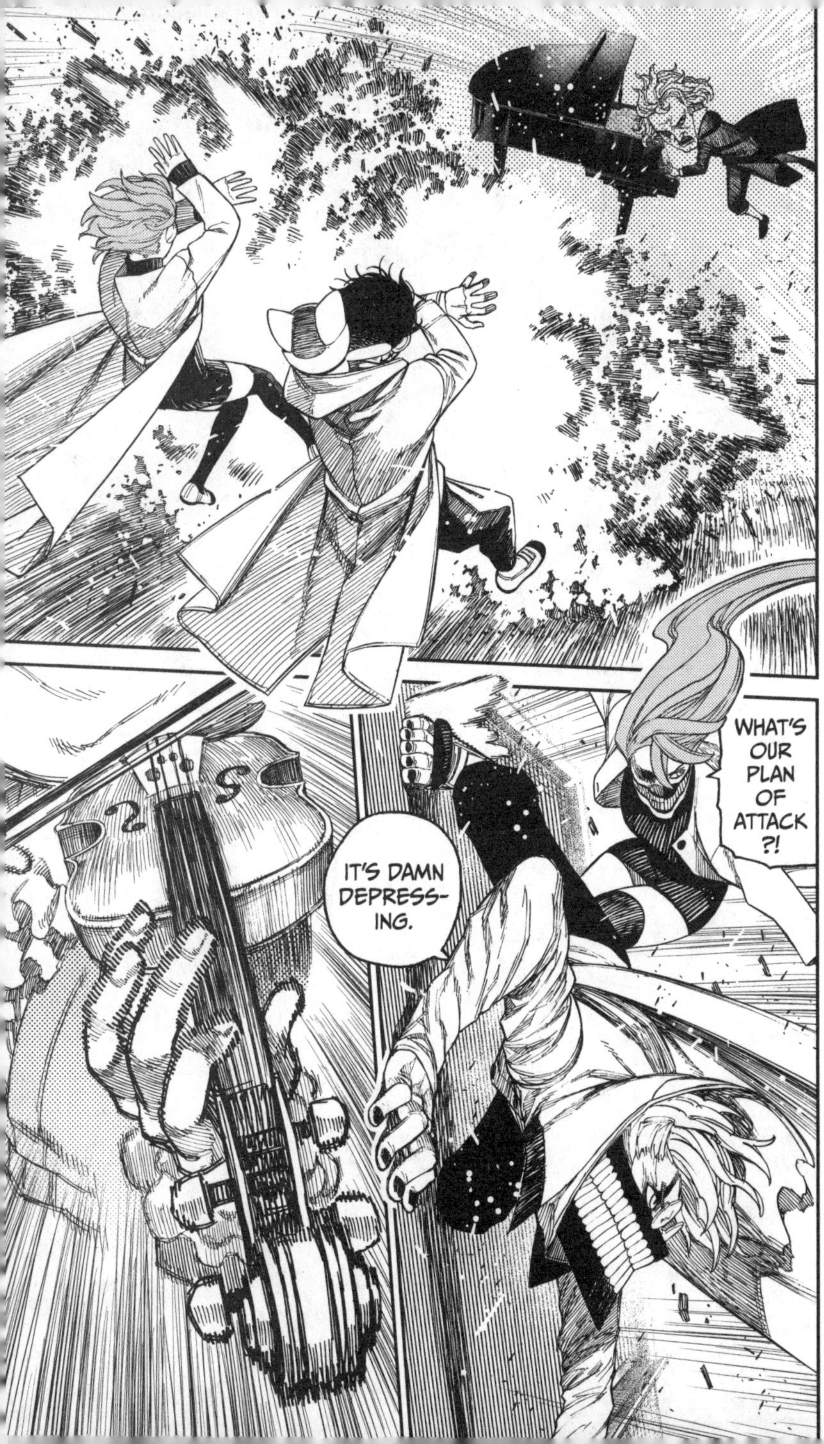
WHAT'S OUR PLAN OF ATTACK?!
IT'S DAMN DEPRESS-ING.

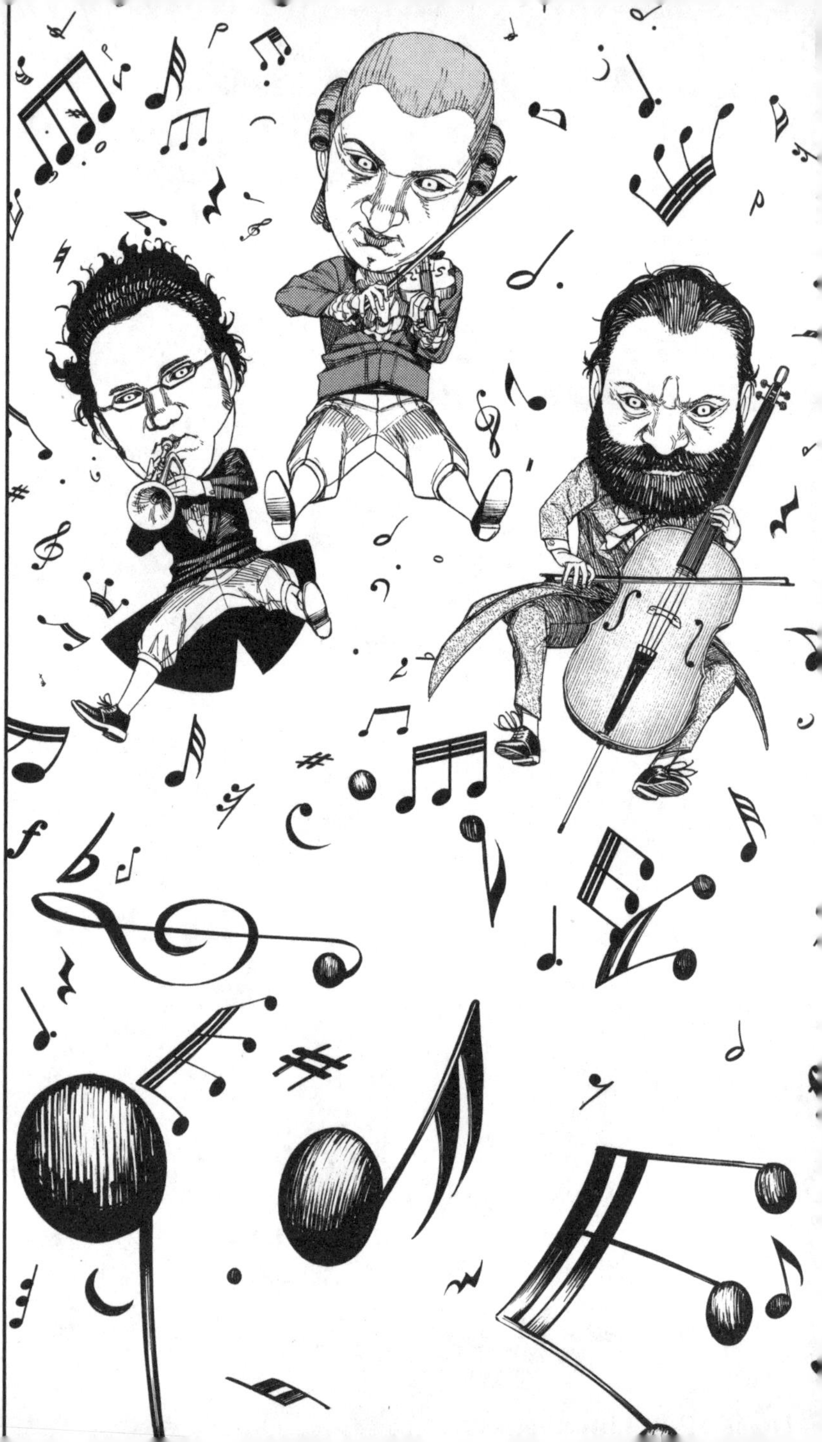

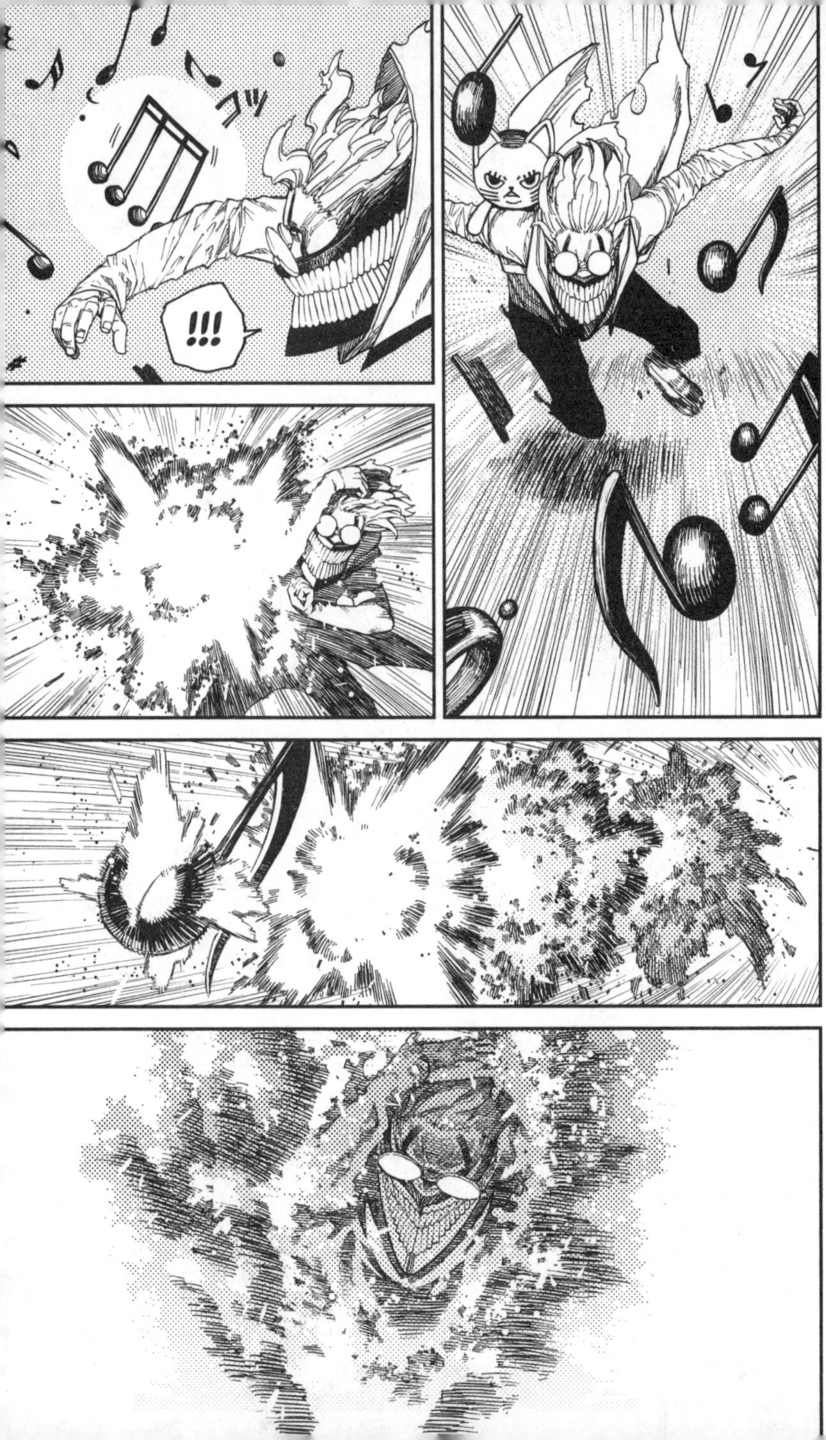
コッ
!!!

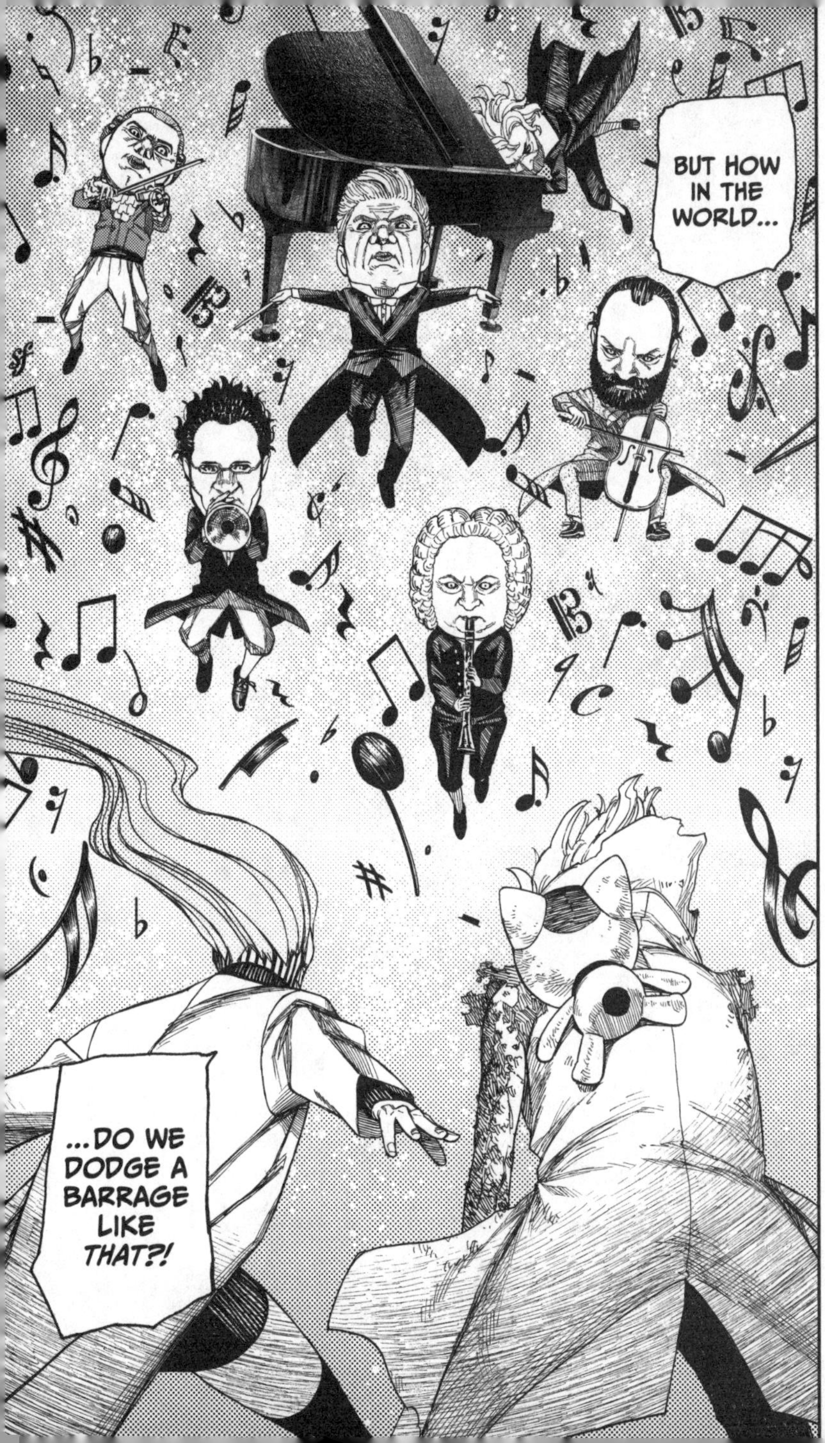
BUT HOW IN THE WORLD...
...DO WE DODGE A BARRAGE LIKE THAT?!

DAN DA DAN

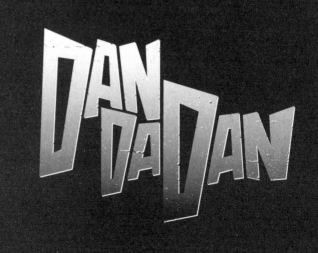

58. Symphony No. 6

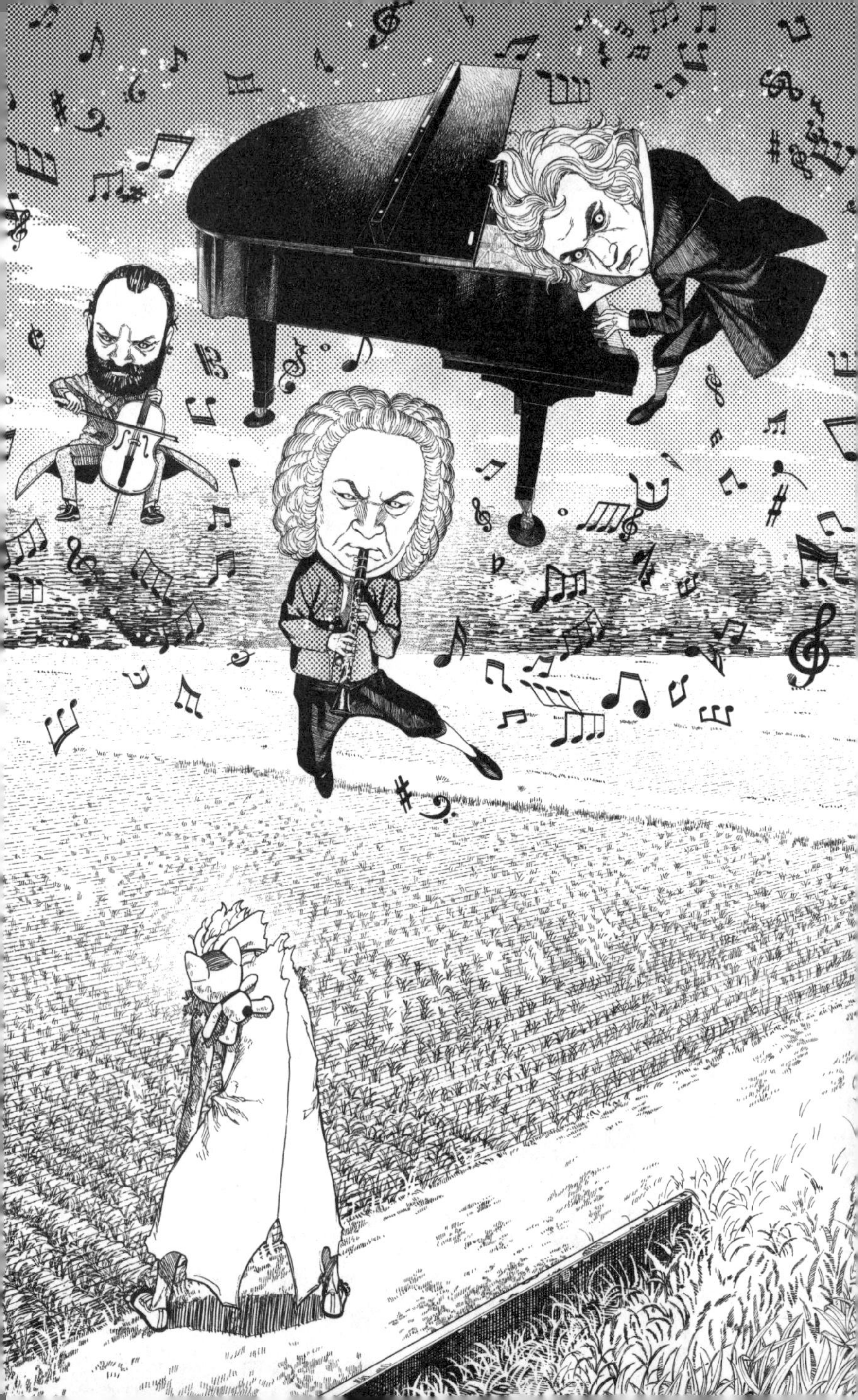

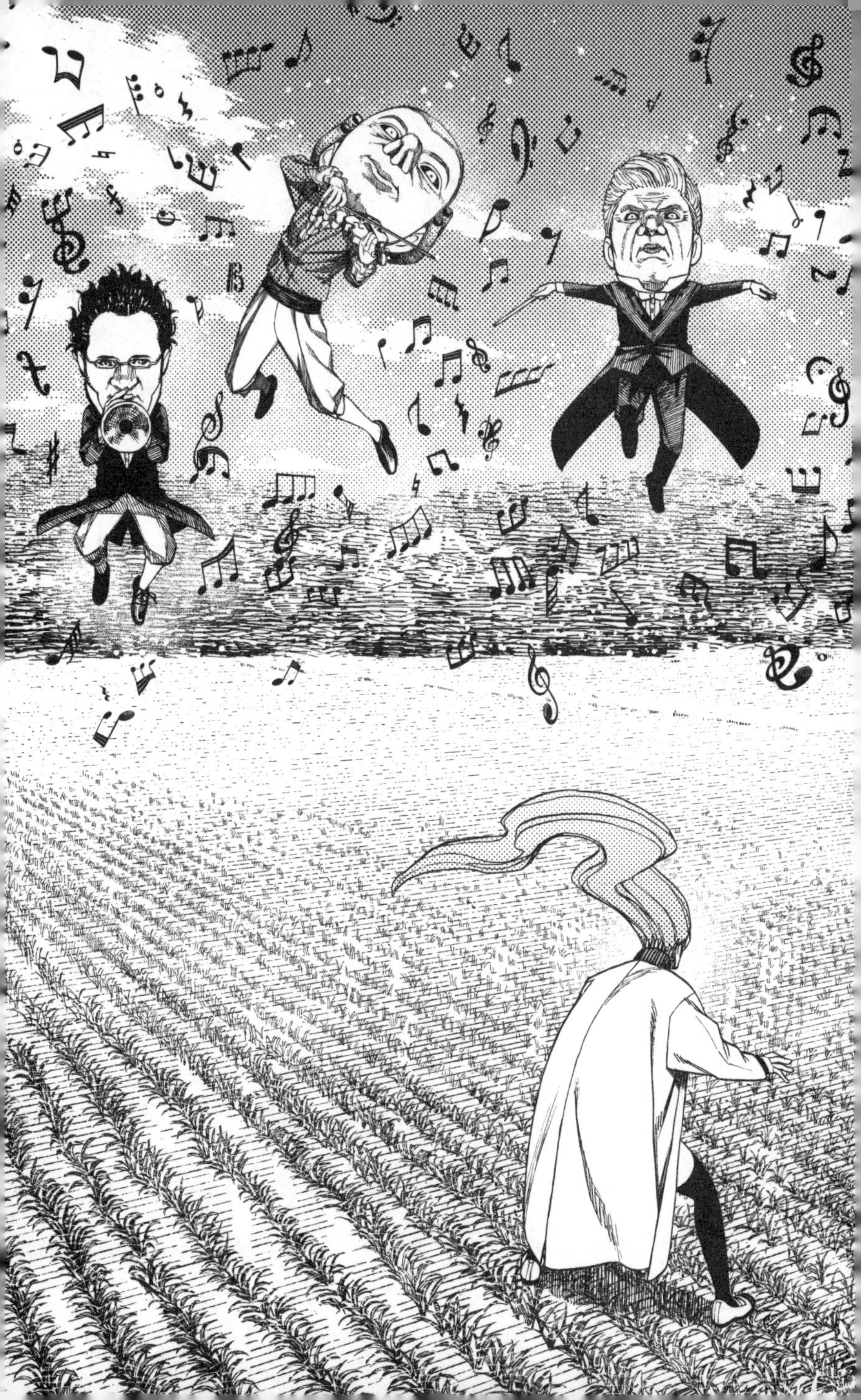

SHE'S DODGING ALL OF THEM!

WOW! AIRA-CHAN IS AWESOME!

TUNK

THIS IS NO TIME FOR ADMIRA-TION!

YOU NEED TO DODGE LIKE THAT TOO!

AND I'M GOOD-FOR-NOTHING!

MISS SHIRATORI! SHE'S INCREDIBLE!

KOFF! KOFF!

HFF! HFF!

I'M NO BETTER!

BUT NOT AT ALL...

BWUH!

I THOUGHT I'D BECOME A BIT STRONGER...

I'VE FOUGHT A BUNCH OF TOUGH ENEMIES...

OH!

...AND I GOT INTO THE RHYTHM OF IT!

IT REALLY MOVED ME...

THERE *IS* SOMETHING! SOME MUSIC I HEARD RECENTLY!

SHIT! NO OPENINGS TO COUNTER-ATTACK!

EVEN WHEN I TRY EXTENDING MY HAIR...

...THE NOTES ARE HITTING IT SO IT DOESN'T REACH THEM!

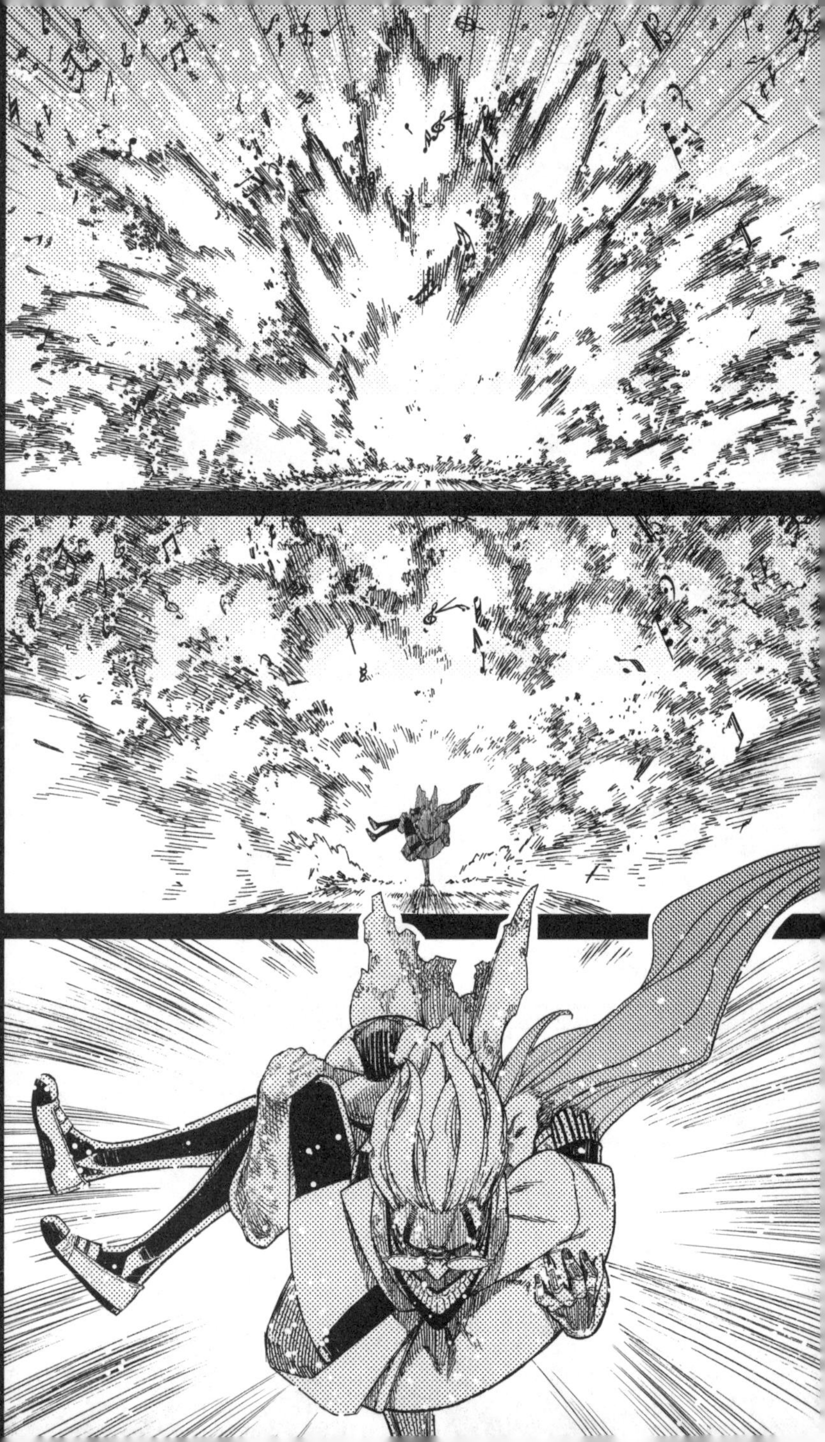

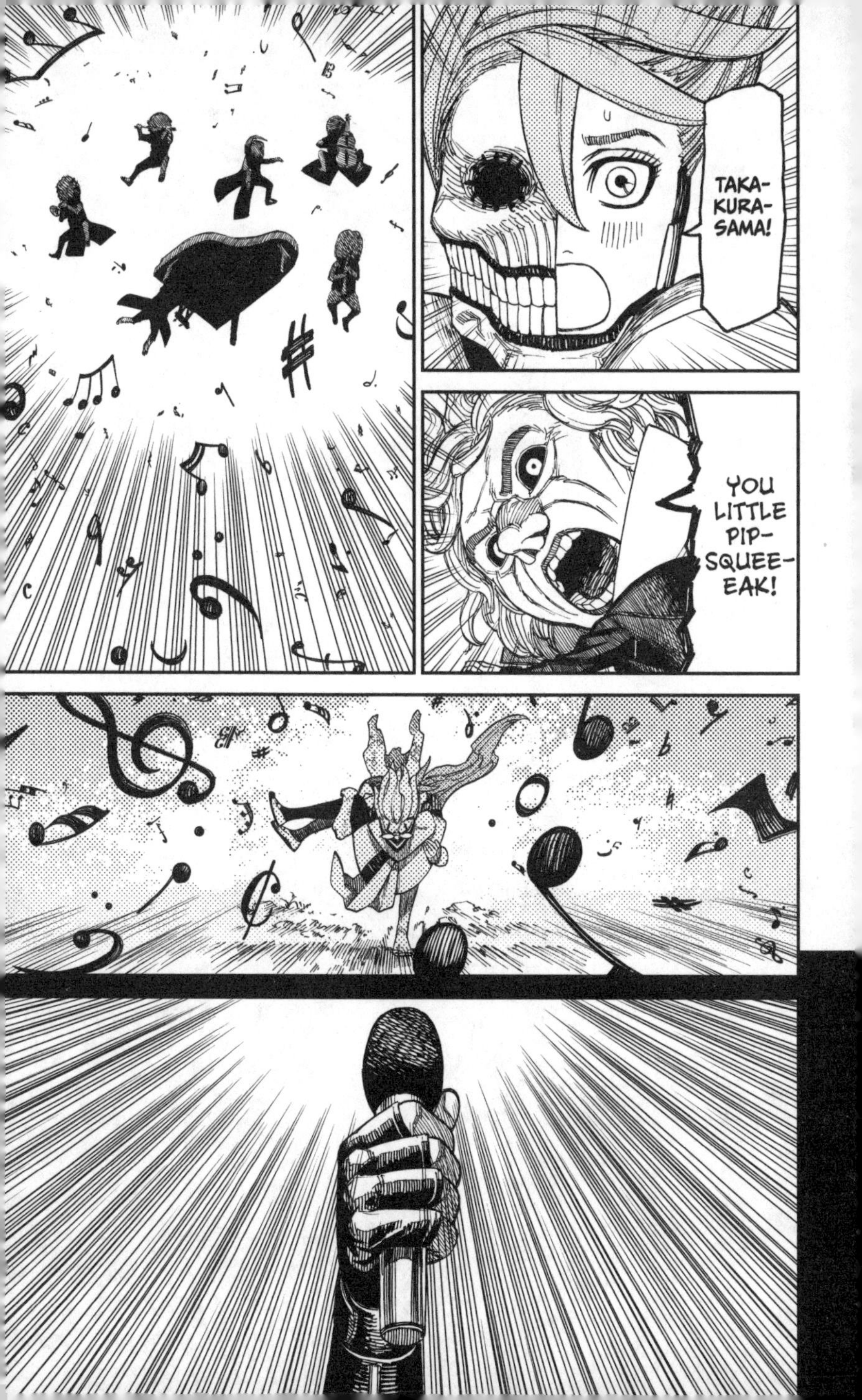
TAKA-KURA-SAMA!
YOU LITTLE PIP-SQUEE-EAK!

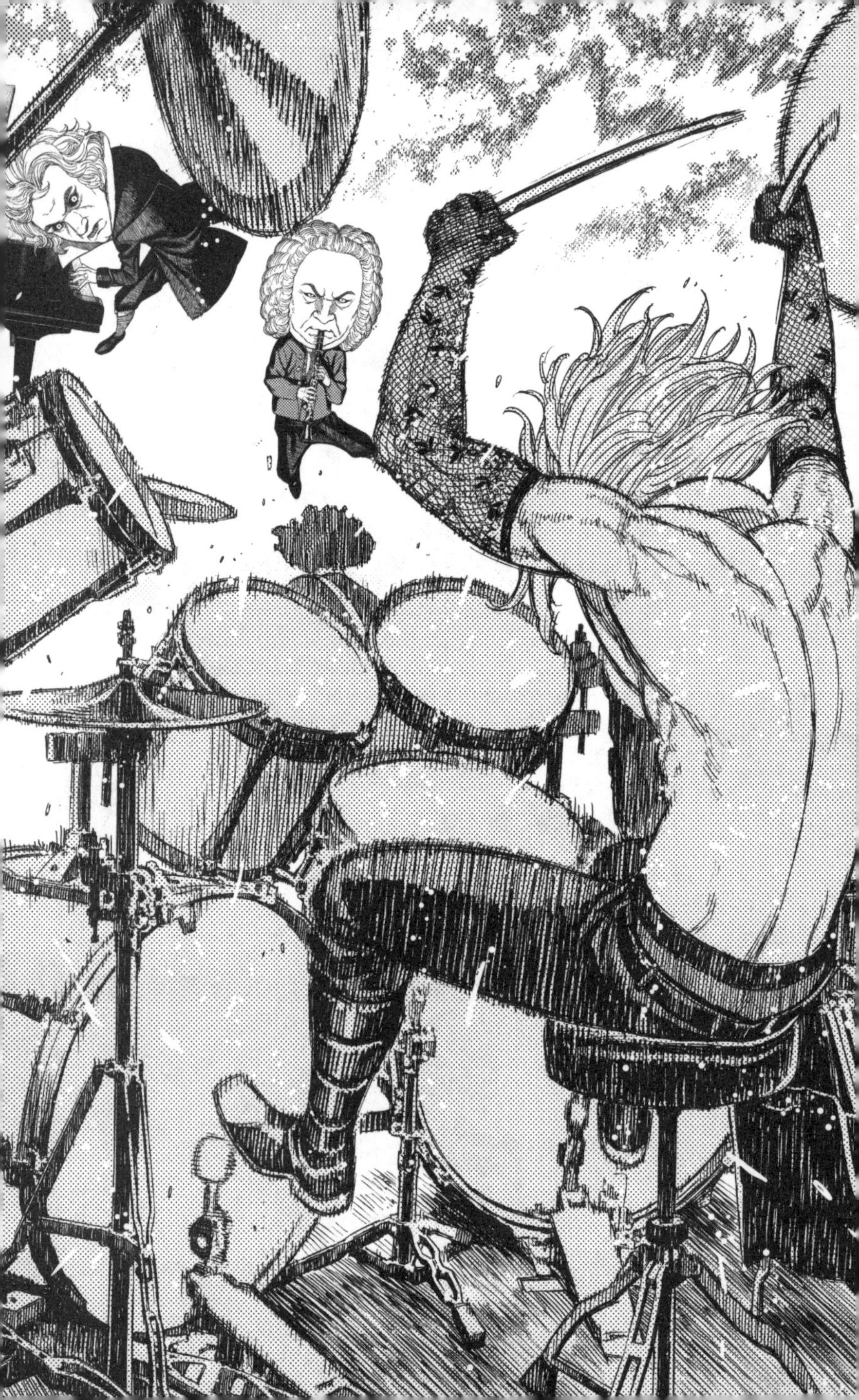

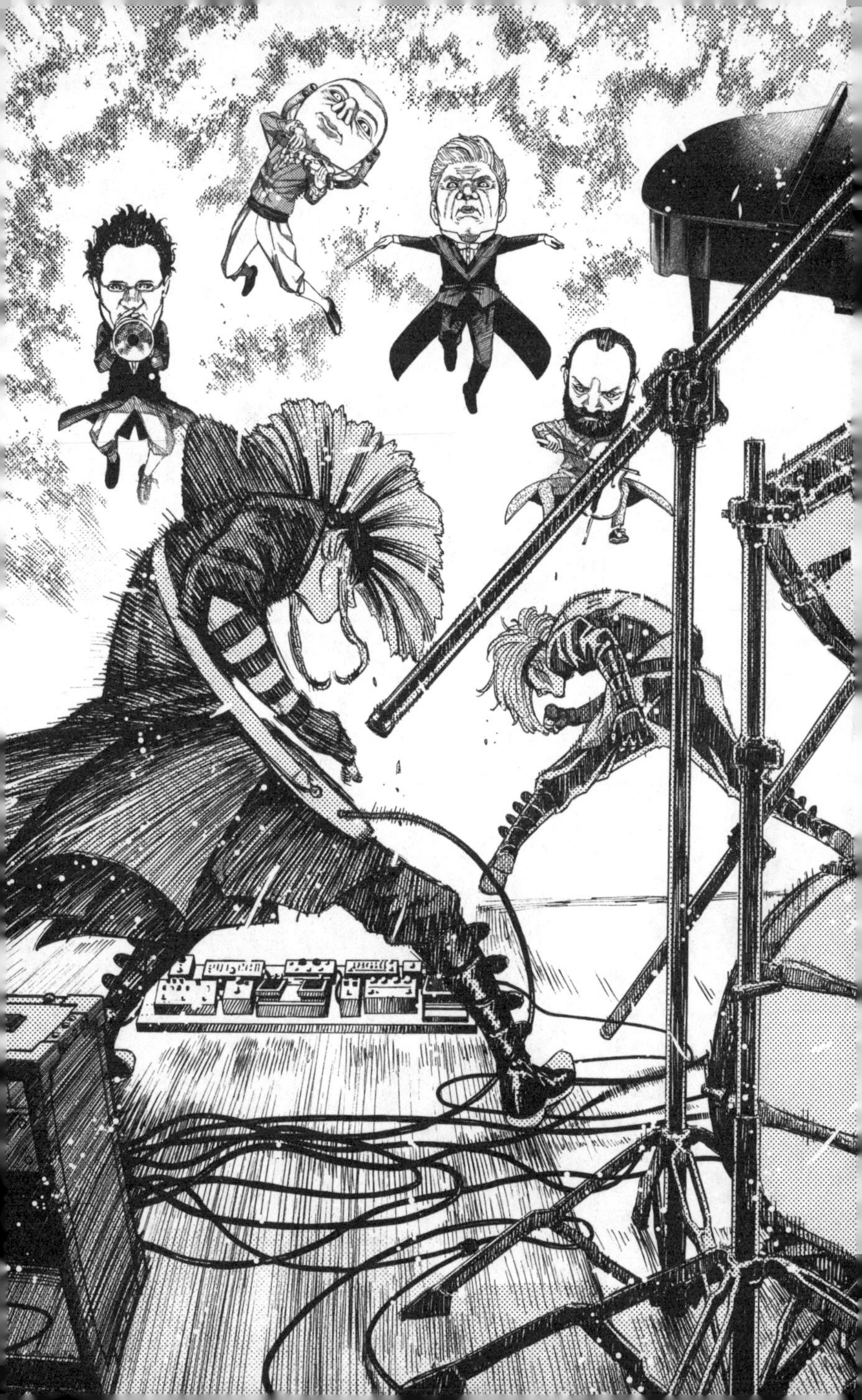

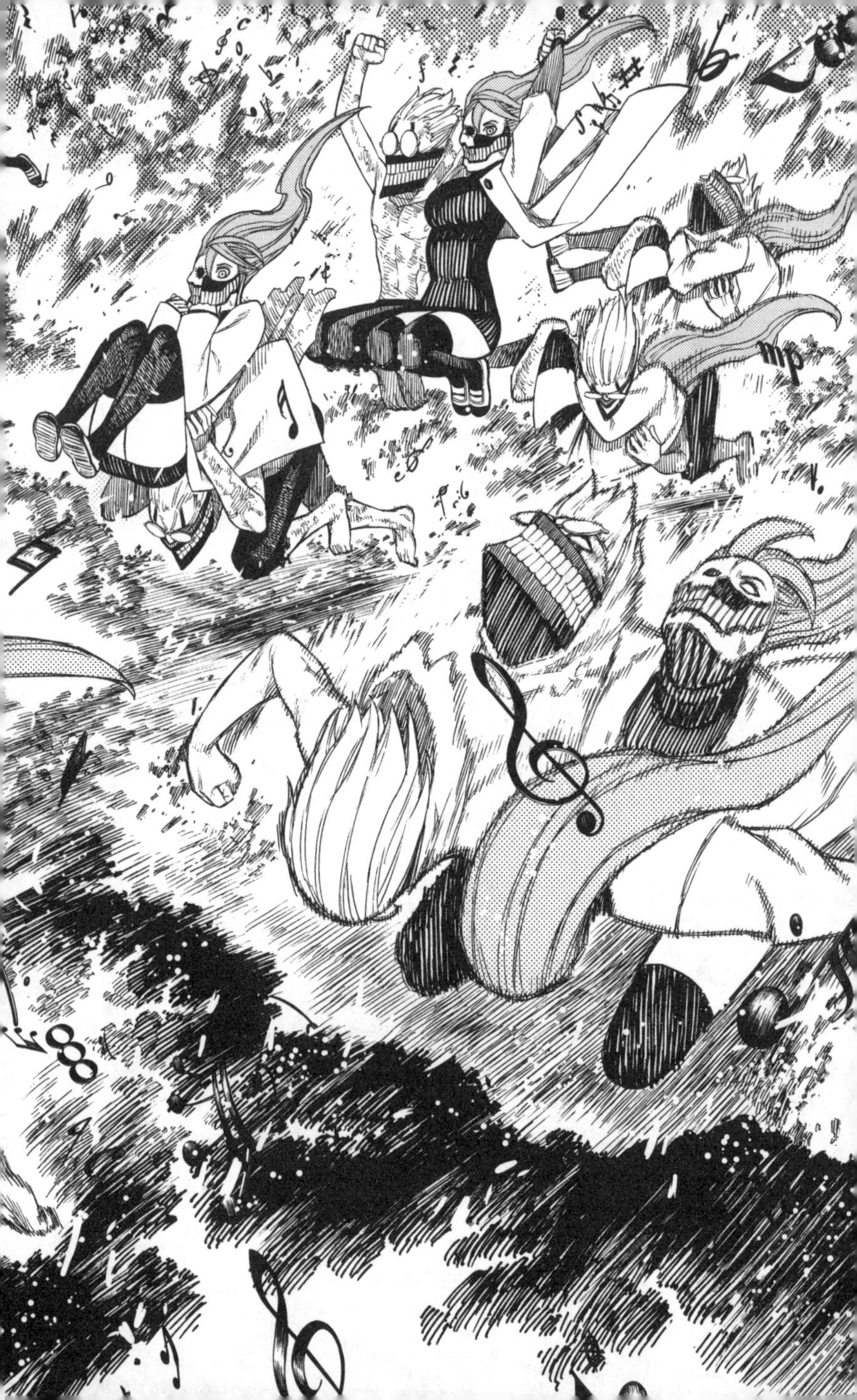

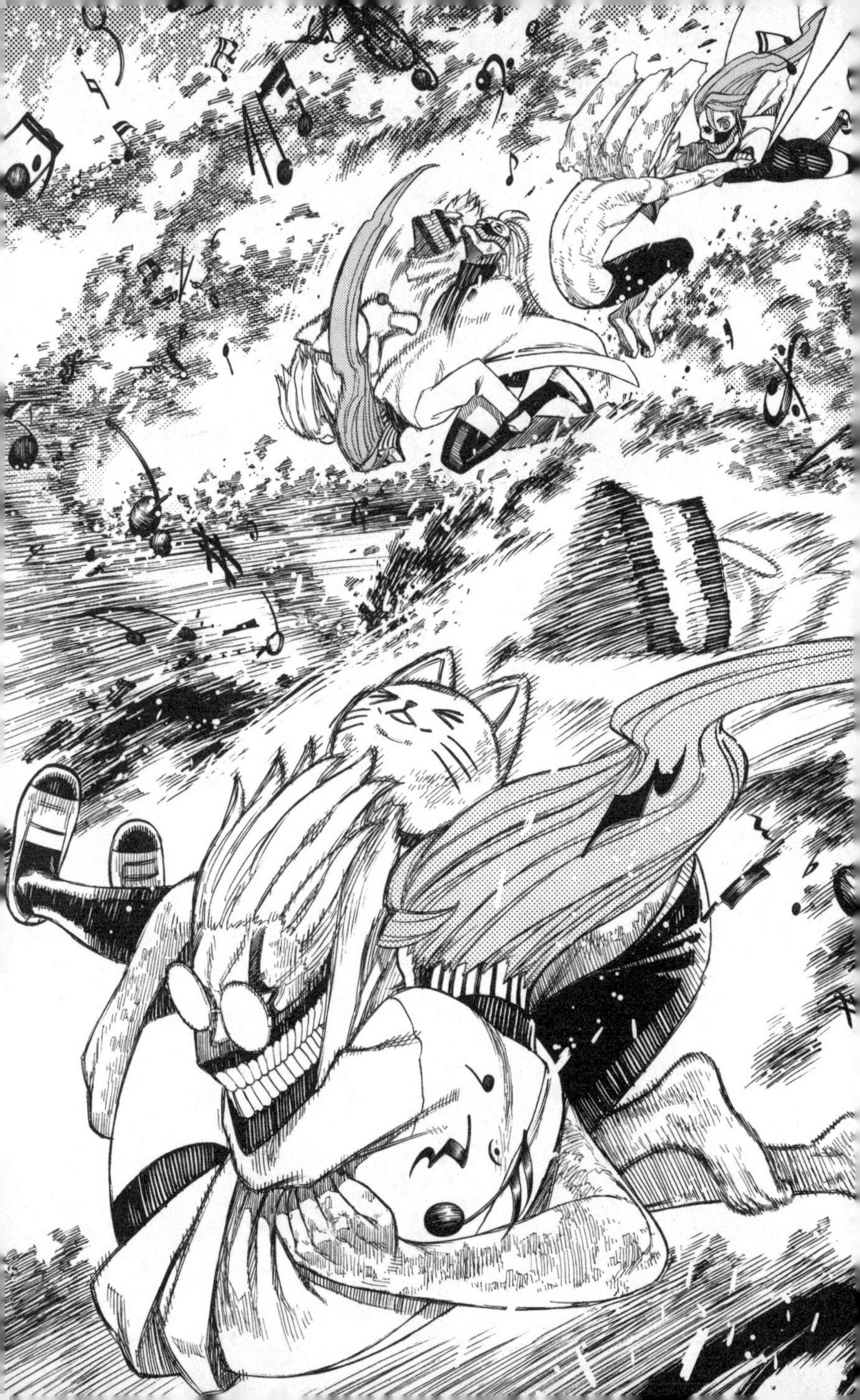

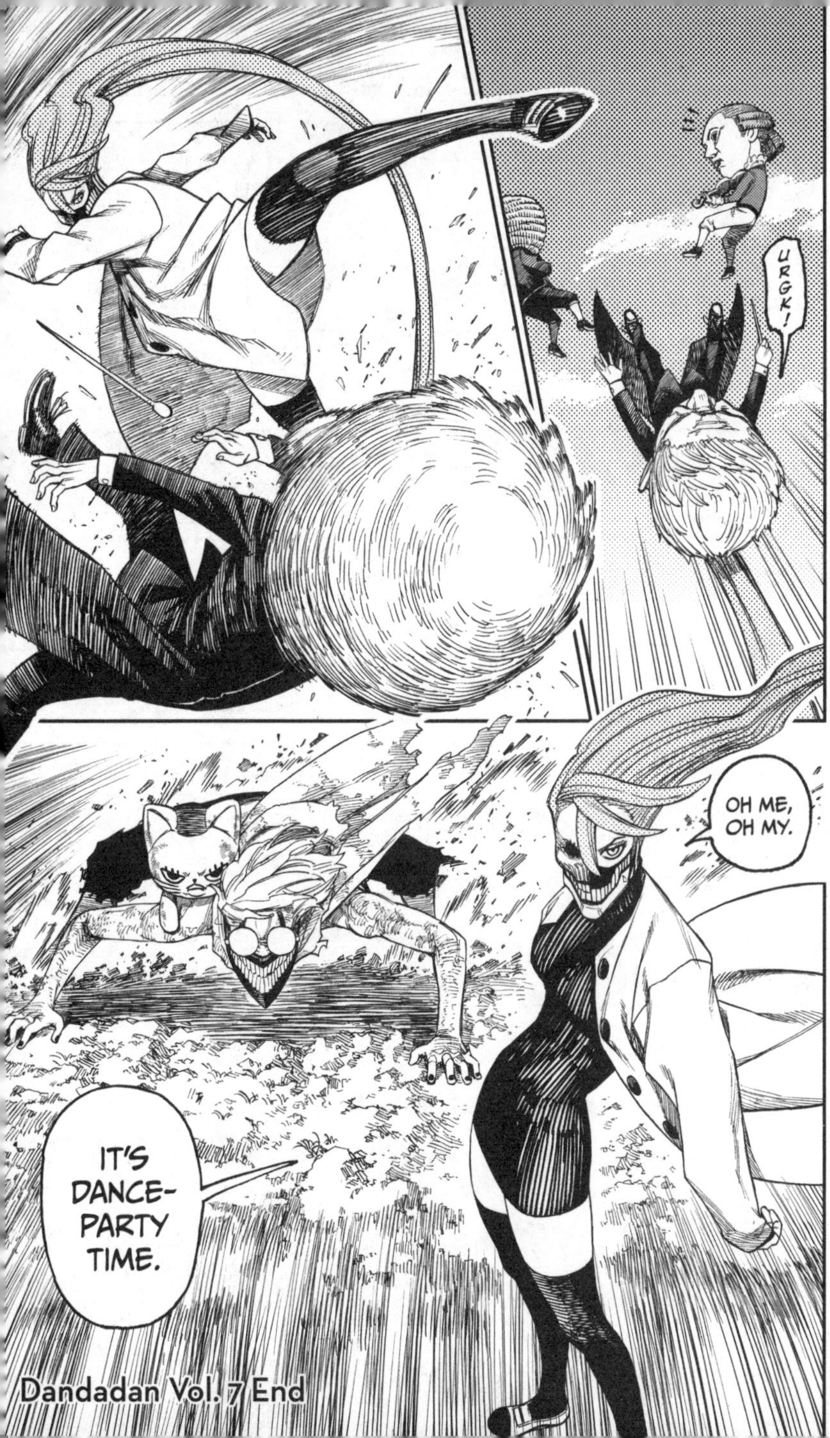
URGK!
OH ME, OH MY.
IT'S DANCE-PARTY TIME.
Dandadan Vol. 7 End

BONUS

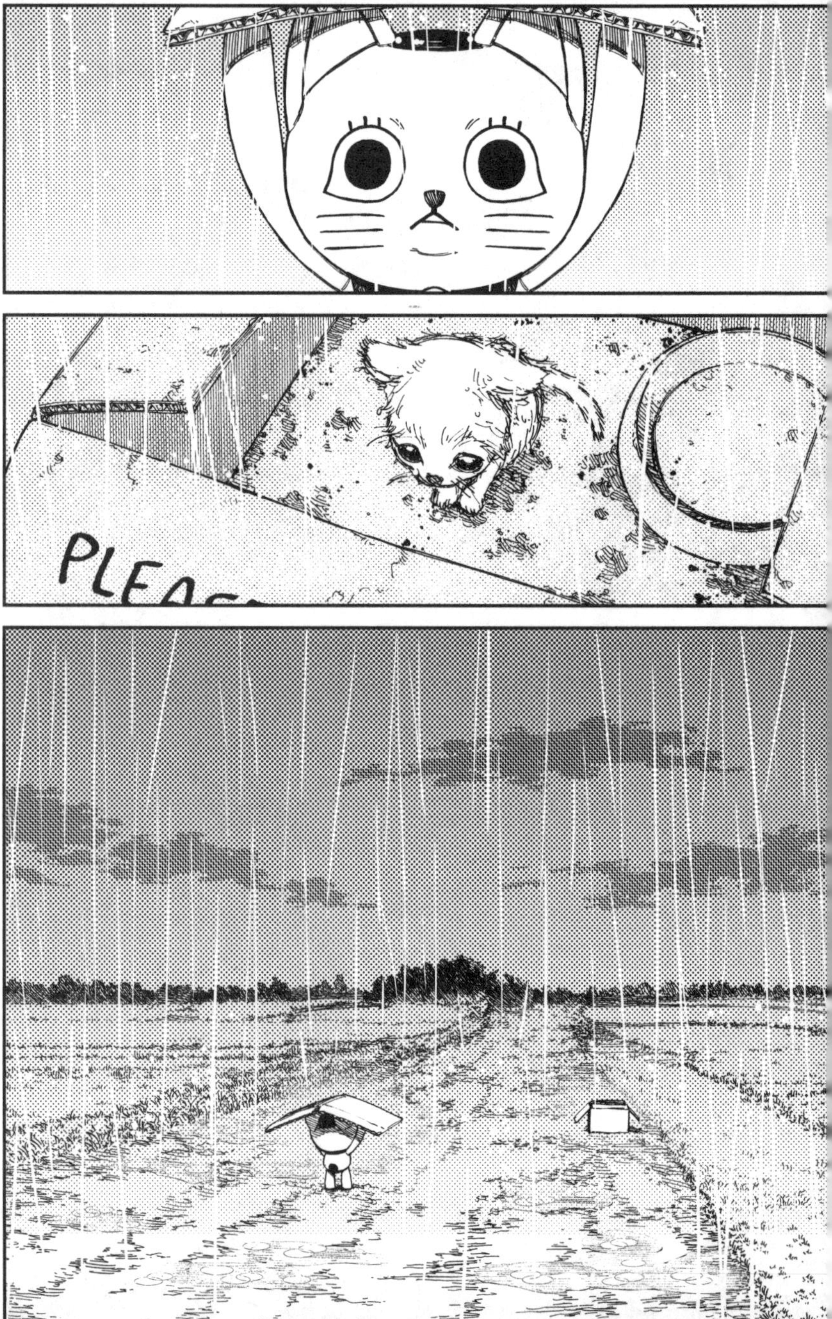
PLEAS

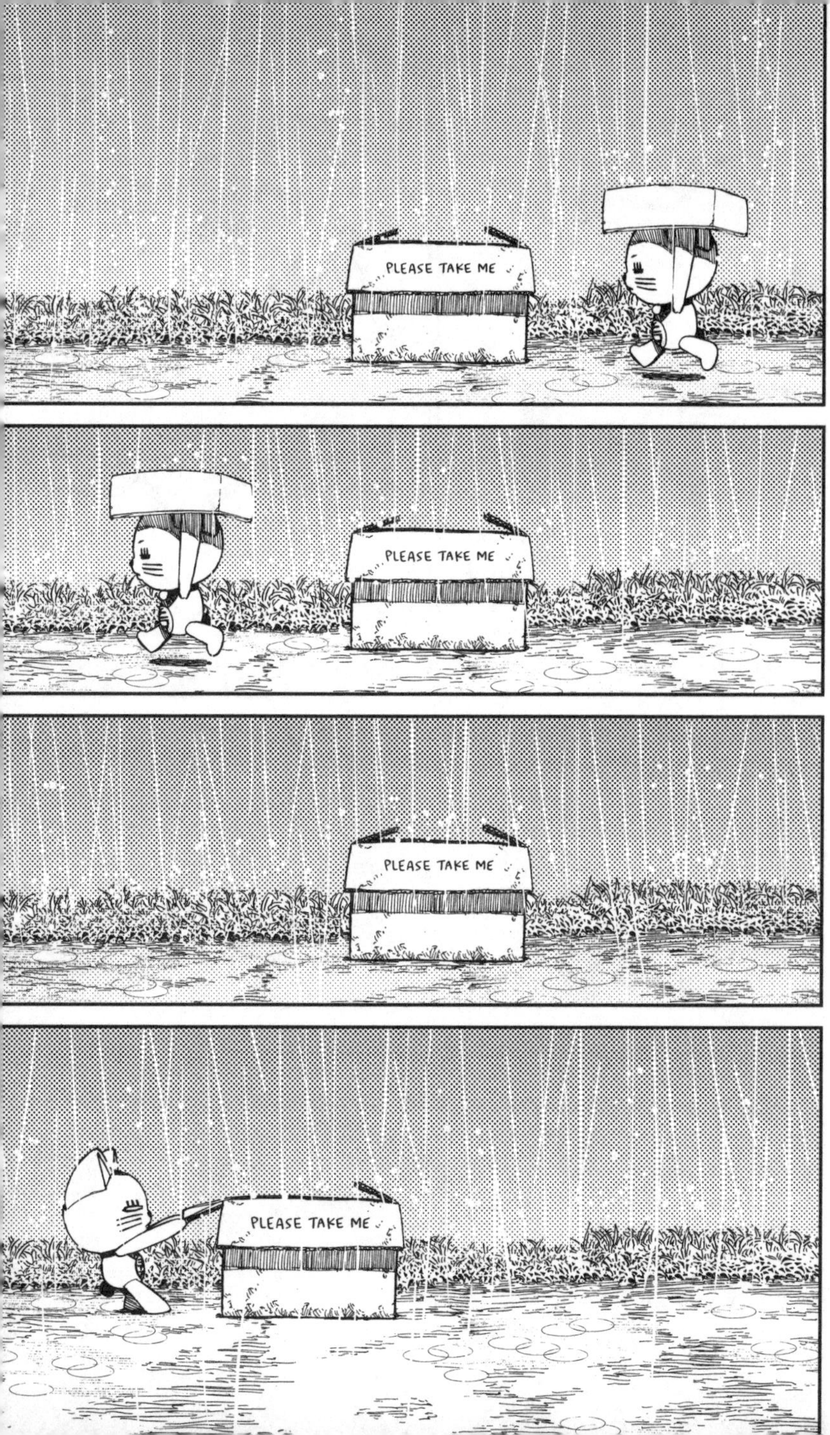
PLEASE TAKE ME
PLEASE TAKE ME
PLEASE TAKE ME
PLEASE TAKE ME

HEY, MOMO! WHERE'S THE MILK?!

HOW SHOULD I KNOW?!

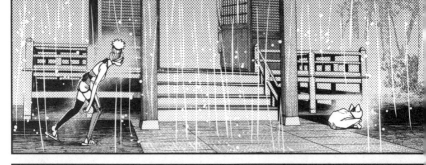

DON'T GIVE UP ON ME, OKAY?

...AFTER ALL.

YOU'RE STILL ALIVE...

End

KITO FAMILY

TYPE: HUMAN (?)
HABITAT: HOT SPRINGS DISTRICT
HEIGHT: 140-180 CM

A MULTIGENERATIONAL CLAN OF SELF-PROCLAIMED GUARDIANS OF A CERTAIN HOT SPRINGS AREA. OPERATING UNDER THE GUISE OF LANDLORDS, THEY BEHAVE OUTRAGEOUSLY AND WITHOUT CONSIDERATION. RESIDENTS AVOID THEM. THEY HAVE CONNECTIONS IN THE POLICE FORCE, SO ANY COMPLAINTS ABOUT THEIR CRIMINAL ENDEAVORS GET COVERED UP.

NAKI

JUMANUEL

JURIA

JUGEMU

JUHIKO

JUICHI

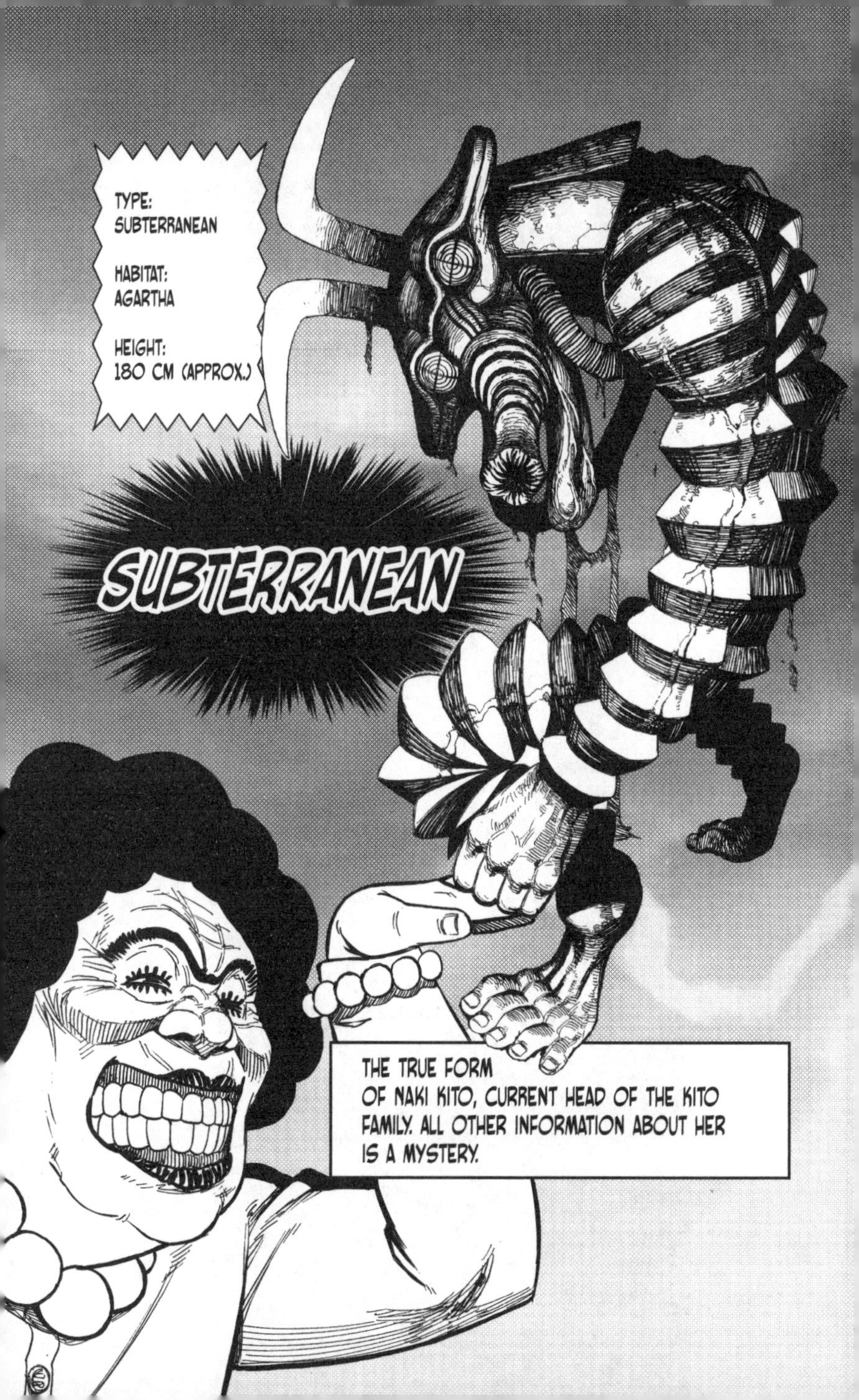
TYPE:
SUBTERRANEAN
HABITAT:
AGARTHA
HEIGHT:
180 CM (APPROX.)
SUBTERRANEAN
THE TRUE FORM OF NAKI KITO, CURRENT HEAD OF THE KITO FAMILY. ALL OTHER INFORMATION ABOUT HER IS A MYSTERY.

YUKINOBU TATSU

I was overexuberant in my chewing of some Black Black gum, and somehow my tolerance for its spiciness has now increased.

Yukinobu Tatsu debuted in *Gekkan Shounen Magazine* with *Seigi no Rokugou* (Rokugou of Justice). He has also worked as an assistant for manga artist Tatsuki Fujimoto on the well-known series *Chainsaw Man* and *Fire Punch*.

DANDADAN 7

SHONEN JUMP Edition

Story & Art **YUKINOBU TATSU**

Translation/KUMAR SIVASUBRAMANIAN
English Adaptation/JENNIFER LEBLANC
Touch-Up Art & Lettering/KYLA AIKO
Design/JULIAN [JR] ROBINSON
Original English Logo Concept/SARA LINSLEY
Editor/JENNIFER LEBLANC

First published in Japan in 2021 by SHUEISHA Inc., Tokyo.
English translation rights arranged by SHUEISHA Inc.

Printed in Canada

Published by VIZ Media, LLC
P.O. Box 77010
San Francisco, CA 94107

10 9 8 7 6 5 4 3 2 1
First printing, April 2024

VIZ MEDIA
viz.com

SHONEN JUMP

ratings.viz.com RATED M MATURE

PARENTAL ADVISORY
DANDADAN is rated M for Mature and is recommended for mature readers. This volume contains language, violence, suggestive themes, and a rockin' exorcism!

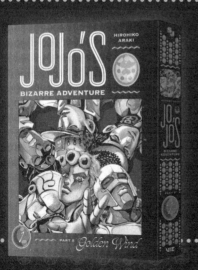

Hell's Paradise

JIGOKURAKU

STORY AND ART BY
YUJI KAKU

Gabimaru the Hollow is one of the most vicious ninja assassins ever to come out of the village of Iwagakure. He's ruthlessly efficient, but a betrayal results in him being handed a death sentence. There is only one hope: travel to a long-hidden island and recover an elixir that will make the shogun immortal and he will regain his freedom. Failure is not an option—on this island, Heaven and Hell are a hair's breadth away.

Even an invincible ninja may not be able to survive Hell's Paradise!

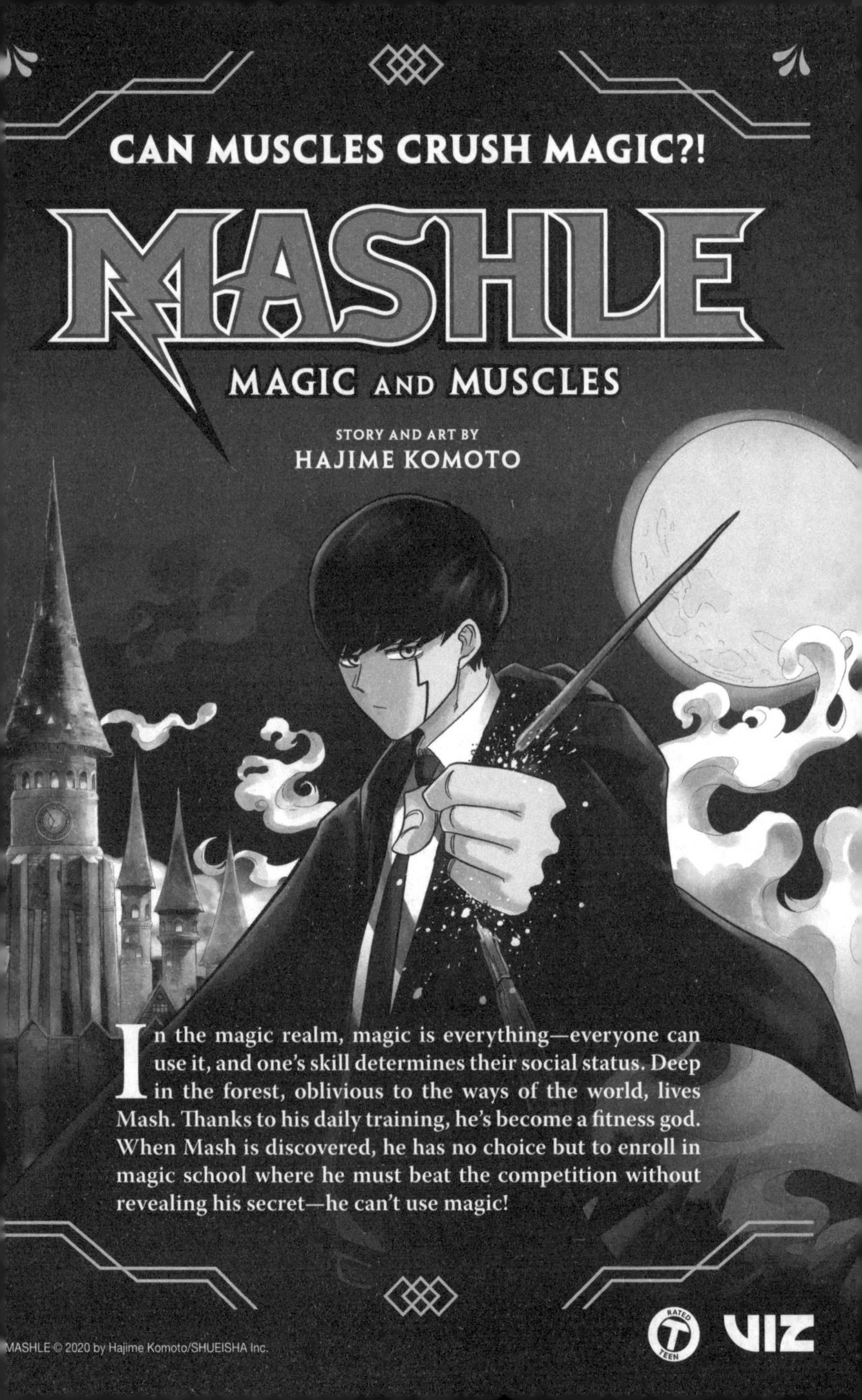
CAN MUSCLES CRUSH MAGIC?!
MASHLE
MAGIC AND MUSCLES
STORY AND ART BY
HAJIME KOMOTO
In the magic realm, magic is everything—everyone can use it, and one's skill determines their social status. Deep in the forest, oblivious to the ways of the world, lives Mash. Thanks to his daily training, he's become a fitness god. When Mash is discovered, he has no choice but to enroll in magic school where he must beat the competition without revealing his secret—he can't use magic!
RATED T TEEN
VIZ
MASHLE © 2020 by Hajime Komoto/SHUEISHA Inc.

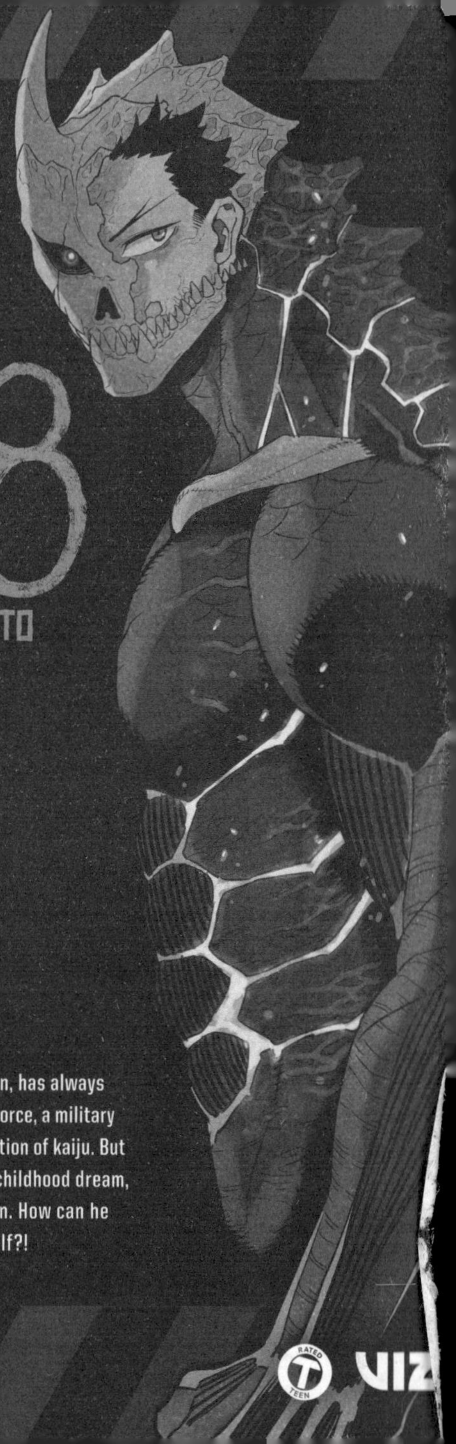

Kafka wants to
clean up kaiju, but not
literally! Will a sudden
metamorphosis stand in
the way of his dream?

KAIJU NO. 8

STORY AND ART BY **NAOYA MATSUMOTO**

Kafka Hibino, a kaiju-corpse cleanup man, has always
dreamed of joining the Japan Defense Force, a military
organization tasked with the neutralization of kaiju. But
when he gets another shot at achieving his childhood dream,
he undergoes an unexpected transformation. How can he
fight kaiju now that he's become one himself?!

KAIJYU 8 GO © 2020 by Naoya Matsumoto/SHUEISHA Inc.

YOU ARE READING THE WRONG WAY

DAN DA DAN

Dandadan reads from right to left, starting in the upper-right corner. Japanese is read from right to left, meaning that action, sound effects, and word-balloon order are completely reversed from English order.

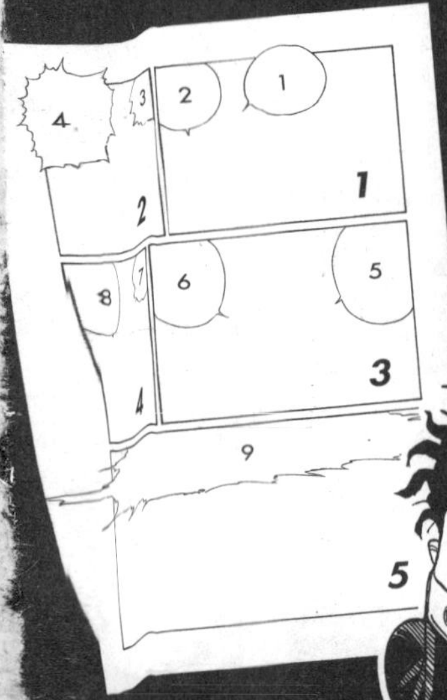
1
2
3
4
1
2
5
6
7
8
3
4
9
5

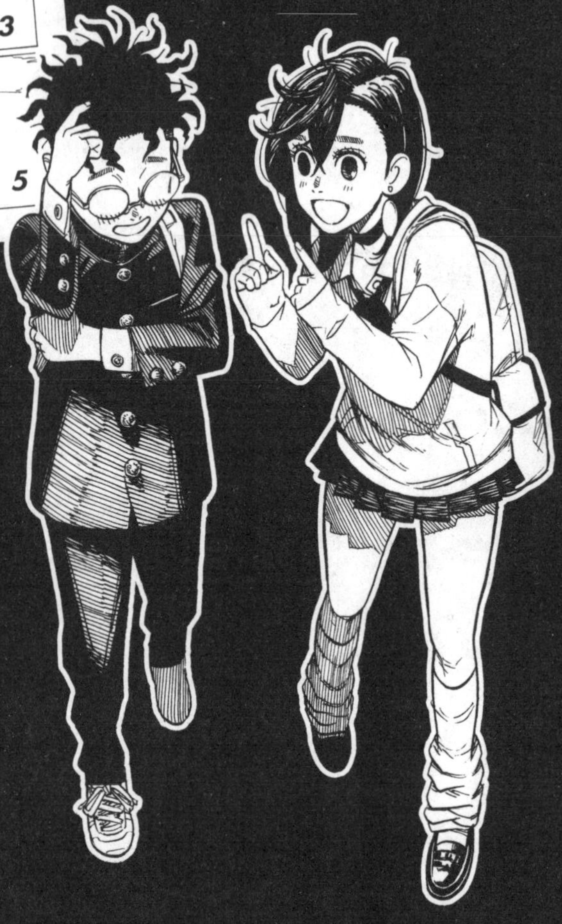